West By North, A Quarter North

Roberta (Gomez) Ricker

Enjoy!

Dear Jean,
What a nice
surprise.
Have fun with
this —

R.

Published by:

Roberta Ricker
P.O. Box 2336 South Portland, Maine 04116-2336

Inquiries & order information: robertaricker @ aol.com
(or use above mailing address)

ISBN 0-9745093-0-2

Revised
Second Printing April 2004
Printed in the United States of America
Morris Publishing
P.O Box 2110
Kearney, NE 68848

Cover Design & Layout
Suzanne Ricker
suzannericker@aol.com

This book is dedicated to:

Maria
A woman who managed to sustain an indomitable Grace and an unfailing constancy.

Antonio
For the gift of an American citizenship.

Bob & Lillian
There was nothing over and above,
nor more nuts and bolts than their marriage,
attention, and love.

Family of Long Island, past and present
For an environment in which every child should be wrapped, if only for a trice.

~~~

Bob
Bellows issued from the "sanctum sanctorum"
Endless rounds of nautical questions,
All of which invaded your time and space.
Answers, *by gorry*, you always had the answers.
Plus that particular brand of dry wit,
The one that continually catches me off guard,
And makes me laugh.
Much obliged "Ole Deah"

Suz
How good is it to have a gifted child who is a willing and interested partner, genealogy researcher, graphic artist, and computer whiz? I've been blessed.

Lin
For the definitive lifelong lesson in constancy.

Cover: Painting *"Family Portrait"*
by Roberta Ricker (nee Gomez)

Title: West by North, A Quarter North:
These are the coordinates which sailing ships charted
from Spain to New England.

Contents

Preface

So—if one does not *remember the past*, one will be *condemned to repeat it.* Is that how it works? That's a rather ominous adage to have hovering overhead for the balance of one's lifetime. Back when I knew all of the answers, I was convinced that the majority of one's personal history was comprised of nuances that were of little consequence—second-hand moments that were systematically disposed of after the fact. Who needed a hoard of faded factoids clogging up the works? Every brain cell that I owned was called upon to help create a life and maintain whatever was brought to the ford.

When my hair finally turned ten shades of salt and *pepp'ry*, an impeded memory became an issue and I went in search to see, if by chance, there might be a few, old, lethargic timelines that survived my youthful, misguided mindset. There they were, sleeping heaps of reminiscence, untold past events and human conditions, which when called-up from dormancy, swooped in like particles trailing behind Haley's Comet.

Pawing through remnants of the several eras that came before me was somewhat like reassembling a broken mirror, piecing polished imageries and tarnished ruminations back together, all of which molded into a reflective mosaic of...cracks and distortions. Not to worry! Even an Impressionistic painting that is viewed too closely will look cracked and distorted. So—I walked across the room in order to get a better perspective, turned around, and voilà. The sum and substance of a nearly forgotten space in time came into focus, the one in which my family moved across the stage with an island community, where they crossed paths with luminaries, and managed a fancy little two-set with several historical events.

Geographically, most of the scenarios took place on Long Island, Maine, a small island that was significantly snagged by history—given a few hard tugs—and then set free to be an island once again. What lies within these pages is an insight into an island community that has metamorphosed at least six times since settled by the Cushing brothers in the 1700's—a peek at a small social unit that has a novel history, and a nonrenewable way of life. Nonrenewable, because out there on the islands in Casco Bay, Maine each generation has been obligated to make its own way with whatever tools were available to them at the time.

Were the good old days actually better than today? It appears that way from a distance, but closely compared and contrasted it seems to me that neither is better, nor is worse. Only the tools have changed. The people part of it, human nature, has remained a kaleidoscopic constant.

Now—how to bring a genre painting into being, the one in which so many had a hand in creating, seemed a daunting task, because along with remembering, writing is not my bailiwick either. Too many words and too many thoughts demanded a major block of attention—all at once. Oral accounts needed to be tidied up, dusted off, and a smattering of family fairy tales parsed into reality. A friend said, *"Choose a single voice in which to write."* Oh dear! As formidable as is the art of writing, these chronicles could easily be the first and last in my lifetime; therefore, to shore-up my lack of literary know-how, no-less than three voices were enlisted.

Little information was available from which to get a clear picture of my family's immigration to this country. Therefore, the first voice that tuned-up did so with a strong historical tone, thereby lying down a foundation onto which the true-to-life characters could settle.

The second voice, which I called upon, was that of an old reprobate, who I dubbed, *Ole Chum*, and who directs a running discourse *with*, but mostly *at* his close-mouthed companion, *Ole Deah*. Islanders, up and down the coast have met these two old men, because they are a collective of every pair ever found sitting in front of an island store, gossiping in island cant about occurrences—as they *"sees 'em."* Their musings are actually based upon true events that took place in Casco Bay, Portland, Maine, and the United States between 1903 and 1918. The gist of their dialogue was gleaned from an old newspaper that had a ten-year run at the turn of the century.

The third voice is the most spontaneous, because I was there. It is my voice, which speaks from what I experienced on the island up until age seventeen, and much of what I discern in general.

Once the base for comparison between the good old days and the nowadays was secured, what did strike me—significant enough to write about, was the atypical way of life that we led, though none of us thought it to be at the time. What was the measure? There was none. There were no TVs, no computers, and no focus groups. An entire fleet of war ships was moored at our front door; and in spite of the unique connection to a war that encompassed the world, we were non-the-less provided with an incredible environment, a state of constancy all wrapped up in a protective community. Somehow, the island made childhood a prerogative for youngsters of my generation—the *Silent Generation*—the one sandwiched between the WW2's and the *Baby Boomers*. The island clearly indulged us in an age of innocence, one that we tarried in for a much longer period of time than today's child is afforded. For that I am beholden. It was a fabulous gift, and a thank-you card is in order. So! I got a little wordy—couldn't fit it all into a greeting card.

New York City – Malaganese Eyes
Present Day

Mary Sue reached for the cab's safety handle to brace herself for another erratic trip through the streets of New York City. In the middle of Time Square the driver interrupted the respectful silence with what she anticipated would be idle conversation, the type that she usually avoided like the plague. Her mind was otherwise occupied with pending corporate matters granting her good reason to ignore any verbal interlopers. Regardless, the cabby's turn of phrase cut through the maze of business minutia with the precision of a surgeon's scalpel. His words were not mundane, a wasted opinion about the weather, or political banter, but came from a place so far out of left field that it took her a few seconds to adjust to their weight. He simply said, *"You have the Malaganese eyes."* Shooting a furrowed look into the rearview mirror she queried, *"Where the hell did he dredge that from?"* She made eye contact with him, and retorted with a curt,

"Excuse me?" Succinctly he asked, *"Are you Malaganese?"* and with that question she realized that the total stranger had pinpointed her lineage in the blink of an eye.

He appeared to be well versed, a world traveler, Greek in heritage as defined by his accent, an individual who needed little prompting to expound. Matter-of-factly, he explained that he once lived among the people of her facial stamp, a people limited to only one corner of the world, the Costa del Sol, Malaga, Spain—and was emphatic that he found her countenance—her look, exclusive to that particular area and no other. His detection was uncanny! Hypothetically speaking, the exercise she witnessed was as though he plucked the first note of a musical composition out of the air, and from that singular clue guessed the name of an entire aria.

For the cabdriver this was a simple exercise. Captured in his rearview mirror were the distinct characteristics of a Malaguenian as evidenced in Mary Sue's smoky black eyes and shining blue-black hair. He was pleasantly occupied by the

Mary Sue (Cady)

response that he elicited from her, and from that she sensed that the study of origins was no more and no less than a game he played to alleviate the boredom of New York City traffic. Yet neither had an inkling of the scope into which this brief encounter had reached.

Her inquisitive nature took charge, drawn instead to the basis of just how he came by that determination. A rush of stories cropped up in the forefront of her mind, stories that her mother, grandmother, and aunts had chronicled over the years, images of the late 1800s, the period in which her great grandparents sailed from Malaga, Spain, and their life on islands off the coast of Maine.

Crunching some numbers reminded her that the earth had spun roughly over one hundred year's worth of seasons since 1894 when Antonio Gomez and Maria Campos departed Malaga for Gibraltar, where they exchanged marriage vows, then made passage to America. Sixty years had elapsed since they lived and walked among a small Casco Bay Island community in Maine. Scattered as they are, the family engendered from their union is fully into the fifth generation; yet in an instant, a cabby in New York City pulled Antonio and Maria back from the relative obscurity of all those passing years.

Had my niece, Mary Sue, been the type to brush off a found-opportunity, had she forgotten to share the novel cabby moment, I would never have been struck by what I saw as a revelation—an affirmation by the world at large that she had retained her identity as a daughter of España. It was a reminder that we belonged to a larger lineal tribe, at one point in time. We hadn't forgotten about those roots, but early on had simply assimilated into the American culture as the melting pot theory was expected to work.

At present, each fifth generation baby barely passes through the birth canal before those of us who are *long of tooth*[1] mount a debate over which side of the family the newborn favors, a behavior that makes the young mothers crazed, and has the in-laws rolling their eyes to the heavens. What to them may seem a petition for ownership of the little darling's pedigree, actually, has the earmarks of a simple search for a filial complexion.

We'd not been versed in our grandparent's beginnings, and were apprised only that Antonio Gomez was from the province of Malaga, Spain, in the maritime, an unabashed adventurer, and Maria Campos, was an orphan from the same area. Now and again, one infant is borne to us with a certain facial stamp, and we are presented with what we appreciate is a fleeting memento of the Costa del Sol, and a moment to reflect.

Turning to a gallery of family portraits that opened to my mind's eye, scanning across an exhibit that furnished the image of every successive generation, I saw a clannish resemblance that tied all of us together carried mostly through the eyes. However, I am of the notion that more comes through ancestral lines than the shape of a nose, or the color of the hair. Environment gave us mannerisms and behavior. What I saw in the portraits was a

---

[1] Long of tooth is the same as being old as dirt.

certain essence, an evolved spirit that hitched a ride with the gene pool, and came through at birth, by dint of what I call a *biological osmosis*, a rational for inexplicable family traits that pop-up, from out of no-where.

The exchange in the New York City cab resonated with my own osmotic connection. The interaction was a nudge to start somewhere, preferably at the veiled beginnings in Spain. Human nature being what it is, there was no doubt that the law of opposites would come into play, the light and dark, comedy and pathos, the sweet and the sour—a slice of the Laws of the Universe. After all, everything that is of the earth has an opposing force, probably for balance, but I can't help but reflect that *Whoever* created these laws had a delicious sense of humor.

Now alert to the obverse and converse of life, I was cushioned from any shock-find, prevented from being blind-sided during the hunt. My father and his sibling circle were the logical conservators of crucial information and parceled out voluminous fictions and folklore to us. Yet, those seemed mere fragments of a larger picture. When it came to substantive information the delivery changed, doled out instead in tiny fits and bits, the conservators unwilling to relinquish any more than was necessary. Interestingly enough, Dad's narratives were the sparsest of all—or had I not been listening?

The ebb and flow of life dictated the inevitable. Dad and his siblings' mortal careers played out, their essence now the base from which our lives have since evolved, the search for a wider filial glimpse now relegated to a quasi-run through history, viewed through lenses that are slightly tinted by a singular point of observation—mine.

Navigating back to the time of grandmother's birth was not an easy span to traverse; therefore, it was tempered greatly by backsliding—all the way into 1871, drawing from the familiar surroundings on these shores—rather than to instantly leap across the ocean to an exotic Spanish culture. Those auras and customs were foreign—distant, and were my grandparent's actuality, one imbued by the ancients of the Middle Ages, of Kings and Queens, of Moors, Romans, and Mid-Eastern influences. Without a bevy of personal anecdotes from which to

16

draw, it read as dry as a bowl of bran cereal without any milk with which to wash it down.

My breadth of view of April 1871 was Casco Bay Maine, off shore islands, fisher folk, cobblestone city streets, waterfront ambiance, and the smell of salt air. Well! What a doofus! Fisher folk—waterfront ambiance—salt air! Barring the absence of a great deal of sun, to a large degree, this describes Estepona, Spain, a small coastal village that lies in the province of Malaga, and the place wherein this all begins. Lest my many observations be perceived to be floating out there in the ether, an acquired montage of anecdotes bore out another observation. Had Maria been less strong, it could well have been an entire family without a legacy—or a soul.

Chapter

1 ...Veiled Genesis

Ice made its way out of the Penobscot River in April 1871, evidencing the end of a harsh winter up and down the Maine coast. European settlers living out on the many off-shore islands had armed themselves with a considerable amount of wherewithal and fortitude to face down the austerity of living through the harsh winter months, practicing it dutifully until they got it right. Spring's thaw breathed a new life into those worn down by the winter doldrums, set their minds off in the direction of renewal and replenishment. Indian tribes would soon return for the summer months where annually they hunted for whale and seal, fished the waters, drying an entire supply of seafood for the next winter season. They left their lyrical language in places like Mericoneag Sound, Sebasco Harbor, Harraseeket River, and Maquoit Bay, lilting words that bespoke of an earlier time when the native Indians were the only people around to tag a name onto the nooks and crannies of Casco Bay. Chebeague Island's English settlers lived in a copasetic alliance with the summering tribes, and one might ponder the success of their alliance, where so many others failed.

Though the English settlers were one hundred years removed, and far from the rule of the Crown, they retained a strong accent that remained a dead give-a-way as to their roots. In New York they dined on raspberries, but out on the islands in Casco Bay, Maine, they savored *rawzbr'ees,* and *blu'brees*, an Anglicized vernacular that has outlasted generations, a signature cant that has come to be known as the Maine accent.

In April of 1871 Stephen,[2] one of the many seafarers in the large Ricker family jaunted along the well-beaten paths to get

---

[2] Stephen Ricker, 1844 – 1928, son of Joel & Melissa.
From genealogy by great-great granddaughter Suzanne Ricker

down to the shoreline. He and the other islanders acquired the long, swinging stride, presumably, to hasten the trek from point A to point B—and on Chebeague that could be a long, five-mile haul. They made it look effortless, after all, most had three or more generations behind them who'd practiced the measured gait in heavy hip boots—long before Stephen even drew his first breath in the arms of his mother, Delight.

Island names, wonderful tokens of their English background were about to be retired, some not used again for generations, some never heard from again. His mother's name, Delight, probably reflected her order of birth and her own mother's mindset at the moment. Likewise, his aunt, Relief's, name could well have resonated her last-child status.

Stephen, and his wife, Melissa[3] were well on their way in the naming game of their own. Their first-born, Robert was six months old at the time Stephen chose to jump feet first into the stone sloop business. He'd recently bought the stone-sloop, *"Swift,"* from Charlie Sawyer, may well have been champing at the bit to get *her* ready for the upcoming season—to test *her* out with a trial run out by the bar that separated Little and Great Chebeague Islands. [i] As he sailed by, there on the bar stood a tenacious and perpetual reminder of his great-grandfather, Wentworth, the first Ricker to step ashore on Chebeague. [4] The aging, lone, red oak tree was a sapling that old Wentworth found in his beet garden on Ricker Head—and on a lark stuck it into the most improbable and barren ground for an oak tree to grab hold—out there on Indian Point. [ii] That it did—and then proceeded to tenaciously hang-on out on *the Hook* for well over one hundred years, a hallmark of the Ricker's genesis on Chebeague; a century's landmark for all mariners, in fact, marked as a recognition point on U.S. government navigation

---

[3] Melissa Wallace – 1848 - 1906

[4] Wentworth Ricker – 1752-1841, great-grandfather to Stephen, arrived on Chebeague Island before the first of his ten children were born in 1778. He may have been a farmer like his own great-grandfather, George, who died in 1706 trying to outrun the Indians in Dover, New Hampshire, a story that was embellished with each telling, though it actually did happen—but **not** on Chebeague as folklore seems to perpetuate. [4]

charts. Wentworth was a retired soldier of the Revolutionary War variety, who stepped foot on the island some months after the war ended, was there when the Hamilton family and others created an industrious and successful fleet of stone sloops.[5]

Akin to the red oak, Wentworth too, tenaciously held onto life for ninety-three years before going to his *great reward*—there long enough to see three of his great-grandchildren born, the fourth batch, in the line of Rickers, to go the distance. Most of the Rickers, from that point on, would measure distance by the nautical knot. [iii]

Traditionally, in the early sloop days, the island was devoid of men from spring to late fall. In May, teenage boys, with their fathers, cousins, uncles, and white, whiskered grandfathers sailed up the coast in their stone sloops, ran out of the quarries in Stonington, Rockland, and Vinalhaven—until the season ended in November. The vessels carried three to five men. Most all were related to each other, some owned shares in the vessel, an investment, which paid a return. Although a small fleet, they became an enormous element in the construction of our East Coast cities—delivering granite for the several Naval Academy buildings at Annapolis, the Board of Trade offices in Chicago, the Washington Monument, and government buildings in DC, and Boston. A considerable amount of granite was made into breakwaters, lighthouses, and forts—locally, Portland Headlight, Fort Gorges in Casco Bay, the lighthouse on Halfway Rock, the breakwater (Bug Light), and Ram Island Light.

Independence Day celebrations enthusiastically consumed the entire Chebeague Island community as it feted the birth of a nation, for which a few islanders, like old Wentworth, fought. Conjointly, they feted the birth of the tightly knitted fleet, a Fourth of July jubilee that was basked-in annually for one hundred years. During those festive days, each stone sloop captain pressed to get the crew home for the Fourth. They ceased work and made a marked effort, usually converging on Casco Bay with every piece of cloth available hung in the masts to hasten a timely arrival—some sloops carrying a thousand square

---

[5] Stone sloops began sailing out of Chebeague Island in 1795.

yards of canvas in their mainsails. Some say that the sloop captains were on the conscientious, stogy and stoic side, ever obligated to their vessels, and diligent in their intent. However that may be, they weren't the least bit shy about picking up the gauntlet if challenged to an impromptu playful race. Crisscrossing, and near swipes across each other's bowsprit in a crisp wind was but a moment of play, a break from the no-nonsense—and a mere inkling as to the extraordinary boatman-ship of its master. Sighting the entire fleet coming through Broad Sound under full sail was ardently anticipated—a part of the revelry of the island, and for those who watched quietly atop the East End Point, the sight never ceased being anything less than breathtaking. However, when November's overcast days turned a slate grey, the stone sloops returned, anchored, and rested in the mud flats off Chebeague for the winter—graceful ladies skirted in ice until the spring thaw.

Throughout the stone sloop heydays, Captain Stephen owned and sailed two sloops, the *Newcomb,* and the *Swift*, but he warily watched a new mode of transportation test the waters and establish a foothold. Islanders who rowed their dories to and from Portland would luxuriate in what crews on sailing vessels called *stinkpots*, coal burning, steam powered vessels—the new passenger vessels that made the several cloistered communities on the islands more accessible. [iv]

While he still had ties to the *Swift,* Stephen opted to help Chebeague Island develop a passenger and freight service. Based upon the same pattern as the stone sloops, shares were sold and they named her the *Henrietta*.[6] She serviced the island, once over daily, but by year's end it became too much for the islanders to support, was inconvenient, in that they had no wharf. To get to and from shore, passengers were relegated to many an ungraceful boarding, or debarkation from a dory. Sunday-go-to-meeting shoes don't take kindly to salt water. It was better than the long row to Portland, or the catch-as-catch-can schooner, but needed to be improved upon. At age forty, Stephen was still young when *stone slooping* completely ceased, and he elected to make five

---

[6] Henrietta 1875

trips a day to Portland for the new boat line on the *Gordon* and the *Alice*.[7] Though piloting passengers skipped a generation,[8] therein began the strung-out history of Ricker men who became captains and engineers of the many passenger vessels in Casco Bay. [v]

Spring of 1871
Long Island, Casco Bay, Maine

John Sears of Boston settled first on Long Island[9] in the 1640s, but was *removed* by the Indians, *probably quite unceremoniously*.[vi] For another one-hundred years the Indians had the place to themselves until the intrepid, young Ignatius Cushing decided to go the distance at his home on the *Westend*, overlooking Hog Island.[10] Time marched on and the York family, too, settled there along with the Cushing descendants. With the birth of a son,[11] in 1816, the York family added to the sparse community that was comprised of only four families.

Whatever the draw to the three and one half-mile island, by 1830, Long Island had the largest population of any of the upper bay islands in Casco Bay.[vii] One hundred forty-six people had set root, was farming the land, and fishing the waters.

Though the churchgoers had yet to raise a building, in the 1850s the bulwark of the Episcopal Methodist Church, settled, hung tough, and was tough—on some of the membership who failed to follow the laws of the church. Most of the two dozen members were faithful to the newly founded place of worship, though one might expect a visit from an elder if thought to be amuck of the rules. It seemed the better part of discretion to attend each Sunday and make penance, add a penny or two to the

---

[7] In the *Merchant Steam Vessels of the United States (1884) p.285,* it lists the *Alice* as built "for" Captain Ricker Command; which indicates that he initially started out on the *Alice* as captain, *not the owner.*

[8] Stephen's sons started out as fishermen. Robert stayed that way, Charles lobstered out on Cliff Island, Gus became an engineer on the *Portland Lightship*, and Ern lived and lobstered on Chebeague.

[9] 1703 London maps show Long Island as Smith Island.

[10] Hog Island is Diamond Island.

[11] York, Capt. Jerry...Born Long Island 1816

offering, one that usually tallied up to fifty cents after the collection dish was passed about the room. Fifty cents a week was enough to keep them in the grapes and ample for the forty-five cents needed for a pint of wine for communion services.[viii]

The island turned an important corner when a private school came into being, pre 1820, most likely, held in someone's home, until 1832, when a school house was erected[12]...designed, also, as a place of worship.[ix] *Adam's Geography* and *Murray's English Reader* expanded their horizons. A third book expanded their inner horizons; one utilized throughout the Portland school system, the Bible, the old-testament. *T'was* a struggle; an average of twenty-five children sporadically attended. Came the advent of Public schooling in 1850, any child living on Jewell, Little Chebeague, Crotch, and Hope Islands was enveloped into the Long Island's district. They attended daily from nine to noon, two until five, all year long, with two afternoons off (Wed & Sat), plus 4th of July, Christmas, Thanksgiving, and three weeks at end of school year. *No wonder it had a hard time getting off the ground.* Children who did *not* whisper, were *not* absent or tardy were favorably reported at the end of the year. Express use of the four-foot hickory stick was to point out lessons written up on the black board. Its ancillary use was to instantly garner attention—with a thwack on a desk, or across some knuckles, a gesture that not only brought all daydreamers to attention, but also lifted the whole class inches off their seats.

A flight of years, on past a considerable influx of people, a score of births, where in 1871, the tide of social convention and tourism discovered the bay islands. Long Island was being thought of in terms of a summer playground for the ne'er-do-wells and *do-wells* of the mainland, and in 1886 the Dirigo House was built on the front shore of the island to serve the need, though farmers and fisher folk remained its core—the heart and soul of the island. *Year rounders* were still thinking in terms of basics, subsistence, and education. A primary school was located on each end of the island, and a third, two-story grammar school

---

[12] First schoolhouse – 1832 Built where the old tower is now located, down across the cow path from the *Westend* cemetery. Me/His/Soc MZ P837.1

was built mid-island.[13] The buildings, unfortunately, were cold as a barn and to harness all the heat from the stove that could be conserved, they strung the stovepipe across the ceiling, venting it on the opposite side of the room. School was called off on dark days—a concern for eyestrain, perhaps? Perhaps!

Spring 1871
Portland, Maine

Up the bay a few nautical miles on the mainland, Portland residents strolled at a quick pace along the ticklish cobblestone footing in the coolness of an 1871 spring day, some with handkerchiefs covering their noses to ward off the acrid smell of rancid smoke hanging in the air. Mule drawn conveyances jockeyed around horse drawn trolleys, and a legion of vendors precariously skirted both in a city that had just picked itself up by the bootstraps in the wake of a raging fire that burnt it to the ground in 1866—an inferno that left ten thousand homeless. In five years time, the citizenry was now back under-roof, more secure that they would never again be as vulnerable to a fire of that magnitude. The city fathers saw that Sebago Lake's waters were piped in, and a fire alarm system situated throughout. Most structures, thereafter, were built of brick, as with the gum factory on Fore Street, [14]a high imposing building expressly located as a fire break should a fire on Munjoy Hill get out of control.

Rufus Deering–*of the old Portland family*, Mrs. Alfred Woodman–*Portland Society*, Charles Payson–*old money*, Ruben Ruby–*a black man*, George Cushman–*bakery business*, noted physicians, and a host of concerned citizens made up the board of managers for a sizable number of charitable organizations. They benefited sick and disable firemen, supported the relief of shipwrecked and destitute seamen. Most were concerned about preventing want, and provided comfortable, decent clothing, and

---

[13] Three schoolhouses. One primary school, located on Fern Ave. (is now the Ivy Hall) Second primary school located at *Eastend.*
The two-story grammar school was located mid island, going east, just beyond the old Navy garage (present fire station).

[14] Hub Furniture Store

moral elevation of the poor, the aged, and the children. Volunteers had as many as thirty districts to canvas, collect, and report. The *Widow's Wood Society, which is still in operation,* furnished fuel for destitute widows in the winter and was supported by every church in the city. A group of doctors formed the *Portland Dispensary* on Federal Street to offer medical attendance to the poor, and twenty-five orphaned girls were housed at the *Female Orphan Asylum.* The *Martha Washington Society* furnished clothes and food to indigent families who were victims of intemperance. Poor houses and poor farms were a part of the time and the mind-set. Portland's *Almshouse* was, unfortunately, well patronized. [xi]

Ulysses S. Grant, President of the United States, thought a visit to the tenacious community of Portland to be important to his political interests, where by now industry had dug a secure toehold. Nearly three thousand cargo ships sailed into the state of Maine, more than Massachusetts. With the exception of New York and Boston, Portland hauled in the largest quantity of sugar, molasses and melado[15] of any port in the union. *Is not the "demon rum" distilled from the above ingredients? It leads one to wonder if the Martha Washington temperance brigade knocked at the molasses factory door for contributions.*

Situated in the middle of a cow pasture at the top of Munjoy Hill, the Portland Observatory actively kept merchants abreast of their incoming vessels, those that when docked would require berthing and stevedores. With a powerful lens in the telescope, the observer was capable of identifying ships thirty miles out; to wit, he would hoist the colors, the merchant's identifying flag to communicate the imminent arrival of that company's vessel. [xii]

Looming over Commercial Street,[16] moored sailing ships *snugged-up*, bow-first into the docks, spars extending high over a street that ran from one far end of the Portland waterfront to the other, from the Eastern to the Western Promenade. Commercial Street was the brainchild of railroad interests, a street that was

---

[15] Melado – Crude sugar as it comes from the pans without being drained, or a mixture of sugar and molasses.

[16] Commercial was built in 1853.

bought, paid-for, and offered to the City as a gift, a much-needed corridor for the railroad to access incoming cargoes. To this stage, Fore Street was the original waterfront, beneath which Commercial Street was built from a foundation of rock filled cribs, and paved with cobblestone, the cast-off, unwanted ballast that was off-loaded from sailing ships just in from a transoceanic trip. The thoroughfare evolved into a hub of commerce that dispersed a lavish supply of cargoes. Ice arrived from Boston for refrigeration. West Indian molasses was off-loaded to make white, yellow, and coffee colored sugar in the factories throughout the city. Waste-rags from India and Egypt made shore as the makings for paper at the SD Warren paper mill.[xiii] Locals swore up and down that the rags from Egypt were mummy wrappings, with mummies in them—mummies that were ground up for fertilizer—which gave a whole new flavor to the adage *"Use it up, wear it out." And to date, a building on Commercial Street, in which molasses was probably stored, has faired well, its original tenant long forgotten, until a recent year—until the sprinkler system was set-off throughout the several floors. To the dismay of the trendy store housed on the ground floor, the molasses soaked timbers began to exude dark, watery sheets of goo that oozed down the walls. The hundred-year old remnant of a time nearly beyond recall was released like a genie from a bottle—for an insurance company to manage.*

Spring 1871
Estepona, Spain

Warm sunlight cast over Manzanares Street in Estepona Spain in April of 1871, cut a swath over the entire rustic fishing village and its sandy beaches. The parade of years paid little attention to the village, leaving it a labyrinth of connecting narrow cobblestone streets that filled with, and emptied of its convivial dwellers in the time-honored dance of toil, pleasure, poverty, siestas, and bullfights—a shuffle choreographed by the incessant heat of the day.

With babe in arms, Maria Gil[17] and her husband Pedro Campos made their way from their home, around the corner to the Church of Santa Maria de los Remedios for their daughter's baptism, a church that sat in the heart of the village. Sweet fragrances of the almond blossoms scented the air, and most likely wafted along with them into the musty ancient cathedral where Father Francisco de Avila Navarro performed the sacred ceremony of spiritual purification, while the Godparents held the three day-old infant over the basin of holy water—echoing promises. The baptismal papers referred to her as Maria Aurora Campos Gil, legitimate daughter, and offered up enough information to clearly illuminate the sanctified moment. As would be expected, both sets of proud grandparents, Pedro Campos and Maria Gomez, Juan Gil and Antonia Chacon were in attendance to grant familial oversight to the occasion. [xiv]

Somewhere in the same village, Antonio Gomez Haimeno was establishing his four-year old bearings, likely with a flair for risk taking. *I say likely, because in his adult years a liberated nature and risk taking was a way of life for him.[xv] Its not much of a leap to envision that his mother and father, Josefine Haimeno and Antonio Gomez had their moments holding down the feisty, diminutive four-year old. [xvi]*

Their surroundings on the Costa del Sol were made up of stacked houses, whitewashed in order to deflect the searing rays of the sun, a white village with front doors that opened directly onto the activity of tiny twisting streets. Back doors swung open to animal pens, and vegetable gardens, a place where barefoot children sifted through herb-lined pathways of thyme, citrus trees, and a few hundred crocuses planted for a bit of saffron. Seaweed, harvested from the shoreline, was put to use to enrich

---

[17] A long practiced Spanish tradition is clearly defined in Maria's baptismal record and in later vital records, whereby Antonio referred to his mother by her maiden name. Maria's mother, Maria Gil, and grandmothers, Maria Gomez and Antonia Chacon were too referred to by their maiden names in the earlier document. Spanish women were not required to assume the husband's last name upon marriage. Women kept their identity—and didn't have to burn their bras to get the idea across.

the gardens and orchards; chestnut barrels filled with sidra, *cider with a kick*, were piled high in tapas bars. A day's catch of cod quickly required salting, or brining while still fresh, and then was hung overhead on racks to dry in the heat of the sun. The annual task of slaughtering a pig brought out each and everyone to lend help in the chore, followed no doubt, by a bit of sidra, *cider with a kick*. Food preservation and preparation consumed most waking hours of the day.

Maria amused herself in and around her family's workplace, especially captivated and entertained by the donkey that was yoked to the axis of the huge Campos Factory's pottery wheel. Traveling countless miles, in endless circles, the animal turned silica sand and clay into malleable masses for the pottery wheel. Maria and Antonio's fathers plied their pottery craft into vessels for water, wine, and olive oil—giving one the impression that both families must have known one another in the day to day of the pottery trade. The village wasn't that big. [xvii]

Each evening, she, her family, and the villagers congregated to watch a reenactment of a ritual that had taken place for generations, that of closing the gigantic gates of the village, the vestiges of a fortified castle built in the 1500s. Their forefathers had done so in defense of the village against coastal pirates in the days of yore when there were pirates plying, pillaging and plundering the coast. Not surprisingly, the ritual became deeply etched into Maria's earliest recollection—so riveting an experience that as an old woman she carried the story forward to her first grandchild, Phyllis as one would a fairy tale. By that point in time—it was. [xviii]

Their lives were simple, filled with a generous ration of spirituality mandated by the Church's ceremonial religious observances. So many, that four-dozen religious observances had a unique dessert or pastry assigned to each holiday, none made at any other time of the year. Sweet things—Spaniards loved sweet things. No meal was complete without a sweet ending. In the everyday commonplace, cuisine was the underpinnings for most family occasions, and it is no exaggeration to state that Spaniards ate their way through a year's worth of feast days alone.

Considering their way of life on the Costa del Sol, it is now intriguing to observe how many of Maria and Antonio's present day progeny now live near a shoreline, work and play on the ocean—how many have been ceded a strong flair for culinary inventiveness, plus the scads that have an incredible green thumb. None have the need—or penchant to cure fish, slaughter pigs, or sit at a pottery wheel, though a potter's aptitude for three-dimensional design has caught hold in a host of family members. They go about their way in their respective careers, occupations that we expect in today's society, but hidden within the ranks, there is the one who sculpts incredible wooden decoys, a carpenter who audaciously takes on most anything with grand results, and a superb hair stylist, who effortlessly sculpts vanity, glamour and good looks. The old family tree has obviously been nurturing every new season of growth, despite its age—without signs of waning.

I nearly fell off my own branch of the family tree with the discovery that Spaniards love a sweet ending after each meal. Osmotic theory, here we come! Now I have the rationale as to why I've led a shameless life insisting on desserts after each and every meal—and may I interject—without so much as a pang of self-reproach. Now, I could have rested on the osmotic theorem and said no more was it was not for the fact that rice and clams in tomato sauce, blood sausage, pickled pigs feet, and eels didn't make it through my osmotic curtain. So I'm not a purist! On my mother's side, the Canadian recipe for hog's-head cheese, where everything but the squeal is stewed together, didn't filter through either.

Spain - Andalusian Earthquake

A potent earthquake, of six-point eight-magnitude rocked the area Christmas day, 1884—the epicenter located not many miles away in Malaga. Shocks and tremors decimated a great portion of the area's homes and ancient structures. Amidst the tumult and traumatic events of the very same earthquake the artist, Pablo Picasso, then a small child was greatly affected and, with his family, survived, but over all, countless lives were lost and wrecked. Terror, fires, and fear sent the survivors bolting out to the fields and away from the falling debris. Amid the pall of smoke and unbridled fires, King Alfonso XIII and his entourage wended their way on horse through endless miles of rubble, intent on bringing comfort to his stricken subjects now living in fields. [xix]

Strong aftershocks hovered beneath the area for an entire year robbing survivors of any sense of safety and calm. Indeed almost to the day, on January fifth, 1885 another immense quake erupted involving a vast area of the Andalusian region. As though they didn't have enough death to deal with, huge fissures ripped through the villages, belching up entire cemeteries as they tore through. Coffins were splayed open, corpses exposed to animals and laid bare to the flocks of ravening birds that hovered over the area. As is usual in devastation of that magnitude, a cholera epidemic spread its tentacles far into the country, with respect to none. Maria was fourteen. [xx]

Her orphaned state was never clarified to our generation, but in view of the cataclysmic upheaval, a plausible supposition to be made is that her parents died as a result of the two earthquakes, or from the ensuing epidemic of cholera. Regardless the cause, it is fact that she and her siblings were left without parents and placed in the care of a grandmother and an uncle, though the children's care was eventually relinquished to an English boarding school in Gibraltar.

New England
1893

A succession of heavy gales and thick snowstorms harassed the New England maritime in January of '93. Up the coast on Vinalhaven, for the first time in six years sailors were walking from their schooners to the shore. Midas Channel Basin from Isle au Haut was packed solid, and Friendship Harbor was closed entirely in January with two feet of the *blasted stuff.* Captain John MacVane of Long Island planned a timely, seven-week trip into warmer waters, long enough for New England to get over the hissy-fit she'd been in since December. He cleared Portland, aboard the three *masted*-schooner, *Grace Davis*, punched his way through the weather, and headed for Puerto Rico to pick up a load of molasses. Vapor rose like geysers off Salem, where overnight, ships were freezing into the ice, so much so, that for five days in a row no ships had come into the harbor. Hyannis was growing a thick icy shoreline, by the minute, and it reached a mile off shore by the time MacVane sailed on by the area. He didn't know it, but on his way by Baltimore, forty coasting[18] schooners with cargoes were imprisoned in the ice, too dangerous and expensive an effort to get them out, therefore, they paid off the crews and the captains went home. The schooner *Leviathan* of Thomaston, reported abandoned while on a voyage from Georgia to NY, was again seen 312 miles from Cape Hatteras, with her mizzenmast standing and decks two feet above water. [xxi]

By February 1893, Portland's streets were plump full of icy slop. They were so plugged that Lieutenant Robert Peary, who'd returned from Greenland, canceled a planned trek through the streets of Portland with his team of huskies, a bit of a public relations tour for the locals it would seem. Imaginably, Portland Police had seen it all, but there was another twist to the colorful and unique jaunt. Peary asked to use the police station to house his dogs, adding one caveat—they must have ice, be able to sleep on blocks of ice–so as to *"keep healthy."* [xxii]

***

Eighteen ninety-three was a benchmark year for Antonio Gomez following a stint with the Spanish Navy.[xxiii] Spain and America were sniping at one another over tariffs with Cuba. Perhaps through the normal barrage of scuttlebutt aboard ship, he learned of an expansion of the conflict, one that could get sticky—and as the events bore up historically—an atmosphere that actually became downright mucilaginous. Early March of '93 he cropped up in the Azores, applied for a passport to America through the Spanish Consulate, which said, *"to New York,"* and through some quirk, or impulse he made his way to the Portland, Maine area, specifically to Long Island, Maine. [xxiv]

---

[18] Coasting –To land along side the sea or seashore.

What drew him to Maine? How did he get here? Why isn't he in the Ellis Island records? [19] *My oldest friend in the world, Susan, a Cushing from Long Island—let drop a salient bit of island lore as though it a foregone conclusion. Everyone knew that a MacVane brought Antonio to the island. Well! I never knew that! This blockbuster piece of information required a mile of corroboration—thus, Susan directed me "thither." Thither, paraphrased, means "miles in that direction—over across, and knock at Harriet's door." "My mother* [20] *always told me,"* Harriet said emphatically, *"of a story the old-timers in my family regularly took up in conversation—that my great-grandfather, Captain John MacVane plucked Antonio off a busy New York dock and brought him to the island, by way of the 'Grace Davis'."* [21]

John MacVane, thirty year old Captain of the 352 ton tern schooner, *Grace Davis*, hailed from Long Island, Maine, born around the time of the Civil War. Like most of the MacVanes, though hardened from years at sea, he was a fair and patience man who revealed a compassionate and speculative side to his salty character. Therefore, at that moment, it was in MacVane's makeup to save wandering souls, thus, he gave the dice a roll, picked up a young Spaniard looking for work on the New York docks, and by doing so, added a peppery savor to the community hash. [xxv]

---

[19] Ellis Island does not list Antonio in 1893. So many immigrants were streaming through Ellis Island between '92 and '94 that they were not certain that all were recorded. Of every large ship, on which Antonio sailed, only one was a passenger ship, the *SS Peninsular*, which was a ship that made regular runs between the Azores, New Bedford, and NY. It logged a trip within the passport's timeline. The Portland newspapers reported the *Grace Davis* arrived in Portland on March 28, 1893 with a load of molasses from Ponce, Puerto Rico. The next reporting of the Grace Davis (with MacVane) is five months later, clearing Portland with a load of coal from Philadelphia. MacVane may have found Antonio within that time frame...or made a pit stop in NY in March of '93. The search continues.

[20] Priscilla (Bickford) Nelson's mother was a MacVane.

[21] John MacVane was Captain of the *Grace Davis* from 1891-94.

The upshot of it all was that, until today, obviously, I never gave much thought to the genesis of our family's Americanization or of my two old friends' genesis through, land owner Ezekiel Cushing, his settler brother, Ignatius, plus Harriet's connection with Captain MacVane. Neither the good Captain, nor Antonio would have given a minute's brainwork to the parallels that they created on a day in 1893, when (I'm assuming) they shook hands in agreement. These were parallels that eventually stretched a century into the future to hitherto abide in Susan, Harriet and me, three "begats" of the island's ancestral tree. The continuity of those tautly stretched lines has the definite earmarks of a genuine, one hundred per cent legacy, which we enjoy to this day. Of that meeting of the two men, I am muchly appreciative.

Antonio sought out other Spanish compatriots with which to help interpret the lay of the land. The Spanish Consulate was handy-by on Commercial Street in Portland, and few short blocks up at the corner of Exchange and Middle Streets, Ernesto Ponce owned a cigar and tobacco shop. Ponce, a man of vision, and a successful Spanish entrepreneur, purchased ten acres of land on Long Island in 1875 and sat on the investment for twenty years. Antonio's penchant for tobacco may have had something to do with their meeting, but possible future employment on Long Island with Ponce was the more significant factor. [xxvi]

The corner stones were laid and within the next year, Antonio returned to Malaga filled to the brim with bravado, turning Maria's head with promises of a castle in America as part of the mix—*true*—to fetch her as he had pledged. It would seem that she too was laying cornerstones, because two years earlier she procured a copy of her birth certificate from the priest in Estepona. These are elements of a well-devised game plan. He housed at the Continental Hotel; she bided at the Scud Hill South in Malaga until their marriage plans were cemented, both working as cooks—likely saving money for the passage.

Maria didn't seem concerned that he exhibited the nomadic trait of the gypsies, lacked a religious practice, and displayed an inclination towards following risky pursuits. With aggrandized expectations swirling in all directions, and *a castle in waiting,* one could visualize that the small, wiry, mustachioed man, with intense black eyes, appeared a mite grandiose and overblown, a trait that her elders could have read as future problems for the young woman. This penchant for wanderlust was not the earmarks of one who would transform into your basic cornerstone of a traditional Spanish community.

Obviously, adventure was intoxicating, and the promise of a new and burgeoning society—an *immense* draw. Against the family's dictum, Maria resolutely stood her ground and married him early in November of 1894 with friends, Cristobal Mendez and Maria Aragon in attendance. The four friends made their marks, as none could write, and the bond between the twenty-seven year old bachelor and the spinster, as she was considered at age twenty-four, was sealed. The action dramatically changed the course of her life, created an unbridgeable chasm between her and her family, a drastic repercussion, serious enough, in that the family shunned her. Someone was certainly irate and decidedly unbending.

There seems more to it—raising the questions: why did the exchange of marriage vows take place at the registrar's office in Gibraltar with two witnesses in attendance? Why not by a religious ceremony held in the church of Santa Maria de Los Remedios in Estepona, with family? This took on the distinct flavor of an elopement, but why? She was not with child. What transgression could Maria conduct in the eyes of her family that created such a schism? Could her tie to the Gomez family through her Grandmother, Maria Gomez, have been a relation to Antonio's family that was within the third degree of kindred? I'm just asking! Were that the case, the priest, would have most assuredly forbade the marriage. [xxvii]

Tossing a reciprocal act of severance back at them, Maria broke with her family. The cargo ship's crew pulled in its lines, and the captain put out to sea. On deck she watched the coastline diminish before her eyes until the Costa del Sol was a faded blue line on the horizon. All that was familiar to her diminished, an entire culture diminished—that which made her what she was diminished—a wave at a time.

The bow plowed the swells on a course towards a country that offered a place for the *"tired, weary, huddled masses yearning to be free"*... Yet neither of the newlyweds was, in all probably *tired*, both much too young to be *weary*, and they no doubt cuddled more than *huddled* on their honeymoon cruise to America. There were ample moments to settle some of what had just taken place, to bring thorny problems into perspective. The Atlantic's enormity inspires awe; its power humbles, and the full turn of the horizon meditatively clears the mind. Depending on the turn of the weather, the sea can also clear the stomach, especially if one was quartered on a deck below the waterline. After weeks of unsteady footing, the American shores would clearly be a welcomed relief for any frayed equilibrium. [xxviii]

Portland – Casco Bay – Long Island
1894 -1895

Their ship merged into a congestion of wooden sailing ships, one of every type—steam ships, billowing coal smoke, and small steam tugs on hand to take on any challenge given. Sailing into the American harbor, disembarking into a landscape of new sights, sounds, and aromas had to have been an incredible moment for Maria as she stepped off the plank into the slur of indistinguishable language, a surrealistic experience, akin to being reborn.

Maria's dependency on Antonio surely mounted throughout these days, because she knew so little English, only that to which she was exposed in the boarding school as a young woman. He acquired a pidgin's worth that he interspersed with two or three other languages, a chopped-up jargon that, over the first months in America, took him where he wanted to go. Timing was everything. Immigration quotas were cut drastically following their arrival. [22] America and Spain were more at odds than ever.

---

[22] Antonio and Maria may have, in fact, sailed into Portland Harbor, and not Ellis Island at some point between their marriage in November of 1894, and before the birth of their first child in the fall of 1895. They do not register on the Ellis Island records in 1894-95

We had a President, here in these United States, who with his family, retreated to Buzzards Bay out on Cape Cod Massachusetts. Though President Cleveland had an impending war, budgets, and a heap of presidential minutia to grapple with, he made himself available to be on hand to attend to the haying at Gray Gables, he, evidently, a gentleman farmer at heart who felt that the business of the country in 1895 could wait until his haying was done. [xxix]

Up the coast a few nautical miles in Portland, Maine, the young immigrant couple cast about for roots, settled one short block from the water's edge amidst the clangor, whistles, and hisses that filled the air—sounds particular to the Canadian National Railway trains as they made up freights at the Grand Trunk rail yard on Commercial Street. This was not a hushed area of the city, by any means. The gum factory [23] across the street from their rental on 278 Fore Street was in full-bore. Amidst it all, their first child, Josephine, was born on a chilly January day in 1895. [xxx]

Yacht Brinwood
Maria & Antonio (back row, left),
baby Josephine (front row)

In the months to follow, Antonio found work as cook aboard a yacht owned by Albert Scates, a *millonairo* from Baltimore. It seemed an opportune time to have a picture taken amongst the crew with Maria, who was well dressed for the camera in hat and cape, and nine-month old, Josephine, gently held by a member of the crew. [24] Was this a fitting photo to send some cynical in-laws in Spain, perhaps?

---

[23] Today, the former gum factory is the Hub Furniture Company.

[24] Ship's protocol - Per historian C. William (Bill) Colby of Spruce Head Island, Maine. A passenger's child would never be posed or held by one of the crew, though they would feel free to do so with another crew member's child. By this, the inference drawn is that Antonio was part of the crew in the photograph and not a passenger.

Thereafter, they move just a bit up-street, four whole elevated blocks from the waterfront, to a place that set in the shadow of a high, imposing, massive stone wall, one which ran the length of the street and served to retain one of Portland's oldest cemeteries. Beside the cemetery, North Elementary School towered over their new rental, a rather quiet, idyllic spot it would seem, but on the opposite end of the house they were afforded one of the most spectacular of vistas on the New England seaboard. Though they saw it through billows of steam from the constant arrivals and departures of steam locomotives, from their windows on Federal Street they viewed seaward onto the main ship channel to Portland Harbor, the very same port into which Antonio had initially sailed in '93.

Several lush islands lay to the southeast, most all inhabited year round. A forest of ship masts crammed the inner harbor. The *USS Maine* lay at anchor on a visit to Portland, and a fleet of passenger vessels taxied back and to on a regular schedule to the islands, all of it a veritable cauldron of commercial activity. In the spring of 1896, Antonio Junior was on the way, but for Maria the panorama of amusements were enough to fill any empty moments, an equitable pastime between child rearing, work, and pregnancy. [xxxi]

On the Fourth of July, the two island steamers, *Sebascodegan* and *Merryconeag* carried nearly 2000 passengers out onto Casco Bay; a good portion of them headed down the bay to a variety show and the fishing boat race on Long Island. Through Antonio's tie to the island, the inference can be drawn that the young family was attracted to the eight-mile turn around regatta. Races for the twenty-four foot category started in the afternoon at 2:17 and returned at 4:04. H. Floyd took the lead and won the $15 first prize. H. Cushing came in a close second to take away the second prize of $10. In the twenty-foot boats there were two Bickfords, another Cushing, and one of those Dyers. C. Johnson dropped out during the first half. [xxxii]

One hundred years and several generations later, the front of the island was packed with commemorating, jubilant onlookers for one of the most recent Long Island lobster boat races. Souped-up, ear shattering, diesel powered lobster boats—with bows high into the air, serge to the finish line—rooster tails shooting out from under their sterns, practically drowning anything in their wake. The fact that a Johnson dropped out of the race in 1896 is a sliver of news that may not set well with a present day heir-apparent, a faithful Johnson entrant, winner in the lobster boat "Dawn." It should be said, that his closest of friends, the descendants of the Floyd and the Bickford families will absolutely revel in the news that a Johnson has not always crossed the finish line. See how they are?

***

In the seventeen years he'd been in the country, Ernesto Ponce amassed a tidy sum of money from his Granite Springs Cafe and cigar businesses on Exchange Street, electing to dump it into real estate, a great deal of real estate. Railroad service, with its influx of out-of-state vacationers and Canadians, had changed the lay of the land. Ponce recognized a found-opportunity when he saw one and purchased large tracts of land on Long Island. He calculated that on a single occasion Long Islanders served two, to three thousand people at one clambake—namely, one that took place when the City of Portland feted a Centennial celebration in 1886. Sixteen cords of wood fueled the fires. Five hundred bushels of clams, and near to three thousand lobsters were consumed in a time honored Indian fashion of steaming the food on the shoreline atop hot rocks and seaweed. But, on the average, upward to two hundred people were seated at a clambake. [xxxiii]

Ponce tested the waters, trusting that this boom would hold up. Subsequently, in December of 1889 he set down plans to build a hotel on Long that would serve the throngs, and eventually added a dining room that seated four-hundred, fitted out each bedroom with horse-hair mattresses, *as opposed to straw*, then advertised—location, location, location. [xxxiv] Carpenter, Claudis Isusi, a Spanish compatriot of Ponce,[25] kept the crew working around the clock to get it all ready. The hotel was built fare and square on the shoreline, with its own private dock, Ponce's Landing, and faced a glorious view of the inner bay, with Mount

---

[25] Isusi moved to Long Island in 1880,

Washington in the far distance. Faint train whistles skipped across the water to perk an ear now and again, their forlorn sound added ambiance to a hushed afternoon, a reminder that the world across the bay continued to turn.

Mineral spring spas were long, established, and very

Granite Spring Hotel, Ponce's Landing

successful in Spain, a known element to Ponce that he used to separate his hotel from all others. The Granite Springs Hotel offered up the medicinal aspects of Long Island's sweet mineral spring waters and hot and cold salt-water baths on each floor as a draw, waters guaranteed to cure all ills, especially kidney disorders. That claim may not totally have been an old snake oil declaration. Though not foolproof, a quick swish in the ocean waters kept fishermen's hands relatively free from infections that they acquired by handling putrid fish bait. The cool salt water of the bay was restorative for tired, aching, feet, and a good plunge, off the end of the wharf, *feet first,* cleaned out the sinus, and freshened up the eyes. [xxxv] *As to the kidney connection—a snake oil mind set may have been in over drive.*

Ponce hired Antonio and Maria as part of the staff of twenty-five, and in doing so, incorporated them into the larger family of Casco Bay Islanders. Antonio felt solvent enough to buy a lot from Ponce on Garfield Street in November of 1897 and within the year a structure was built. They waited, like others, to be accepted, although proverbially, any person not borne to the islands waited a considerable period of time to be wrapped in the mantle of islander. *In some cases the jury is still out!* Neither coercion, nor legal tender, nor even marriage could make it happen. Logically that left lineage as the common denominator to secure one's place, but even being born there did not guarantee success if an individual was not able to bond, or acquire an affinity for the *rock* and its surrounding waters. That inclination must come from within.

Maria's newborns came into the world sporting beautiful dark eyes, their little faces diminutive reflections of those family members pictured in a red velvet photograph album, the one she carried with her from Spain, carried every place that she went. In spite of the chasm and the geography that lay between she and her family, the babies' given names reflected an abiding respect and affection for those still residing on the Costa del Sol. It was an endearment that she did not carelessly heave out with the dirty dishwater, but honored with namesakes: Josephine Mary named after Antonio's mother, Josefine—the middle name, Mary, after her own mother, Maria and her grandmother, Maria Gomez. They again covered three bases with baby, Antonio Manuel,[26] after Antonio, and *his* father. *We could stretch it a bit, and interject that one of her grandmothers was Antonia. Nicely done!*

Maria & Antonio with children (l to r) Alfred, Josephine and Antonio Jr.

By February 1898, Antonio applied for citizenship, a wise move in view of the kindling Spanish American War that was about to break open. President McKinley asked for over one hundred thousand volunteers to fight against Spain. Antonio did not answer the call and began to refer to himself as an American merchant seaman, rather than a former member of the Spanish Navy. Generally, he found it not a good time to be a Spaniard in America. Passions ran high over the quickly executed war, one in which Teddy Roosevelt and his Rough Riders fought and gained prominence. In his speeches Roosevelt charged that they would *"drive Spaniards from the Western World."* Spitfire that he was it was doubtful that Antonio was going to be driven anywhere, particularly by passions inflamed by rhetoric. He had other plans brewing; work at Fort McKinley,[27] boats to rent, and fishing

---

[26] Young Tony was a junior. His middle name was Manuel. By that I am led to believe that Antonio Senior was also Antonio Manuel, though I never saw that on paper.

[27] Fort McKinley was manned during the Spanish American War.

parties to tend. Their third baby, Alfred, arrived and the country went to war. [xxxvi]

As fellow Spaniards they were reciprocally attached to the Ponce and the Isusi families by a common background, comforted to speak a common language while they assimilated the new. Adeline Isusi was at hand, living just down the street. Thus Maria unpacked her bags, hung her hat, and dug in. The wee ones settled into a more orderly life—for the moment.

Industry took one giant step forward with a newfangled invention, one that would impact this country and the world forever—the automobile. In the country's Capital, the fifty-third Congress proclaimed the first income tax law offered as unconstitutional. *The "fifty-third" was extraordinarily well read, constitutionally that is.* [xxxvii]

The island's white beaches and characteristic fishing village activities were notably similar to the shoreline of Estepona, though in Spain the high sun affected a siesta-like quietude.[28] Warm seasons on the coast of Maine created just the opposite. Hotels, boarding houses, and cottages sprung up all over the shorelines to serve the well-heeled clientele. Bathhouses peppered the several beaches, a nook where the ladies could change into bathing suits. Women *dasst* traipse and flaunt around the island in flannel swimsuits, *a creation, which by the way, had twenty-five times more material sewn into it than today's spandex.* The heavy garment was designed with long sleeves, long skirts that hung below the knees, over long black stockings, and when wet, dragged heavily around the ankles. You see— sunlight, at that time, was considered dangerous.

In all reality, summer was short, ten weeks on the outside, hardly around long enough to call it a season. Vacationers made the decision to leave—but the cues came from the forces of nature. As early as August the ambience of the island began to fluctuate. Amidst the tall dried grasses, nature cultivated a

---

[28] Tectonically speaking – I studied a map that depicted the continents, back when they were connected, millions of years ago before they drifted apart. Maine and Spain shared the same space – were interlocking pieces, like in a puzzle.

multicolored carpet of white Queen Anne's lace, splashes of red Indian paintbrushes, wild blue asters, and yellow ragweed. Breezes brushed over the fields, slipped through drying leaves in the trees with a hiss and a whisper. Apple orchards bore fruit, marking time for the coolness to make them perfect. Not to be ignored, beneath the kitchen window, trilling crickets emerged as harbingers of the cooler sun, heralding the summer's end.

To entertain those guests waiting out a late summer vacation, hotels concocted blackberry parties. Cooks, like Maria, collected the ambrosial bounty from the guests, then served them at the evening meal in golden baked meringue bowls, and again, atop cereal in the morning. Granite Spring's cook, Mrs. Ross, when asked for her spice cake recipe, replied, *"Oh! I use just a handfull of this, and a smidgen of that. I never measure."* They never had to measure; they were culinary wonders.

Blame it on the autumnal equinox, depleted funds, but whatever the motivation, everyone's lawn furniture was pulled in close to the cottage, windows were boarded up, and the sun-tanned entourage departed for the season. Few summer residents ever passed through the portals of fall into the first frost, or were seldom on hand to enjoy the trickster season, Indian summer, let alone see their cottages blanketed in snow. They had been summarily and seasonally dismissed by bit of isolated terra firma and its surrounding Atlantic waters.

At last! The end of the wharf became freed up from the crush of people, horses, buggies, and the mountains of baggage. Now the vexations of the shoulder to shoulder boat ride on the hour-long steamboat run to Portland flitted away with the exodus. A native islander might be seen stretched out on an empty bench taking a nap during the off season, lulled by the vibrations of the steam engine, woken just in time by an intuitive alarm in the slumbering brain as the boat made its approach to his island.

Ever aware, especially of an exodus, the year *'rounders* emitted an involuntary sigh of relief when the last cottage was buttoned up for winter layover. It is best described as a seasonal sigh, a deep, long, exhale, that usually signifies that something has finally been accepted. In this case, it was the unadulterated solitude that dusted over the empty, white sand beaches, dirt roads, and piazzas, leaving solitude to fill the vacuum left by the fray. Fall triggered a more simplistic period that added a temperate quality to the community. Seasonal reparation, a payback of sort, was awarded back to the island.

With forty-two weeks ahead of them until spring, the first on their list was to reclaim shortcuts and paths that meandered through backyards as they moseyed by shuttered cottages which, despite the owner's absence, resonated an essence inclusive to each family. Dormant properties stood suspended in time, changing little from year to year, inside or out. The natives didn't embrace the seclusion—nor were they afraid of it. They simply knew how to do it. Each family settled into the predictability of family and old comfortable neighbors. The transition from summer to winter was much like donning an old, warm bathrobe after the constraints of a tight corset had been unfettered.

In retrospect, the Gomez family, who were establishing roots on Long, and the Ricker clan, deeply entrenched on Chebeague, may have vaguely known *of* each other through an occasional trip to Portland on the *Gordon*—maybe not. That mile-wide stretch of chilly waters that poured in from the Atlantic, separating Chebeague from Long Island, might just as well have been an ocean's worth. Islands were born out of the same molten rock, but each one manifested very different characteristics, as did the natives.

Chapter

2

...A November Gale Off The Beaufort Scale

Storm of '98
Captain Robert Ricker

Extraordinary maritime abilities fell to young Chebeague mariners who were spawned from the original settlers of the Hamilton, Ross, and Doughty families—an ability as natural to the Rich, Calder, and Dyer boys as putting one foot in front of another. So tied to the ocean were the pack of Rickers that some said the *whole of them* had saltwater running through their veins. Webbers and Bowens, Cleaves and Longs—all of the stalwarts of Chebeague sailed and fished with the old, and young salts who lived out further on Cliff Island, but interestingly, none were apt to mingle much with the other islands in those days. This was due, in part, to the span of water between them, due some to social engineering. Both islands were quite cloistered, as *dry as a bone*, and as anyone who has been in a conversation with any of the native sons would agree, so too was their wit. They *dasst* partake in anything that hinted of *gamblin'* or the *liberal flow of elixirs* as was known to exist over on Long Island. They *dasst* for good reason. Patriarchal guidance steered them with a stern threat—to thrash any son who stepped ashore on *them hell and be damned dens of iniquity*. Be they a Littlefield, a Hill, a Curit—or any from the community's family who dared entertain the thought—a father's word was sufficient incentive to keep them from taking a dry run across the *Sound.*

Before first light, Stephen Ricker's young fisherman son, Robert, strolled around the back yard with his first cup of strongly brewed coffee in hand before heading down to the shore, waded through the grass, checked the bottom of his hip boots for dew. He smelled the air, and gazed at the sky. If his boots were lightly dampened, he and his crew set sail—confident that a fair wind would be present for the labored row that each of the laden dories would have when tracking back to the schooner. Now if the boots came up *too* wet they got a very early start, say two o'clock in the morning. Heavy dew foretold of a chance of heavy winds in the afternoon. In the normal course of events, there were mornings that his boots came up absolutely bone dry. There would be no fair winds, no trip, and no fish.

Forecasting weather was, obviously, not a science, nor was it daily forecast for them. Nonetheless, the more seasoned men were fine prognosticators of the weather who relied on the color of the sky, and the smell of the air. They amassed their own brand of information, a compilation of *wisdoms* stored up from a time when they could barely walk. Halos around the sun and rings around the moon, those *sun* or *moon-dogs,* translated into portends of storms, as did the tiny, crawling, white caps, *cats paws*, which crawled atop the water rather than rolled.

Wind direction was by far the most important element, but all tolled were short predictors. Mother Nature had a perverse sense of humor, and at times was not adverse to baiting fishermen with one condition, and then backing the weather in on them. Older men forewarned the snot-nosed kids of the family not to set their lobster traps out in the early spring until the seals had pupped. Mother seals never gave birth until the last storm passed. *Presumably, that law of nature still holds true.*

Long Island, Portland, & Boston

On the Saturday after Thanksgiving in 1898, each island household cleared the dirty dishes from the supper table following the time-honored baked bean supper. A hunk of salt pork-fat flavored the molasses sweetened beans, a tasty spread for the slices of steamed brown bread laced with raisins, the bread a crowning touch to the humble meal. One could bet a week's wages that baked beans graced ninety-nine percent of the dinner tables. Even those who didn't like beans may have been forced to admit that the aroma was a pleasing bid-welcome in any house on a Saturday afternoon. Women, from the *Eastend* to the *Westend* of Long Island, would have made a mental note that the drying bean pot forebode impending weather. Baking beans were affected by changing atmospheric conditions, dried out quickly, requiring more additional water than usual if a front was moving on through. And too, they would have made a note to save leftover beans and pork fat to spread on toast in the morning. Once the bean pot was set in the cold back hall, the chore of readying their Sunday-go-to-meeting-clothes for church in the morning needed tending. They would not want to give an impression to the church congregation that they *be* a bunch of ragtags.

New England adhered to rigidly maintained mealtimes where everyone said grace before a mouthful was taken. Why! A pocket-watch could be set by the daily event. Usually, Sunday dinner stewed away on the back of the stove while they prayed and were preached to from the Good Book. Later in the day, a modest supper was served at six in the evening. It signified the end of their day of rest, one in which hard labor yielded to the *"Thou shalt not"* law of the Commandments, one that capitulated to the blue-laws laid down by the State, which ruled that all business come to a stand still on Sabbath Day.

That particular Saturday evening would have been unremarkable for Maria once she bedded-down the babies, three year old Josephine, Tony Jr. nearly two, and Alfred six months old. She had no church to *ready-for* in the morning. There was no Catholic Church on the island. The couple was likely to spend the evening in the lamp lit kitchen, not yet ready to settle in for the night as early as the other islanders. Their inner time clock remained aligned to siestas at noon, last meal at nine PM, and bedtime at midnight, a predisposition that was built into their marrow and passed on through the genes. In houses up and down Garfield Street, islanders digested the newspaper. The weather column in the last edition reported: *"A slight disturbance"*, in Michigan moving southeast *"with a fall of barometer of two tenths of an inch."* Another depression coming in from the Gulf of Mexico was moving to the South Atlantic coast. The report said that the conditions *may* result in a heavy storm. [xxxviii]

With that, they'd bank the kitchen cook-stove, seeing that enough wood was chopped to last the inclement period. The entire island community was so inclined, because no one wanted problems at the height of a storm. Well-water iced over much too heavily for the drop of an oaken bucket to break-through, leaving only one source—the newly fallen snow. Kettles filled with snow lined the counter; others congregated on the stove, melted down for bathing and dishes. Moisture from the slow steaming pots cut the dry air of the cold, wintry night.

In Portland, a crew on a cargo ship went in search for the ship's mascot, stem to stern, high and low for a cat that had taken up residence aboard, one that regularly sailed with them. It deserted, had jumped ship. [xxxix]

On Saturday night in Boston, passengers paid the dollar fare and boarded the elegant side-wheeler *Portland* for the nine-hour trip up the coast to Portland, Maine. She pulled away from India Wharf and left on her normal seven o'clock run. Some say the departure flew in the face of good judgment. At that moment, not many in New England were aware of the impending convergence of two large storms about to bear down on an unsuspecting populace. A large storm had developed over the Great Lakes and was now making its way East on a collision course with a Northeaster that had gathered enormous strength as it slammed up the Eastern coast from Cape Hatteras. The resulted convergence of the two systems formed an immense low pressure that caught New England unawares.

In spite of the high winds, by 9:30 Saturday night the *Portland* reached a point off Cape Ann where a lighthouse-keeper on Thatcher's Island saw her before the gale set in full force. Captain Ruben Cameron of the fishing schooner, *Grayling*, last sighted her at midnight north east of Thatcher's Island. *It is surmised that her possible plans were to head back, bypass the unforgiving shoreline of Massachusetts Bay, and seek the lea of the Cape Cod hook.*[xl]

***

Before the storm made its true presence known, out at sea, other hidden dramas were played out in the fishing grounds as the storm swept into the Gulf of Maine. Late that same Saturday afternoon the young Ricker brothers, Robert and Charles stood on the deck of a fishing schooner warily eyeing the clouds coming in from the southwest. They ruminated over the clear indications of an impending *nahsty-blow*. Robert directed that the dories be retrieved, stacked and lashed on deck. Seasoned to bad conditions he knew better than to batter his men and the vessel in an attempt to make it to shore, ergo, they would ride it out as they had done before. Most vessels that went-down did so in an attempt to make shore in bad weather. Schooners were strong and able vessels with a capacity for with-standing most anything, including *No'theasters,* as was the crew, but as the system moved closer, Ricker's barometer gave notice of an unbelievable event. If the reading *be-true*, they were in for a terrible ordeal. The barometer plummeted to an extreme, a foreshadowing for the young captain that this one was *comin' in a hell and a hoopin'*. So under the circumstances, Ricker had the crew batten down the boat for mountainous seas. They'd carry only the storm staysail—that is if the winds didn't go over sixty-five. Everything on or about the boat that could move, would, unless wedged-in or tied-down, which included a man on deck.

***

Back on Long Island, water in the hand-blown glass barometers climbed quickly up the delicate glass necks, bubbling down onto the drip pans at their bases, an inaudible occurrence that would *not* have gone unnoticed. Most assuredly, it would have been taken-in with a wary eye. Lace curtains tended to billow from the searching winds; a sure sign that the shutters should be pulled closed to keep the wind and the cold at bay—if, in fact, a family had shutters. Unmindful of the late hour, a man might take to the back door stoop under a swirl of snow, light a pipe and ponder skyward for a bit before catching a few hours of sleep. As with every night, this was a chance moment to throw a few more nuggets of coal or sticks of wood on the fire for good measure. The last chore before climbing the stairs was to haul a

49

rug up against the doorsill in order to keep the snow from eking in around the sill, from collecting in diminutive drifts just inside the door. Sleep would be restlessly acquired, for in the early hours of Sunday morning the wind struck the Maine coast with a blast, a blinding snowstorm that hit with a vengeance.

For several miles off shore, seas churned up foam in the high winds, a sign that spurred some to visit the shoreline, to tie their boats fast. At one a.m. Sunday, the chief of the weather bureau ordered the storm Northeast signals *"be hoisted."* The most catastrophic of November gales in New England's history was upon them, and building force. Homes up and down the coast were *unroofed,* barns blew down, chimneys toppled, houses floated off foundations by tidal surges. New England residents were in grave jeopardy. Hundreds would perish in the tempest.[xli]

Families hunkered down while deep howling winds washed over the island during the darkness, an unsettling din for those sequestered in their own homes. Gusts shook the rafters, and tore at the roofs, resulting in a fair amount of floor pacing throughout the night by those dwelling within. For the second time in one decade Maria and Antonio experienced nature in an extreme, an awesome power, and an intimidating reminder of those larger laws set down by the universe.

Heavy snowfall changed into hard-driving, horizontal sheets of mixed ice and heavy snow, the type that stuck to tree branches and weighted them to the ground. Many toppled under the burden of nature's harsh pruning device. The same sticky snow would accumulate on the rooftops in weighty drifts, adding to the anxiety. An elderly neighbor, living alone, would have to be checked upon at daybreak. This was a given.

Salt spray, lifted from the cresting waves, rode the wind to saturate the island. High tide, the critical period for everyone on the seaboard joined with its ally, the tidal surge, in playing the turbulent game. The ocean's excessive power and unbridled wrath tossed boulders about like marbles in the thunderous wave action, and as though rancid tasting, wooden lobster traps, and mounds of debris were spit far up onto the upper reaches of

Andrew's Beach.[29] *Were someone able to stand at the top of Rohr's Hill, an unlikely event at the height of the storm, they would have witnessed surging water lapping at its base, an uncommon occurrence in the history of the island, but one noted in storms of a much lesser intensity.*

***

In the early morning hours of Sunday Ricker's sixty-foot vessel was riding the same seas as was the doomed side-wheeler, *Portland,* relegating the crew to be unwilling participants in the fight of their lives. At this point, all sails were lowered, because no canvas could stand in a *whole gale* gone amuck. Fire in the potbelly stove below-deck was presumably vulnerable to water that washed down the stack, snuffing the coals. Air, full of ice, forced them to double and triple-layer woolen clothes. In the cramped sleeping quarters the men braced themselves so as not to crash into the overhead and it is a given that they grabbed onto some sisal, tied themselves into the bunks so as to prevent being thrashed to pieces.

Up on deck Ricker worked to keep her bow into the waves, having reinforced his efforts early on by setting off a sea anchor[30] that he hoped would keep her end-on and headed into the seas. Secured at the helm, held hostage and at the mercy of building seas created by those, God awful, deafening winds, there was little a man could do but to count every seventh wave and brace for it. They swore that the seventh wave was always bigger than the other six, but gave no explanation for the superstitious overtones. *At that point, it may have served them better had they had a seventh son of a seventh son aboard.*

These were young and hearty men in their twenties, but the rugged, steady winds, and hours of constant pounding jarred their bodies and jolted their stomachs up into their gullets. Hewie Newcomb was convinced that they were going to die and

---

[29] By the 1940s, Andrew's Beach was renamed Southside Beach.

[30] Sea anchor – (Drift sail) On a sailing ship exposed to the wind, if a sea anchor is set forward, made fast by a hawser, the vessel moves to the leeward faster than the sea anchor. The resistance brings the vessel's head to the wind.

was harassed unmercifully for verbalizing his fear, a castigation that other crewmembers inflicted on him, without one sting of conscience. Cousin Hewie had to be careful lest he be considered a Jonah. Sinking was not what Ricker had set out to do on this trip.

No one slept; all were on edge, and frozen to the core. The entire crew was on *watch and watch*, which called for half the crew to be on deck, half below, in short rotation. Thank God for the short rotation or they would have frozen had they not moved about. Within the whiteout conditions, the air was full of ice, the wind coming from the northeast, gusting to over seventy miles an hour. Brother Charles kept a vigil on deck alongside Robert, mindful that either could be knocked overboard or freeze in their boots. Words bellowed, one to the other, were snatched away by the din, by winds that reached force twelve.

Visibility shut down to zero. Mountainous waves mercilessly pitched the schooner from one to another. She strained to make it over the crests of the waves, only to shudder and crash down the backside of another watery mountain. Ricker's foremost concern was pitch polling end for end, or breaching the never-ending walls of water, both of which the vessel came near to doing too many times. She brazenly tempted the elements while Robert's instinct and adrenaline worked to keep her righted, but he actually had no control of their destiny; all were now pawns of a *Divine Superintendence*—and they knew it.

Thirty-hours crept by at a snail's pace, an eternity until the conditions finally began to moderate, and although the wind subsided, the seas remained riled. Exhaustion drove some to sleep, but only for short kinks. They likely awakened to a sense that their inner-time-clock had been spent, used up a *dite* more than they wished it had.

***

Inconceivable as it may seem, once daylight arrived, islanders living close to the shore bundled up and with heads into the wind ventured out at the height of the storm to parts of the island overlooking the water. Those with an impulse for drama went to the backshore, where traditionally the *most* drama took place. Despite the whiteout conditions, this seemingly foolhardy constitutional was a must for some, and actually treated with a great deal of circumspect. These were prudent people who knew their limits, knew that the island was not going to wash away, and knew exactly where to witness the most dramatic scenes being played out around them. Nature did not disappoint them.

Though the drumbeat of menacing music, today we chart storms on the television, from which a reporter dramatically broadcast warnings to evacuate the islands, stay indoors, buy batteries, be in a fright, and especially—to stay tuned to this channel. Notwithstanding—I will wager that in the next big, bad, tempest—standing high on a bluff, out on the back shore of each of the bay islands libertines will continue the age-old introspective—quiet witnesses to the irascible side of Mother Nature. It is her generous dose of actuality—an age-old elementary reality check.

***

For those who were capable of getting to the Franklin Wharf in Portland, the overdue status of the *Portland* had nervous relatives in a panic. The downed lines of communication from Boston threw up a deafening silence while the New England coast was pummeled for a good part of two days. Everything was socked-in, brought to a standstill by the snow and ice that encapsulated the region beneath its high drifts, a storm that physically rearranged the coastline, destroyed a city's worth of man-made structures, and ultimately changed the life's path of a legion of people.

At Simington Cove, a fleet of eight vessels hove-in from the storm, but by Monday morning was pared down to a fleet of one at anchor. The others were at the bottom. From Sunday, three a.m. to Monday, three a.m. seventeen inches of snow fell, while in New York they were measuring it by the foot. Monday afternoon, the Portland newspaper reported the overdue status, and the feared sinking of the *Portland*.[xlii]

The side-wheeler made it to the Cape, but not to safety. At five a.m. on Sunday morning a life saving station heard four faint blasts of a ship whistle, a distress call. The *Portland's*

53

white oak and hackmatack structure was in all probability now terribly compromised as she continued to pitch battle with the adversarial wind and the angered sea. The grand lady was lost in the onslaught—as were all one hundred ninety-two souls aboard. A gold pocket watch that was found on one of the recovered bodies had stopped at ten o'clock—the approximate time that all was lost.

No one survived to describe the final, harrowing moments, yet anyone who has sailed on mountainous seas will be inclined to fill in the spaces. The ever-present law of opposites most assuredly rode the waves in tandem, heroism with cowardice, level heads along side of the panic stricken, and the hopeful in the company of those in despair. Astonishingly, in that type of vacuum, heroism, composure, and faith surfaces much more often than does cowardice, panic and despair—cropping up where it is least expected. Human nature has a solid history of an extraordinary capacity under the worst case scenarios. Hence, one could almost guarantee that there were individuals on the "Portland," who were able to look into the face of mortality, and through pure selflessness, wrap a fellow shipmate in solace—up until the last. The "common man" is anything but common. On the contrary, he is a mosaic of complexities, a doctoral candidate from the school of the "Divine Superintendence."[31]

* * *

Communicating to each other with an economy of words and hand signals, Ricker's crew bandied back and to, astonished that it all held together, and that they were all still alive. Each one harkened back to the way the vessel thrashed and pounded, but especially about the strength and intensity of the storm. It was a *Christer*, they so named it; not as a cuss, but because of the fair amount of prayer that was probably sent up

---

[31] www.noaanews (Story 9716) In August of 2002, one hundred and four years after the sinking, NOAA located the *Portland* with a ROV (remotely operated vehicle), three miles north of Cape Cod in Stellwagen Bank National Marine Sanctuary, where she had settled in her final berth—beneath the wrath of the November Gale of 1898.

for serious consideration. Winds finally shifted into the Northwest, and only then were they able to secure the deck and affect necessary repairs.

Although they were ragged and worn down, as soon as the wind allowed, the vessel was rigged to go under sail. Thrown miles off course, Ricker had to mark time until the trailing clouds passed over, to get a fix on the sun, to re-establish the boat's position. Interestingly, in spite of the misery that they had endured in the past thirty-hours, their greatest concern actually had more to do with the families back on the island, and the distress that each household was experiencing. *It would have been in their make-up to think in those terms.*

Chebeague, too, had endured its share of the storm's wrath, and to compound the state of affairs, they were worried sick about the unknown fate of the island's fishing fleet. *Chebeaguers* haunted the East End Point, each wanting to be the first to sight sails approaching Broad Sound, to be the bearer of good news. At the tender age of nineteen, Anniebelle,[32] Robert's wife of just eighteen months was far too young to be wearing widow's weeds. The storm plagued at her imagination as she grappled with the growing fear that their three-month old baby girl might never know her father.

A considerable amount of time would elapse before families knew for certain whether the schooners had survived the *seas*; therefore, it was vital that the crew make way for Chebeague lest they walk in on their own memorial service. It would not be the first time in the history of the island that an overdue fisherman appeared in the church doorway—just as the minister was making a rundown of his upstanding attributes—a living ghost made privy to his own epitaphic data.

Once the battered schooner was at its mooring in Coleman Cove, the men dispersed. On entering the kitchen door, one can be fairly sure that the family men hugged their wives a little tighter than usual, although it should be pointed out that they were not prone to let anyone see those flagrant shows of affection.

---

[32] Anniebelle - Annie Mabel Calder b. Sept 1879

Their old man, Stephen, had experienced some winners out there in his stone sloop days, but had never faced down a battering as severe as had they. All that he taught had come into play, but sound instincts, and sheer bravery sustained them through the worst of the worst, and although they survived to tell these stories for decades, this storm would wrest a measure of youthful infallibility from each of them.

All tolled, the fishing fleet finally set at their moorings on the *Westend*, welcomed back without fanfare, swapping stories with each other around the potbelly stove at the fish shacks, a scene of great long arms flailing in the air to describe their brush with mortality. Coastwise, countless vessels were lost in the storm and they were told that on Orrs Island the wind mowed a twenty-five foot swarth through two hundred yards of dense woods, a sign, it would seem, that inside the storm, an intense squall line also moved quickly through the area. [xliii]

Camaraderie was rarely shown by wordiness, but rather in a facial expression, a nod given as the duckbill visor was readjusted on the head, the quick strong grip of a handshake, or a *wump* on the back. Each man's strengths were as vital out there as was the timber of the vessel. Quietly listening to others, Robert's brother-in-law, Silas Calder,[33] reached over, opened the stove's door, picked a hot coal out of the burning nuggets with his callused fingers, laid it on his pipe until it was sufficiently lit, then deposited it back into the glowing embers. It took years of lobstering to create the thick, hard calluses on his hands, those tough enough to handle hot coals. For the most, it took years of harsh conditions to callus over the realities of fishing for a living. Hewie Newcomb met his own mortality in that storm, didn't much care for the likes of it, and never again went fishing.

They were a-breed-unto-themselves, faced Mother Nature right up front in the delivery of a continuous, grueling task, but it was not in them to tarry long ashore. Most required just enough time for the softness of their women, to make repairs, set on stores, and head back out. Just two days of hand lining from the dories would give up an acceptable yield. The seas were

---

[33] Silas Calder, brother to Anniebelle

becoming passable again—their thoughts turning away from the matters onshore, shifting instead towards the oracles in the sky, and the vicissitudes of the sea.

Today on the waterfronts and out on the many islands throughout Maine, the intent has not changed a particle—not a whit. The present day fleet of men on gill-netters and draggers carry on with a deeply infused audaciousness that invariably places them in the vice of adversity. It's built into their makeup, runs in the genes. Each pursuit between fishermen and the fish is a gamble; the clash between fishermen and the elements is an open-ended crusade.

***

High drifts of snow provided a perfect insulation for Antonio and Maria's bare bones home—likely, *a build-as-you-acquire-material* type of structure. Conjecturally, it was buried in drifts, with a narrow path shoveled to the street so that they could connect up street with old Sam Marston and his wife Lydia, or down street with Claudis and Adeline Isusi and their two girls. Bill and Martha Merrill were hard at it on the lower side of the Isusi house clearing a path to their horse, the well, the woodpile, and the

Horse driven snowplow

outhouse. Next door, Vincent Mountfort fortunately had two strong, older boys, Vincent Junior and Frank, at hand to dig them out. At some point, everyone on the street connected with each other. A blast of weather seemed to knit neighbors more closely together.

One might assume that nine months hence—up and down the entire northeastern seaboard, the birth statistics took a giant leap. Not surprisingly, before Long Island had shoveled out from under the avalanche of snow in December, Maria was with child again. More weather made-up on the heels of the *Gale*, which left a small window for work for anyone on the island. The job shoveling out ahead of the horse-plow was available for any able bodied man who was ready to take on the backbreaking task.

***

The national average income for a family of five, in order to simply subsist, was $1.36 a day.[xliv] Ponce expected Antonio to honor their agreement of '97, as well he should, the one in which he would pay Ponce two hundred dollars a year for three years, after which the property would become theirs. Antonio had to come up with fifty-five cents a day to honor the agreement, but by the spring of 1900, Ponce bought the property back from Antonio for one dollar, *and other considerations*. This strongly indicates that Antonio had either not earned enough income, or had shelled-out fifty-five cents a day for something else that he found to be of more value. [xlv]

Once the weather broke, Ponce began to develop properties, and over the years started several summer homes on Garfield Street, each one earmarked for summer rental. Angelo Louis and Matilda Althea[34] were Maria's fourth and fifth borne, respectively. By September of '02 the small bare bones home was filled to overflowing. The crunch was on. Antonio needed a new plan. By '03 Antonio put down his hammer and nails and turned to fishing for a living.

---

[34] Angelo Louis is the name on the birth certificate, though throughout his life, he went by the name Louie. Matilda was nicknamed Tillie.

3

... 🐟 Ole Deah & Ole Chum's 🐟 Grapevine

Every island has an Ole Deah and Ole Chum who've known each other since they were snot-nosed kids, who've been on the earth more years than their great grandchildren can count, and last they looked, betwixt them, are related to everyone on the island. If you've never met them, I must introduce you to the two old curmudgeons. Ole Deah never speaks a solitary word, never gets a word in edge-wise around his partner, Ole Chum. They enjoy a daily ritual get-together in front of the island store, in the same spots overlooking the comings and goings of the passenger boats, fishing boats, and anything that catches their interest. Their musings are based on fact—on how it actually was before there was electricity, cars, and phones. They are the island's "All Seeing Eye." Not much ever got by either one of them. Ole Chum does all the raving and ranting. He's finely honed the art, and is wicked good at it. Ole Deah puffs on his pipe, nods a great deal, and is a sounding board for his old friend. That's probably the reason they've been close partners for so long.

🐟 Fall 1903 🐟

"Told ya! Bound ta happen Ole Deah—BOUND ta happen! Cleave's Club is become some notorious since Napoleon Bonaparte Chase took it ovah. Ayuh, ayuh—he's a piece of work all right. Turned it into an open bar, then went and got raided on Friday night at 9:00 p.m. Alst I know is four Portland sheriffs strutted right up to the door and seized a half-barrel of beer—closed them down right there on the spot. Wun't he pissed! News spread fast enough. Everyone and their uncle knows they've been awash in liquor up there—sold more in that club than all others combined. Course—people's been havin' a hissy fit ovah it since he opened. Really now—that friggin' gamblin' was costin' a few some real money, yes suh—hard earned dollars. Hard earned!" [xlvi]

Summer's greenery faded into the earthy colors of fall's foliage and it was at its peak by the first day of October '03. The area's residents handed over the dollar-fifty it took to buy into a foliage trek to the White Mountains, to view it from the most spectacular of all vantage points. Other parts of Maine were blanketed in rural fairs, the first of August in Topsham, very popular and well attended, with more to come before the fair season ended. On the second of October, faithful followers jumped a train and headed west for the popular Fryeburg Fair.

At the dinner hour the following day, foliage was the furthest thing on the minds of a large number of foot passengers, or of little interest to the commuters sitting atop twenty-five horse-drawn vehicles, and most assuredly not paramount to the eight trolley cars worth of people collected on each side of the Portland Bridge. The gridlock was created by, and at the mercy of a sloop drifting broadside towards the draw, a bit of drama to take home for dinner table chat. Two majestic six-masted schooners had hove in at anchorage, a sight many might not have taken time to gander at had they not been a captive audience. Over there at the Randall & McAllister dock, they watched Light Ship #74 as she readied to head out in the morning, returning to its station after three months of overhaul leave. She was still taking on 10,000 gallons of fresh water and 75 tons of coal. Every seam had been caulked and tightened, her smokestack and reversing gear shortened, but her foghorn would be the most noted improvement. The old three-tone didn't cut it, evidently, didn't transcend the miles, but the newly installed single tone horn would be heard ten miles in any direction. It is doubtful that many, stuck on the bridge, had much interest in the ramifications and innuendoes of a single tone foghorn. Their collective interest lay in the eventual outcome of the derelict sloop.[xlvii]

Portland's City police arrested 259 people in the month of September, 169 of them for intoxication, and a dozen or so each for larceny, assault, and safekeeping. The remainder divided equally among deserters, truants, and those who ran away from home, which are all tantamount to the same thing. They hauled in the insane, the vagrant, the nightwalker, and those in danger of falling into vice. Evading trolley fares and uttering obscene words got a few an overnight in the pokey, and cheating by false pretenses, and keeping a disorderly house pulled in a few more. Portland's *finest* was busy. Several thousand soldiers assigned to the vicinity may have somewhat affected the lay of the land—so said the Police. [xlviii]

Church notes from Henrietta S. Cushing (Nee Dyer) [xlix]
1903

Weddings, twelve in all this past year, of which Charles MacVane married Lillian Doughty, Gott Doughty married Nettie Johnson, Ruben Doughty married Alice Blanchard, and Fred Ross married Nelly Johnson.

🐟 Ole Deah & Ole Chum 🐟

"Nother winter out from under us. Ju-das Priest! Wait 'til Ponce and the other hotel owners hear this one. Well, mister-man, those new regulations the Harpswell lopstamen drummed up ovah there are gonna smart some. Listen to this! [1] They made up an agreement startin' this very summah of '04. Listen now! Listen! From this point on, they wun't haul or sell lopstas under ten and one half inches, measurin' from bone of nose—to end of bone of middle tail flipper—fixed by law. Gwaaad! That's been on the books since 1895. Who ever paid attention to it anyhow? Know what it sounds like to me old stock? Someone in Augusta's 'bout ready to change them minimum measurements on us.[35] Mark my word—you wait and see. Hotels prefer steamin' up them small, undersized chicken lopstas at the clambakes anyway, y'know, the ones that cook up in a minute. They don't like 'em gawmy. Summer complaints won't care how

---

[35] Maine Lobster laws-1895 lobster laws defined legal minimum and maximum size regulations for lobsters. The law *was changed* in '07 to four and three-quarters, bone of nose to center of rear of body shell.

big they are, long as they get to go to a clambake. I'd wager it'll prubly start costin' 'em more than the twenty-five cents apiece. Ever think you'd see the day?

Got an ear full when I tooled down to Harpswell. Took a squint at the lay of the land over at Eagle Island. Lieutenant Peary, you know that fella that's been perambulatin' Greenland—well—his summer cottage is near to finished. Gave a lot of work to the locals. They're even usin' wood that's been washed ashore, as well as stuff hauled-in.[li] Only house on the island 'ceptin' for a small caretaker's dwellin'. A world of difference from that God forsaken, frozen terrain he's been lured to in the Arctic. Hauled back a ten-foot long narwhal horn from the last exploration—he did. First one ever seen in this country. Has it on display out there. Don't he bring back some of the damnedest rigs? [lii]

Rain's been persistent though, ain't it? Prubly is why they sunk that seventy-foot drain all the way down Garfield to Island Avenue to stop the washouts. Should drain away some of the excess. Land is squishy up above there—like some people I know—AND right thick with mosquitoes. Ain't seen nawthin' like it for years. Ayuh, they been wicked fierce all ovah the Bay.

One more rainstorm old tout and we're gonna see a riot Downfront. The whole-of-'em are complainin' 'bout rocks, washouts on roads 'n hills. Makes drivin' them buggies and wheelin' a mite treacherous. Hawses are having a hell of a time negotiatin' that hill over by Cushin's Pavilion.[36]

Mosquitoes 'bout carried us away at that baseball game over on Chebeague last month. Rain held off long enough for Long Island to tromp 'em. G. MacVane, E. MacVane, Henry and seven others—who wun't MacVanes got 'em eight to five on Chebeague's own turf no less. Good bunch of ball players. Don't care what they say."

---

[36] Cushing's Pavilion stood where the VFW hall is now located.

62

Church notes from Henrietta...1904

~The Reverend Felix Powell's church was filled on Baptism day with the Clarke, MacVane, Doughty, Johnson, Wallace, and Horr families to name a few. The number of residents spiritually insured by baptism numbered seventeen. Four more couples were married, and six more residents died, two of which were children. [37]

~July 16th A Mr. Kennedy of New York was bathing on Saturday and was drowned.

~July 24th A child of Winfield Horr came very near being drowned on Sunday from a boat near the wharf.

~The residents bought a hearse.

~June Eight babies were born into the community including a daughter born the 22nd to Ruben and Alice Doughty.

~Little Merty Delmer born to Gott, and Nettie Doughty on the 25th

~And born to she who was Cassie Cushing, a daughter in August.

~July of '04 brought a terrific thunderstorm to the vicinity — doing a great deal of damage.

William Horr's house (down by the Methodist church) was struck by lightning and burnt to the ground. No one was injured.

After baling up a fair crop of hay, in the fall of '04, island and mainland farmers wailed into the fall plowing and ditching, put the final touch to the vegetable gardens, covered some over with hay, storing most of the vegetables in a root cellar. Parsnips, left in the ground, turned sweeter after the first deep frost, though by spring were too pulpy, good only for the cattle. The women, as usual, were out-straight canning and preserving. Their labor over

---

[37] Baptized: Mrs Alice Clarke, Edna Clarke, May Clarke, Elsie Clarke, Caddie Dorsey, Miss Adah Doughty, Lottie Fowler, George Griffin, Mrs Jennie Horr, Mr. Jacob Horr, Julia Keating, Addie MacVane, Lillian MacVane, Janie Wallace, Hattie Wallace, Raymond Wallace.

the wood cook stove had just started. Coastwise, sword fisherman also hauled in a bumper crop. The annual contest broke records with a single 530-pound catch, a second recorded at 500 pounds.

At sixty-six degrees, the weather stayed fair for the five thousand people who poured out onto Peaks Island for the Labor Day close-out, many of them from Boston and areas served by the Grand Trunk railroad. Peak's baseball game was nearly canceled, the other team a no-show leaving a quickly put-together ragtag team to play Peaks; the final score, Peaks—23, Ragtags—03. Though the island was buried in humanity, no scurrilous activities caught the attention of the extra police that were called in to service for the day. Visitors headed for the popular Gem Theater, which was running at full tilt before closing for the season. A troupe of bicyclist exhibited a *"startling"* routine in another area of the island, and the Boston Balloon Company made two parachute ascensions, one in the a.m., one p.m. But—where, in the whole of Casco Bay, did they scrummage up the *"serpent"* that was blown into bits by a mine-throwing expert? *Did anyone get a squint at the creature before it met its demise?* [liii]

Ole Deah 🐟 🐠 Ole Chum
Labor Day – 1904

"Finest kind suh—finest kind! Warm for Labor Day. Be happy when they stop that infernal dredgin' for that new steamer. Be impossible to keep it dredged enough for the *Machigonne*. She's too deep—keeps groundin' out. Everyone knew she'd have truble comin' down the Diamond Roads,[38] 'specially at Threfethens. Don't it make me cringe to see her comin' when it's low tide—*right hairy* on a dreen. [liv] Been nice if management had asked the opinion of the down the bayers before they bought her, or at the very least conferred with their own captains. Daow! Don't know if they could lump together an ounce of common sense between the whole-of-'em.

---

[38] Diamond Roads – Channel between Peaks Island and the two Diamond islands.

Went and lost a good man this August of '04—Claudis Isusi. Well thought-of by ev'ryone, 'n not just sayin' that—just cause he's dead. Ponce i'll miss 'im awful. Been with 'im since dirt was invented. Some say Ponce brung 'im ovah from Spain. Ayuh, down heah since '80, anyway. Gotta go a far piece to replace a man like that.

God, ain't that's one handsome schooner out there? Handsome! The yacht *Pinafore,* I think they call her—b'longs to that big Civil War General, what's his name? Ayuh, that's it—Chamberlain—ole Joshua of the 20th Maine. [lv] *Man of the Cloth* wun't he? S'pose that bunch of fishermen and lumberjacks he had in tow fightin' them Alabama farmers had to tone down their profanities a mite. He'd be in his mid seventies by now, wouldn't he? Ole war wound is still plaguin' 'im, you say? Look at the pile of people he's got aboard. I'd guess that he's goin' ta Lower Goose—likes it down there for some reason. Read somewhere he's thinkin' of buildin' it up—resort of some kind. He'd best take a slow tack down through there. A big mess of whale's been rusticatin' out 'round the bay. Late for whale to be in these parts ain't it? Whata ya 'spose is holdin' 'em heah?

Awful tired today. Need some of that *Swamp-root* they's selling uptown to get me goin.' Been up since four o'clock helpin' with that conflagration n' came home lookin' like a chimley sweep. Right—ayuh, the old Latham place, right up in back of the Fern Dale cottage. Henry Horr's owned it for some time now. Nah! She was so far gone they just let her burn herself out, right to the last clabbid. Tough news to hand 'em on a holiday. Nope, nope—they haven't a clue yet. He and the wife are still out there on Bustins enjoyin' the end of the summer. Well suh! Before we go any futher, shouldn't someone tool out there and let Hen know his home burnt down to the ground last night? You ain't gonna let he and the Mrs show up and find it that way are ya?

Take these off my hands—'nother pile of them church notes for your ole-lady. I'm goin' home—need a short kink. We'll bunch up later."

Church notes from Henrietta...1904

~Sept 5th   Henry Horr's house burned.

~Sept 15th Orin Horr's house burned.

~Little Minnie Horr was baptized in September.

~Minnie Horr [39] died on Monday the 26th.

~October - Revival services were held at the church for the entire month with five ministers on hand to share in spreading the "Word."

~A Gloucester fisherman ran ashore on Crow Island bar. Boat badly damaged.

~Nov - The five-month old child of Ruben Doughty died.

Halloween put the community to a test in the fall of '04, was the proving ground for hobgoblins to see just how far they could take mischief making. In the quiet of the night, porch steps were *besmeared* with rotting cabbages. Gates, somehow, unhinged themselves, and then found their way into the bushes. Dead cats were hung on doorknobs. In Portland, pandemonium broke loose with bell pulling, pea shooting and—several more dead cats hanging from doorknobs. Uptown, a gang from Munjoy Hill rolled barrels away from a construction site and stole a hokeypokey cart[40] staving it all to pieces in their romp down Myrtle Street. In a session of the Municipal Court, Judge Reynolds charged four boys with—playing football on Sunday. Each was fined one dollar. Dead cats and malicious mischief did not land them in hot water, but messing with those Sunday blue laws was serious business. *One has to wonder where and when the practice of hanging dead cats on doorknobs began—and when it ended. It does seem odd that the clock would run out for so many cats—all on one night.* [lvi]

Though the poor-farm produced tons of hay and produce, *Portland's Almshouse* had run its course. A Committee on Public Buildings was days from opening the new city-owned facility for

---

[39] Minnie Horr was an infant.

[40] Hokeypokey carts were ice cream vendor wagons.

the poor. Unfortunately, those connected with the *Almshouse*[41] were seen as *"utterly out of sympathy with the new building—that they cannot do the good work in it—therefore, will retire, resign, or run away."*

Portland's City Fathers appointed a Committee on Smoke to work through an ordinance against the dense pall that hung over the city, a combination of air rancid with sulphur from coal burning stoves, trains, and wood smoke, then took time to put out bids for lighting on Long Island. Special officers in the Portland Police Department marked an increase of young girls, as young as fourteen, charged with street-walking at an unseemly hour down on Commercial Street. One was locked up in the lodging room *"for deep meditation"*, after a fatherly lecture upon the evils of waywardness. The backside of the coin to progress and industry had sashayed through the door and too had settled-in. [lvii]

Presidential election rhetoric saturated the newspapers, making no bones in its front-page editorials about the paper's leanings, sniping at the conservative Roosevelt in each edition. The day before the election, in which nationally, fourteen million were expected to vote, the *Eastern Argus* slipped one more positive statement in for its favorite candidate with headlines: *"Landslide for Judge Alton Parker—who should sweep the country. Sure to have 273 electoral votes."* The following day, the headlines read: *"Election went as indicated on surface. President Theodore Roosevelt—who swept the country yesterday."* Sweep? Swept? Sure to have 273 electoral votes! It surely took more than a dustpan's worth of votes to make up the difference between the two contradictory headlines. *The reporter, who initially coined a landslide for Judge Parker, was obviously in denial.*

***

---

[41] Almshouses were privately owned poorhouses.

🐟 Ole Deah & Ole Chum 🐟
Puttyin' Around

"I see this fall where that shipbuildin' company went belly-up in South Portland, abandoned that four masted schooner our own Capt'n Stewart was havin' built. He reared right up—renounced all claims to it. Wasn't gonna get stuck with a half-built vessel. Don't blame 'im. Buildin' so many with steam engines these days that in time he'll prubly not be sorry. It's an omen for sailin.' Day's comin' to an end, I say.

Take a squint ovah there. Considerable comin's and goin's at Ponce's Hotel—just opened for the nineteen *and* 05 season. Are you payin' attention to me? Added a casino, bowlin' alley, dancin', pool, and billiards this year. Gamblin's gettin popular again. Tryin' to draw 'em away from Cushin's Pavilion. I dunno if theys gamblin' up there too. If there was, old Ignatius would roll over in his grave and old Ezekiel just might come right through the roof 'n Charles will have ta pay for the shingles.

Hear how much Ponce is gonna charge for that eight-room cottage he built up the road above the bak'ry? The one 'cross from the hotel. *A hundred twen-ty-five dollars* a season! Gotta give the ole Midas credit—but—the twenty-fifth of June, John Bickford opened his new place, Casco Breeze House—built it right in spittin' distance of Ponce's—has a café—no set meal time like the others—serve ya any time of the day. Heard he even built in a toilet closet. Tacked on a fish market too. Opens July first. Won't make any money off the locals—that's for damn sure. Fish guts—toilet closet—ledge—phew! Air's gonna be some ripe over there 'long about July. We'll hav'ta appoint a committee on stench b'fore the summer's ovah.

Speakin' of appointin', wunt that a smart move hirin' island boys as summer police. Snagged Asa Littlejohn, one of the Horrs, William, and two of them Woodbury boys, Edward and James. Good choice locals. Specially talented if they were hellers themselves. 'Course I ain't intimatin' they was. Imagine it'll get sticky arrestin' a family member, and it'll come to pass. Some implant from Portland ain't gonna have the inside straight on everybody. Them boys have grown up into it, have the cut on it all. Smart move—yes suh! Wicked smart move!

Jasus! That was a little too close for comfort, wun't it? Scared the hell out of me. William Merrill better think twice 'bout keepin' that high-spirited hawse of his. Nearly bought-it when that thing took a fright. Went overboard down off Ponce's, hauled William with it. Trapped him under the wagon. Just like a tomb. 'Nother of them Woodbury boys, Frank, and that pint sized Spaniard, Tony Gawmez[42] dove in—plucked William out—secured the wagon while the hawse swam ashore.

Not gonna believe this—two hours later, the hawse did it again, only this time it went down over the embankment. What do you s'pose keeps spookin' that poor devil? Gotta hand it to the creature—freed himself up of the wrecked wagon, swam ashore, galloped away, at least 'til it ran out of land on the far *Eastend*. Them two children playin' in the road were lucky mister-man. Jumpt out of harm's way just in the nick of time. You don't s'pose it had anything to do with that earthquake cummin' on? Wouldn't be surprised! [lviii] You feel it? I was up and about when it hit at the crack of dawn—bout 5:15. Lasted only about ten seconds, but sure did rattle things. Ayuh! Cut quite a swarth I heah. Well now, you look at the way these islands are all set in a row, right on the edge of a million-year-old lateral rift. Say they got reports from Kitt'ry—way up into Banger. Were plagued here with eight of 'em in the 1700s. Only one reared its head in the last century, heavy shock back in '58. Animals will let us know if we're to worry.

Peary's about ready to make way again to find the Pole. He's sure hellbent. Ya know, he hired Tony Gawmez. Nope—he's taken' his caretaker, Percy as cook n' is' leavin' Gawmez to caretake Eagle. [lix] Tony's been pesterin' Peary to go on this one, and there's Maria with them six kids and another biscuit in the oven. What the hell's he thinkin' of? Aah—he needs a slat right up the side of the head. Peary prubly told him to go pound sand anyway. Ayup—Gawmez already moved ovah to Eagle with the

---

[42] Antonio Gomez

whole kit and caboodle—Maria, kids, and chickens.

Lookie! City officials showed up—finally! Call themselves the Committee on Lights—a little dim if you ask me—like most politicians, always givin' us what they want, rather than what we actually need. Gotta dog 'em—Dog 'em! Lookin' at whether the good-barrister Looney needs a gas light in front of his place. Another would do some good on Beach Avenue, and three's needed awful bad on the whole stretch of Fern. Fern's the one that leads to Fowler's Beach. Damn right! Dark as a pocket at night—all those pine trees—makes the hair stand right up on the back of my neck.

Speakin' of Fowlers—back in June they removed the Ocean Club to Judge Gould's house on Mount Hunga, right up there beyond the beach. Rhor is buyin' the old clubhouse. What's that all about? Why do they call it Mount Hunga?[43] All's I know is word of mouth since a time aftah old Ignatius Cushin'[44] settled in the mid-1700s—less than a smatterin' of people here at the time. Some family starved to death up there durin' a hard spell of winta. Had to have been a massive amount of snow for that to happen. Hard to imagine livin' out heah in those days. Mount Hungah's always given off a different kind of quiet up there. Ayup! Different kind of quiet.

Run that by me again. Gracious—you don't say! Bathin' by the moonlight at Andrew's Beach—hah! Gettin' a little risqué ain't they? Them devils—skinny-dippin'! Ain't the first, and dasst I say, won't be the last.

You had Henrietta's notes in your pocket since WHEN? Ain't you numma than a pounded thumb? Don't care if they's old. Don't want to miss any juicy news."

---

[43] Mount Hunger is sometimes referred to as *Jerry's Point*. Actually, Jerry's Point is on the south side of Mount Hunger. Per Susan Longanecker, Jerry's Point is named for Jeremiah Griffin.

[44] Ignatius Cushing...brother to Ezekiel who purchased the land in the 1700s...ancestors to Susan (Cushing) Longanecker. Susan and her husband are the proprietors of a bed and breakfast—"The Cushing Homestead" PO Box 266 – Long Island, ME 04050

Henrietta's Long Island Church notes
January 1, 1905

~January first. Beautiful and warm.

~ January 11th Hattie went to Boston.

~Warren Woodbury very sick at this writing with typhoid fever - he is at he Eye and Ear Infirmary in Portland.

~Seven children were born, in September:

~To the wife of Reuben Doughty, a son born.

~To the wife of George Morton, a son.

~Five couples married, nineteen were baptized and the Reverend Powell is having repairs on the Church to enlarge the main room. Two week revival in October.

~Five islanders died, including one baby.

~Warren B. Woodbury succumbed to typhoid. The Portland Police attended in body to the number of 30, as the deceased was a member of the force.

~Little 10-year old daughter of Mr. Williams from spinal trouble.

~April 2nd First run day-boat on Casco Bay Line.

~April 23rd Harpswell line - First Sunday- boat.

~May - Mr. Winfield Horr built a grass fire near his orchard. It spread with great force, got into the woods. They got it under control at night. In the morning of the 11th it sprang up into the woods. They had to call for assistance from the City. The fireboat #7 and water boat and a tug came. They worked from 2 o'clock until after 7at night.

~June - Etta, daughter of Edwin Clark fell down stairs and broke her arm.

~The Day Brothers have erected a building at the West End for their popcorn business.

🐟 Ole Deah & Ole Chum 🐟
Summer's End

"Hear me out now! Last year, in "04, William Horr's house burnt down from a lightenin' strike. Then last September, Henry Horr's place went down, then Orrin Horr's. Now it summah of '05 'n Winfield had a grass fire get away from him. Cryin'shame. After readin' those church notes 'bout the Horrs, I'm thinkin' they'd best start collectin' beach rocks and start buldin' their houses with good ole solid stone and mortar. A pail of water and a broom is all that is between any of us and a runaway grass fire. Knock on wood. Heard that came from sailing ships at sea. Sailors had nothing between them and the deep briny so they knocked on wood for good luck. Ain't it odd how something like that carries on.

Committee vote on lights went quick enough, didn't it? Noticed, they took care of their stomachs first—dined at Cushin's hotel—prubly lopstahs. Ya know the Indians usta use lobsters for fertilizer in their gardens and ta bait hooks? The old timers considered them "poverty food" and served them to prisoners, indentured servants and children. Ain't a speck of poverty in that Committee on Lights, is they? Eventually got to the business at hand—eventually. [lx]

Who's that over there at the Cushin' Casino?[45] Follow my finger t'where I'm pointin'. Yep. Must be Charles rebuildin' that chimley of his—blew down in a heavy gale last winta. Poor man's had some awful luck with blow-downs. Squall came up and blew some bathhouses away too. Seems ole Charlie's got his-own black cloud, but his is full of wind.

Look—look! There goes the committee on lights. Fetch a blat at 'em b'fore they get out of earshot. They might like to take a quick walk up to the barn to see the new twin calves born to Cushin's cow. First twins ever born on the island—to a cow. Precious! You seen 'em yet? Awful cunnin'!

---

[45] Cushing's Casco Bay House opened in the late 1880s

72

Roll your hip boots up Ole Deah. Palaverin's dense t'night. A-w-w! They's all agog about one single local steamer that carried four thousand people last week. And whhh-y-y-y are they fussin' so about derelict hulls becomin' such a menace along the coast — as though they'll fetch up on any of them real soon. Now—they got their undies in a knot 'cause the apple crop's gonna be light. Wish that's all I had for worries, though I have ta agree. Really — them dried apples will never turn out the same kind of pie as fresh apples Ole Deah—don't care what anyone says.

Take this newspaper off my hands. Filled with more crap than I wanta digest. Tellin' us that a hobby can lead to madness and that heart disease is brought on by nightmares. They ever stop to think that any sleepin' brain ain't gonna do well if the heart ain't circalatin' properly? The way they write 'em, it's hard to tell the real news from the advertisements. All they're doin' is hawkin' some snake-oil. ^{lxi}

Don't know 'bout you but, I'm 'bout ready for a little mug-up.[46] Been remiss gettin' over to Day's Spa, that new stoah Arthur built right next to Clarke and Griffin's. Might have somethin' new we've never partook-of. You interested? Well! Get the lead out, will ya? I'm starvin'."

---

[46] Mug-up - A friendly cup of coffee, a snack.

*View of "Down front" from
Ponce's Landing*

Chapter

4

...Rite of Passage

Eagle Island, Maine
Present Day

Eagle Island is one of those outer islands, seems out there, all by itself. It's made up of high bluffs, a stand of trees, a small beach, and precipitous, craggy ledges, and measures possibly one quarter of a mile long—would take little time to perambulate. From it one can make out Harpswell in the distance, other islands, including Cliff and Chebeague, and takes in the great long stretch of open-sea out to the *East'd*. Its claim to fame was to have been the summer residence of Rear Admiral Robert Peary, the man who discovered the North Pole.

It was early fall, a rather blustery, but lovely September day for the trip from Portland down the bay on the local tour boat, *Fish Hawk*. Young Captain Frappier eloquently spun the history of the bay through the speaker system, and I sat in total disbelief that I was on a tour boat. Islanders don't go on tour boats.

My older sister hatched this plan, presented it to me as a birthday gift. She discovered that I'd never traveled to Eagle Island to visit the Peary Museum—and for fifty-seven years I'd managed to play hooky from a rite of passage through which everyone else in the family participated. Of the twenty-five tourists aboard, only Ann Marie and I had knowledge that for a short period, after the turn of the century, Eagle was also the summer and winter home of some not quite so famous adventurers, our grandparents, Antonio and Maria Gomez.

We sailed on by Long Island, the island on which were raised—where the community, towards which we continue to have a boundless affinity, abides. We reconnect with them a couple times a year—similar to a bungee jumper who springs back to the point from which he originally vaults—a good way to recondition our frayed tethers. We were heading into an area that we rarely, if ever, traveled—either as children, or as adults. Mind you—it is only a few miles from Long Island to Eagle, as the crow flies, but it seems so far out to sea, and so very isolated. Though the sun deposited its warmth all over the bay, the wind was up, covering the water with cat paws. Ann Marie and I attempted to converse, but the pitch of the engine chewed up our words, reason enough to sit quietly and absorb our surroundings. She smiled each time I turned her way; she has such a beautiful smile—one that entices reciprocity.

I took-in an infinite amount, as would be expected of someone that was raised in the area, which created a mental dialogue for an audience of one. Coming around the *Eastend* point of Long Island, I looked across to Chebeague at a big, white, house on the western end, a benchmark of sorts for most of us, or is it the owner, the venerable fisherman who lives there, who is the benchmark? For a good portion of his years, that man would be right over in that direction—right there at Chandlers Cove— making certain that the *Sirius* was right up to snuff—*Sirius,* the brightest star in the constellation, and she *was* one of the brightest fishing boats in the bay in the fifties. He went out in some of the most God-forsaken weather! 'Course, she was bigger than most, near to fifty foot. S'pose his wife was jealous of her? Nah! A smart woman never competes with a boat. I shut out the whine of the engine, the barely audible dissertation by young Captain Frappier, and switched to a comparative thing between the present moment, and a late summer day in 1905, when our grandparent's traversed the same waters towards Eagle.

Today's chop would have been a bit much for a dory, and I wondered how long it took them in whatever condition they chose to make way that day. It may not have been a dory, but instead Admiral Peary's motorboat, though it would not be in Antonio's makeup to be on an island without his own form of transportation. He may have been short and snarly, but he was also wiry, and as tough as a pitch knot. Their approach to Eagle Island was the same as ours, and unlike the sprawling changes on land over time, the passage of ninety-five years between our separate voyages hadn't changed the seascape but by a fraction.

What they saw, we saw, although—out there, on *The Hook*, on the bar between Little Chebeague and Great Chebeague I scanned for the lone oak tree—old Wentworth Ricker's red oak tree. It was gone! A wonder, I thought, that it survived the near two hundred years it did. Hurricane Gloria decapitated it. Moments before it happened, Mr. Ballard, then owner of the property was standing a few feet away, scanning the furious skies for a low flying jet—until he realized that the low, wailing roar that he heard mingling with an eerie scream was coming from forty-feet up the trunk in the massive oak's branches. At that moment, the entire top snapped off the trunk and was carried off in the powerful arms of the hurricane winds. The century's old lookout, obviously, did not go very quietly into the night. Without it standing sentinel, it was somewhat akin to having a button missing on a shirt.

I remember back when I had all of the energy in the world, when claming *The Hook* came easily. The haul was always choice—that is, if the Chebeaguers didn't catch us on their territory. Someone invariably sauntered off the big island—out onto the bar at just about the time the huge hen clams began to show up on the underside of each clump of mud. They were polite about it, as were we and because a young spark, by the name of Ricker, accompanied me—the mess of clams that we had dug up to that point went with us on the row back to Long.

Actually, the trip from Portland on the *Fish Hawk* was a forty-five minute cool-down from today's accelerated world, and short, moderate swells batted at the tour boat all the way out through the sound, right up until it pulled into the dock at Eagle Island. There was a strong likelihood the island would shed some illumination on the volumes of family narratives and embellishments that had been passed onto us, enough to fan the flames of inquisitiveness. The boat danced into the wharf and deposited us into another place in time, or was I just being notional?

Not middle aged anymore, *unless I live to be a hundred and fourteen*, I was old enough to feel relatively connected to my grandparent's era. Islands hold onto vestiges and remnants of past eras as change ever so slowly filters into the fabric of a community. We may even cover ourselves in those remnants from time to time so as to be able to relate to another generation's ethics and ideals—which is exactly what I did.

A seasonal shift came on the breeze, a particular fragrance of drying grasses, the sour smell of fallen leaves whetted by the rain, all of which mingled and drifted with the salt air. It is a discernible scent that triggers a process—one peculiar to islanders—a mental preparedness for *wintering*. The behavior has an eccentric overtone to it, but seems absolutely normal to one, who must live on an island, and it should be added, a trait from which we *are rarely* ever weaned—no matter where the domicile.

Each island is enveloped in a different aura, yet this one had an air of familiarity about it, probably because everything was grey and weathered, as are so many structures that have long been exposed to the elements. Eagle stood still in time, totally untouched by the advancing years, the lay of the land still whispering of Mrs. Peary's horticultural endeavors. Here was an example of horticultural genealogy at its finest, pedigreed peonies, familial foxgloves, *begets* from a century of self-propagation.

By nature, islands are onerous, terribly exacting, and necessitate considerable effort. Living on them is the same as having a relationship with a fascinating friend, but one with difficult traits. Because the relationship is rich and entertaining, difficult traits are overlooked. When the rapport is positive, it is a dedicated alliance between the rock—the stock—and their heirs and assigns forever. Difficulties seem to melt away and are pardoned in lieu of whatever the individual draws out of it. Conversely, when the connection is negative, just the sound of the whistle of the last boat on a frigid January night can develop into a case of *precipitatory anxiety*, the *daddy* of anxieties.

Although my perspective was a far cry from that of the Peary family, I recognized and related strongly to the attachment that Admiral and Mrs. Peary had with Eagle Island, and in general, to the essence of the relationship that people have with all of these islands, a rich subject of many a ruminative conversation. Islanders have titles and deeds—some passed down for centuries, but people never take possession of the property on which they reside. On the contrary, it is the island's mystique that ultimately claims ownership of the individual. By the sounds of it, Eagle had most assuredly claimed Peary.[lxii]

September's sun was still very warm and shot reflections off the water, clear out to the horizon; a moment to savor, but my mind was in a mode to view it from the family's experience. With the water so close in proximity to the house, the vulnerability of the place was self-evident, and gave off a measure of a lighthouse keeper's solitary reality. Through years of island living, I had chocked-up a little experience, but it was no preparation for grasping the logistics of living out on Eagle. The images of an old woman were immediately supplanted with that of an energetic young Maria—settling her belongings—fixing her mind, initiating the children to the ways of Eagle.

Initially, the appearance of a castle-like structure, on top of which the Peary cottage was built, caught my attention. White and yellowish-orange lichen covered the face of the stone, a sign that the foundation had been there awhile—a good long while. The first thought that came to me was of the castle that Antonio promised Maria before they left Spain—such a romantic notion had this structure turned out to be the one he had promised. The fact is that in 1909, long after Maria and Antonio had moved from Eagle, the Admiral expressed great concern about erosion, which prompted him to shore-up the immediate area surrounding the cottage with huge walls of island rocks.[lxiii] On the ocean side of the house the impression remains that a castle is under construction, that the crew is having lunch, and that the gang will be back momentarily. I wonder if the thought about the promised castle ever flitted through Maria's mind when she was out there.

David Chaney, State of Maine Park Service Director of Eagle Island, spent some important moments that day with us in deep conversation about our family's tie to the island. The meeting was fortuitous in that he had a great deal to offer and was willing to clarify so many of the disconnected stories. David directed us to visit the museum—was a bit insistent; a surprise awaited us in the west bastion, a circular room with seven casement windows, each which wreathes a glorious view of the bay. He didn't say what we were supposed to find, but there amongst the other caretaker's photos we found a picture of the wiry pitch-knot, Grampy Gomez.

On the other side of a thicket, the three-room cottage in which our grandparents lived was off limits to the public. Understandably, it was housing for the park employees. Chaney made an exception for us, a waiver, which we so appreciated at the moment. He led us through the back door—then five steps through what was originally the kitchen—which placed us into the living area, facing the front door. Five more steps and we would be out onto the rocks. There was not enough room in there to change your mind, let alone house nine people—yet it did.

The quarters were well lit by the large floor to ceiling windows, allowing the room to extend, visually, onto the rocky shore and towards each sunset. The kitchen had been somewhat expanded by knocking out walls, though looking down at the floor I saw clear indicators where the inside walls were originally situated, an area that would have been unbelievably small for as many children as they had at the time—a true test of maternal engineering. Ann Marie ran her hand across the windowsill, letting it linger. I knew what she was doing. She was the fortunate one who toted some memories of Grandmother Gomez to this visit and she became immersed in being in the same space. Chaney's private tour brimmed with priceless nuances, priceless, as was his dedication.

***

David Chaney
died tragically in a car accident the following spring,
and having met him only once,
I felt the enormous loss for his family, co-workers
And the *Friends of Peary's Eagle Island*[47]

***

---

[47] The Friends of Peary's Eagle Island, PO Box 70, Bailey Island, ME 04003

Polar Preparation

Roosevelt—as in U.S. President Theodore, was the name Lieutenant Peary christened his newly commissioned ship. She hailed, not from his homeport of Portland, but hailed out of New York, simply because New York put up the money. The paper reported, *"Downeast people hung back with their grip tight on their purse strings, so there was no alternative than to hail her from NY."* [lxiv]

In June of '05 he was heavily involved in readying the vessel for *her* first voyage to the Pole, another emboldened attempt for him and his crew. Moored off Eagle Island, the ship sported a two and a half-foot thick hull, and an engine built into the design of the ship to aid in maneuverability, to assist in breaking through ice during the years ahead. Huskies that were kept on the uninhabited Flagg Island were brought aboard. Word was that the dogs, bred from white and gray wolf stock, had not faired well in the warm summer climate, nor were the majority good petting stock, although Peary had his favorites. One can only imagine the howling that rose from Flagg Island, a sound that rode more than one breeze to awaken, or lull to sleep those Pott's Point insomniacs with an open sash.

Antonio rowed from Long Island family, tightly packed together in the dory, out through the sound, out around the farm on Ministerial Island to begin year 'round work in the late summer of '05. The natural harmony was broken only by the rhythmic sound of oars at work inside the oarlocks of the dory, a cadence set off by the counter rhythm

Moving day - Eagle Island

of water slatting against the boat as it gained distance a few feet at a time. Idyllic as it seems, the air, as like as not, resonated with the chatter of six children, ages one to ten years old— compounded by the squawking of some very traumatized chickens.

A merchant seaman by trade, Antonio was an adventurer by nature, and beholding to none, which translated into a man with an ongoing agenda, one that placed him in the most opportune situations to advance his independence. On June 24th he had been within inches of snagging the gold ring when he made the trial run on the *Roosevelt* from the Cape Elizabeth lightship to Halfway Rock Light. The reporter aboard thought his application was a shoe-in with his background as a diver, rigger, and all around seaman (ship), and wrote: [lxv]

"At the wheel when the new Peary ship Roosevelt was making her trial run from the Cape Elizabeth lightship to Half-way Rock light, there stood, a part of time, an under-sized, swathe (swarthy) complexioned, bright eyed man whose deep interest in everything that pertained to the ship was the subject of comment of many a guest. The man was Antonio Gomez, nicknamed 'Tony,' who will probably make the polar trip with Commander Peary. His application for a place on the Roosevelt as a diver, rigger and all-round seaman, is under consideration and, judging by the friendship shown him by the gallant commander, Tony is hoping not in vain.

Tony was born in Spain, 35 years ago. He has been in America so long, and likes it so well, that he couldn't be hired to go back to his native land. He lives at Long Island, in Portland harbor, lets boats and takes out sailing parties in summer, has worked on the government reservation at Great Diamond island and occasionally dons a diver's outfit and does a submarine job. He takes naturally to water and doesn't care how deep or how cold it is.

Commander Peary, who has a summer home down the bay, took a liking to this wiery (wiry) little Spaniard and has utilized him in several ways. Tony was invited to go on the trial trip and he made himself generally useful from the time she cast off her lines until she scraped the muddy bottom in her labored docking at low tide. 'She good one,' was his enthusiastic reply when asked by Mrs. Peary for his expert opinion on the sailing qualities of the Roosevelt. 'I lika go wid heem,' Tony remarked to a reporter on the trial trip 'I no care for de cole. She be 40 below zaro I no care. I lika Misser Peary. I no fraid go where he weal taka me wid heemself.'

Tony has a wife and 'seex small boy'[48] at his humble home on Long Island. Mrs. Gomez isn't enthusiastic over the prospect of her husband being away from her a year or two, and risking his life in the Arctic, but she has entered no determined protest.

He is handy at the helm, having been employed on several big yachts. He has a great record as a life saver (lifesaver). He carried in his inside pocket on the Roosevelt's trip, and exhibited to several interested parties papers certifying to his saving of eight lives of persons who, at different times and places, were on the point of drowning, or in immediate danger of capsizing.

Five years ago, when a sailer (sailor) on the yacht Brinwood, owned by Albert Kate (*Scates?) of Boston, Tony rescued two boys, one 11 and the other 13 years of age, who had fallen into Boston harbor, from a wharf.

While sailing a yacht of John Blanchard, Boston, he saved the lives of Mr. Blanchard and family, by keeping the yacht afloat in a big blow, which seemed sure to capsize her. It was with the greatest difficulty that he navigated the craft to a place of shelter. It was Mr. Blanchard's own statement that without the cool-headed mastery of Tony the yacht would have turned turtle.

A year later Miss Hamilton, asleep on the deck of the yacht "Esther," in the early morning, rolled overboard. Tony was on watch and seizing a rope that was made fast he plunged into the water, and rescued her before the occupants of the berths could get on deck.

Two summers ago he saved the life of Frank Andrews, 65 years of age, who fell from a dory in Long Island sound, and was unconscious when taken from the water. Last summer Jack Emery, a boy, who was playing on the whaff (wharf) at Ponce's landing, Long Island, in the evening, fell off. Tony jumped from the wharf, caught hold of the boy and swam ashore with him.

Tony had six years of service in the Spanish navy, and was a quartermaster when (*) his service expired. He doesn't care for the navy, he says, and since the battle of Manila bay and the sea fight off Santiago he has been content to pose as an American seaman, rather than as a Spanish naval veteran.

---

[48] Antonio and Maria actually had four boys and two girls.

Some said that Commodore Peary told him that he couldn't go on the expedition because he had so many children, a logical rational. But he also spoke of Antonio's inclination to stretch the truth more than most, though he must have trusted him somewhat, because he was comfortable leaving the island in the care of the man. The explorer had much on his mind in that time, a stressful undertaking of Herculean proportions. He instead chose his caretaker, Captain Percy, as steward, and hired Antonio in Percy's stead. The *Roosevelt* tacked out of view of Eagle Island, and sailed up the bay—without Antonio.

Portland Harbor
June 31st – 7:00 PM

Whistles, tugs, and steamboats bid the *Roosevelt* following seas as she cleared the harbor and sailed out passed Portland Headlight for New York. By Sunday she lay at anchor, laid a whole week in New York while she was *coaled*, after which stores were put aboard before leaving for Cape Breton Island up off Nova Scotia. Commodore Peary spent Tuesday[49] with Mrs. Peary on Eagle. Both left by rail on Wednesday for Cape Breton with plans for him to meet up with the *Roosevelt* on Friday, then onward to the ship's proposed winter quarters north of Greenland. The plans were timely. A northeaster hit the Portland area on the last day of July.[lxvi]

Antonio Gomez

A magazine kicked around our home for years, one somewhat like a Hampton Magazine, which contained an extensive article depicting one of Peary's expeditions and included a full-face picture of Antonio[50] as part of the article. All of the other photos were of the Arctic expedition, distant shots, and groups of people, dogs, snow, and ice. Until his death, Antonio swore up and down that he went on the third trip. He was practiced at swearing—up and down. Did he embellish on a truth that took

---

[49] July 18,1905
[50] The faded picture remains a part of a childhood scrapbook.

him as far as Halfway Rock? The picture, in the article, stands on its own, leaving us with the question of why, if he did not go, was it a part of the article at all?

Schooling by the Tide – Birthing on the Ebb
Eagle Island 1905

Antonio and Maria's encounter with Eagle Island was a profound one. In the early nineteen hundreds the differences between the Peary and Gomez families obviously rested in each one's social stratum. High profile individuals were revered in the manner in which movie stars would eventually be idolized, and now the immigrant family lived mere feet from a family that had gained world prominence. Though absent for years at a time, it is my impression that once home with his family Peary found this island to be a source of strength, his anchor, a place where he recharged. Contrasted, Antonio was champing at the bit, comparable to a ship dragging its anchor in a gale. He may have had a large brood, but he obviously would have left them to fend on their own if offered the shiny brass ring.

Judging by today's standards is not fair. Therefore it is best to try to recall if it was normal back then for families to fend alone for years at a time. In the maritime shipping industry it was certainly the case. Mariners were absent for seven or eight years at a time. Mrs. Peary certainly did so, with two children. She had a family unit from which to draw, and a certain financial security. Maria would not have had the anchor of family or the financial security. The Commodore was wise in his decision.

The main cottage stood high on the northeastern bluff—privy to a panorama of subtle and exceedingly dramatic changes in the sky and ocean, its chin stuck right out there waiting to be cuffed by any low pressure that had punch. It set atop an island so small that all elevated points of land were within spitting distance of the water's edge, and was exposed on three sides to the open seas, leaving the backside protected by a stand of trees. Whether the positioning of the main cottage was mathematically, nautically, or analytically based, the result was absolutely plumb—shear creativity on Peary's part. Structurally, it appeared as though he set it precisely on the inter cardinal points of a compass rose, and there was something metaphoric about the way the cottage appeared as a pilothouse with the island as a ship's superstructure, an apropos concept for its worldly dwellers. For all of the ambiance that the island exuded, its remoteness laid down a different set of rules from which all had to play.

Mrs. Peary often entertained family and friends, created a flurry of activity up at the main cottage, a place, which unfortunately was built without the amenity of a kitchen or dining room. Therefore, it was necessary for the family and guests to have meals served a few hundred feet away, at the caretaker's cottage. This situation could well have spawned overtones of high comic relief. Obviously it mattered not how well the food was cooked, balmy or pristine the day, dining at a three-room cottage that housed two adults and six active children must have been noisy and vexatious. Shortly thereafter, plans were set in motion to build a kitchen onto the main cottage. [lxvii]

Nine-year old, Josephine counted her blessings for the company of someone near her age and encountered a natural alliance in the Commodore's eleven-year old daughter, Marie. The boys found the two girls a bit too snooty [51] for their liking, though at their age, any girl would have been considered too snooty.

Island fascinations are ageless and are gender blind. The moment that the children noticed the receding water, the mysteries of low tide chimed-in a quiet ritual for the snooty and unsnooty, a shared activity, one that would bring all participants to a commonality of disposition, forgetting botherations. It is a ritual into which every island child on the coast of Maine is initiated. Skooched for hours on their haunches in the small tidal pools, they searched as though prospecting for gold. Baby crabs, with legs flailing under close inspection, scattered beneath rocks when scrutiny had run its course, let loose to return beneath havens of seaweed.

---

[51] "Too snooty" was Tony Junior's wording. Josephine had a different recall.

Plunked in the middle of a meadow of slippery seaweed, the natural progression for the children was to then proceed to popping contests, vying to see who could produce the loudest snap from the round bubbles of rubbery rockweed, while they swapped stories, ideas, and possibly even song. An important, but rare find, one in which their mother and father would show interest, was the edible, dark, red algae, known as dulse. It had a strong earthy taste, was loaded with minerals, and once dried, was wadded up like a plug of chewing tobacco and chewed. The earthy part took some getting-use-to.

The boys struck up a small fire down in the crevice of a rock; the rest collected black periwinkles, and another found a small container, filling it with salt water, and set it atop the fire to boil. By this joint venture they created a nosh that took the edge off an empty stomach, but it took the patience of Job to pick a tablespoon's worth of cooked periwinkles, let alone a mouthful, a kind of activity that held the children's interest for a good long time. White periwinkles, though prettier, were taboo. Lore relegated them as inedible; an important piece of information that was passed down during the initiation rites without any explanation as to why they were not fit to eat. *The reason was never made clear, to this day. It was certain that there were no warning labels on the outside of each white periwinkle, but then neither was the "red tide" a coined phrase. Were red tides in existence in 1905?*

Once the prospecting and the seafood nosh ran its course, they took to the slopes, to the raspberry slopes on flattened cardboard boxes that took on the guise of winter sleds. Fine thorny raspberry branches produced a slippery slope as greasy as any icy incline, and when it came to negotiating the bramble-covered escarpments, Marie Peary played as gleefully as did the others.[52]

Late fall arrived on cue, as did the exodus of the Peary family. A curtain of silence dropped all around them, creating the aura of a hushed early morning, twenty-four hours a day. But for the cries of gulls circling the island, the racket caused by crows plaguing at each other, and the resonance of the incoming and

---

[52] Tony Junior spoke often of this activity and of Marie Peary's participation.

outgoing tides, stillness fell over the stationary prow and its keepers, who were left to watch over the empty house. *Was the Peary cottage available for the caretaker's family to use in their absence? That information never passed by me, but it would not be a surprise if Antonio did so—regardless whether permission was granted or not.*

Maria had four weeks remaining in the pregnancy of her seventh child, yet it was time to prepare the older children for school on the mainland with teachers Mildred Hamilton, Eva Wentworth, and Evelyn Gammon, sending them off in a dory each day with a plethora of directives. Alfred pushed the dory off the water's edge and lept in quickly before his shoes and pant legs became too wet. Young Tony manned the oars. Big sister shot directives from the bow, as a big sister is wont to do, and at age six, Louie took in all the politics. Harpswell Neck was a two-mile row where they joined fifty-four others, ages five through twenty-one, in the two-room Schoolhouse #18, that is, when they had enough light to do so. School was called off on dark days. The school budget afforded each of the teachers a wage of seven dollars and fifty cents a week for teaching the Pott's Point and Eagle Island broods.

Capricious weather played into this; oft times forced the children to seek refuge on the uninhabited Haskell Island, a halfway point between *Pottses* and home. A signal fire, built at the mouth of a *cave*,[53] was the prearranged beacon to let their mother know that they were safe and just waiting out the inclement conditions. When weather conditions became snarly, the trip back to the island totally impassable, Harpswell Neck residents opened their homes to the children.

Town of Harpswell - Annual Report:

Law stipulated—absences of one half day or more was a violation and stated: "All persons having children under their control shall cause them to attend school as provided in this section, and for every neglect of such duty shall be punished by a

---

[53] Cave is the word Tony Junior used.

fine not exceeding twenty-five dollars, or shall be imprisoned not exceeding thirty days."

Harpswell elected a truant officer, who when notified by the teacher of a pupil's absence for six or more consecutive sessions during any term, hauled the habitual truant away to the State School for Boys or the State Industrial School for Girls.

Now, here's a good one! When a pupil lost, or destroyed school property, the parents were notified and if the loss was not made good, it was included in the *next* bill for property taxes. If an act even broached defacing school property the truant officer *doubled* the cost. *That was creative!*

Seventy years later, whenever the aged Tony Junior talked about the two-mile row, he stood a little straighter as he narrated the tale, wearing his oldest brother birthright as one would a medal, and deservedly so. All one had to do was to survey the distance between Eagle and Harpswell from the Peary cottage's upstairs window to understand the near to insurmountable feat the children faced each day. Yet, make it they did. "We didn't drop out of school, Tony crowed, we dropped in." [lxviii]

October 1, 1905

Late on a school day, a Thursday to be exact, the children once again beached the dory onto Eagle Island's shore. Supper hour was at hand, the area around the house hushed, their nomadic father off tramping around somewhere, possibly fishing off George's Bank. Normal movements within the cottage were not discernible as the children climbed the rocks and clambered towards the small front porch. Once inside, they fully understood why their mother had not greeted them as usual. She was in labor.

Too small in stature to reach up onto the cook stove, Tony Junior moved a box over in front of the oven door. From atop it the eight-year old stoked the fire and prepared a meal for the others. Maria called upon Josephine to assist with the delivery of her baby brother, *my father, Robert (Bobby)*.[54] As they all slept, and as morning drew near, a light frost carpeted the island. [lxix]

Henrietta's Long Island Church Notes 1905...

Oct   *Mr. Zoeth Rich, Senior died at his home, buried at Eastend Cemetery,* [55]

Oct   *Bonaparte Chase has bought what is known as Mariners Clam Cake house and is going to erect a dwelling for himself at Fern Park. Mr. Rhor having bought Bonaparte's house for himself.*

Nov   *Clubhouse burnt.*

*There was no mention in the notes of Bobby's birth.

Winter 1905 -1906

Though the children were probably pressed into service too, part of the caretaker's duties was to gather and cut wood for the Peary family's summer supply. Wreck wood and broken branches that were deposited on the tide were hauled back to the woodpile to dry, except for the wood that floated in the water for too long a period of time. That they passed over, because it was

---

[54] On our visit to Eagle, David Chaney informed us that one of the Percys, (father or son caretakers), told him that a baby was born to Maria on Eagle Island. Portland City Hall birth records include all of the Gomez children, except Robert Peter. He is not found in the Harpswell or State records.

In that unique sphere of influences, it is not surprising that the infant was named Robert, after the dignitary, perhaps a hallmark for the child, given with attributes to which he could aspire. Bobby was given Peter as a middle name, for Maria's father, Pedro Campos.

Jo, Tony, Alfred, and Louie were born in Portland, Tillie and Johnny on Long Island in '02 and '04. Mid-wife, Mrs. Sylvester delivered all, but Jo and Johnny. To date, there is no birth or death record of the tenth child that was born sometime between 1900 and 1910.

On Tony Junior's date of birth record in 1897, the line where his name should be written is blank. In the top left corner a state employee wrote *"d.o.b. Alfred."* It looks like an afterthought or a guess made by the state employee. On another that has Maria and Antonio as parents, is written the name *"Michael"* and the dates are that of Alfred's birth.

[55] Oral history: Zoeth was run over by a boat off the buoy station at Little Diamond.

waterlogged, pulpy, and too full of salt, the type that only smoldered and smoked-up the place.

The foundation of the caretaker's cottage would have been in need of insulation. Leaves, weighted down by fir branches, would have been the conventional insulator, because the same searching winds that blasted leaves out of the trees also searched up through the floorboards.

Not certain where Antonio was seated in the annals of self-motivation, one can only assume that he followed a semblance of a lobsterman's winter-output. Seasonally, Casco Bay lobstermen broke loose from a tether that forced them out of bed long before dawn each day. One would have thought it the time to slough-off or lie torpid for the winter. On the contrary, when the lobsters migrated out into deep water late in the year, the gear was hauled-in, traps were repaired, new ones built. Buoys were made from large bottles or wood, and the boat's hull was scraped of barnacles, and slimy growth. Trap-heads required mending, new ones knitted, a shared winter chore, but mainly men knitted them. They sank nails into a stud in the wall over by the cook stove, on which a twine was anchored—hauled up a chair—grabbed a wooden needle full of twine and knitted away a winter season. It was a good warm place to work and bide awhile as the good-woman cleared away the dinner meal.

Antonio's fishing trips likely yielded food for the table, and in his absence, the boys hand-lined for fish off the cliff with long handmade poles. Jigging from the stern of the dory, on the way home from school would make a trip worthwhile. Fish made up most of the menu; consequently, it was opportunistic to be at the dock in Harpswell when a fishing schooner arrived back in port. The catch had already been sold off in Portland, but the clean up usually produced some stray monkfish, whiting, pollock, and cusk, all considered trash fish. None brought in a penny a pound and was usually free for the asking if found beneath a coil of rope. Another place to ferret out fish was the pen boards, a space down below deck where the prime fish—haddock, cod, and hake were sorted by specie and size, a place where a few might be found stuck between the boards.

Around Boston they referred to dried-cod as Cape Cod turkey, on the Costa del Sol, Spain, *bacalo,* but the very same preserving process was used on both shores. Antonio gutted, boned, heavily salted, but did not skin the fish—tied them together by twos, by the tail fins, and flung them onto the clothesline to dry. Why the gulls didn't ravish the unprotected supply on the clothesline, and how the simple salted process prevented maggots from taking hold, is a mystery. God knows the flies tried! Maria reconstituted the leathery pieces of fish in water, changing liquid three or four times, shredded it finely and made it into recipes for fish hash, fish cakes, or Finnan Haddie, which was creamed cod over potatoes or rice, with an egg sauce.

Chickens necessitated care, a coop, chicken feed, and crushed clamshells, which provided calcium to harden eggshells. Her elementary test for freshness was to touch each end of the egg to her lips. The side with the air pocket was cold. Therefore a cold temperature on both ends meant the inside of the egg had shrunk, had set too long. Traditionally, on Sunday night, she served up a big platter, heaped with rice, topped with ten or twelve fried eggs.

Rather than use the chickens for meals, waterfowl graced the table, a bit fatty, and fishy tasting, although when stuffed with apples, were choice. On many occasions they ate coot—many, many an occasion. Generally, islanders ate coot during lean times—though the recipe that one island shared with tourist, revealed disdain for the bird, and revealed a dry wit. "*First,* they said*, remove the oil bag—parboil for 24 hours—bake for 24 hours, then throw it away."* Not to be a copycat, another island's recipe varied slightly. *Simmer the coot for several hours with a piece of driftwood. When done, throw out the coot, and eat the driftwood."* It is safe to say that coot was not an odds-on favorite as a main dish.

Jan   Very warm day

Feb   This community received the painful news of the death of Captain Jerry York of So Portland. Capt York was born at Long Island August of 1816

April   First Sunday boat Casco Bay Line

10th   Terrible snowstorm – 15 inches of snow

23rd   Heavy snowstorm

The year's greening[56] came off late in '06 because of a fierce snowstorm in mid April, followed by more heavy snow towards the end of the month. Once good weather set in, they all scoured Eagle to find the tender fiddlehead in its unfurled state and to dig dandelion greens before they flowered or else they cooked up as bitter as...well...there is nothing as bitter as dandelion greens that have flowered.

In Maine's short growing season, a garden took considerable thought, not sown until the chance of a frost was gone at the end of May. Her method for keeping food on the table was to pickle perishable foods in vinegar or salt, to cure and dry meat and fish for future use. But it was her chickens on which she relied. When there was no feed, they pecked the edibles off the ground. *These days, they call it free-range chicken.*

Clam hoes and hods are a wonderful conversation piece— strategically located beside the fireplace—just for a nautical effect. On Eagle, the two implements were crusted with mud, more at home at a low tide, hopefully a dreen-low that exposed mud flats not usually accessible. The smallest of the Gomez children thumped along over the mud, an important job that provoked the clams to exude air bubbles, therein exposing its whereabouts. With feet straddled directly over the air holes, the stronger of the boys dug into the sludgy mud with the clam hoe, turning over big clumps of it between his feet while the others situated themselves directly beneath his butt and plucked all of the clams he unearthed. A few quahaugs and razor clams found their way into the hod—tough eating, but when ground up for

---

[56] Greening-To dig for dandelion greens.

clam cakes had a high flavor. For good measure, they grabbed a few mussels that hung off the rocks just below the water line—easy pickings, easier than digging clams in the freezing temperatures, and just as edible. In the mainland gastronomic circles, mussels were considered a poor country cousin to clams, a morsel upon which they vehemently looked with disdain. Islanders often shucked them there on the rocks and ate them raw.

That divined drift—the lobster migration, reoccurred punctually, barring a glitch in the lobster's internal clock, one that could be caused by extreme water temperatures or major storms. Two centuries earlier, lobsters actually crawled the shoreline in profusion, a phenomenon that took place when the Indians summered on the islands—easy pickings at any tide. No such luck for the Eagle Island troupe. They set off single traps a few feet from shore, sufficient for the family's needs. October lobster meat was nutty tasting, shells hardened, and filled to capacity, but most islanders savored the heightened sweetness of the smaller lobsters that weighed a pound, and under.

Old timers would roll over in their graves to see the world of haute cuisine dowse a lobster's delicate flavor with wine, garlic, scallions, and balsamic vinegar. Were the balsamic from a vintage hundred-year old bottle, it still would not impress them—one bit. About as far out on a limb as they would go, was to serve up a simple, but top-of-the line recipe for baked-stuffed lobster—a "secret" island recipe.

Towards the last of June, Mrs Peary arrived back on Eagle with the children and a maid to see the cottage put-together for the '06 season, and then left for Washington, DC, to escort her mother back to their island retreat. School closed June twenty-second, which meant that Jo, Tony, Alfred, and Louie were now freed up from the daily trip to Pott's Point each day. Shoes were slung aside, the wee hours of the morning spent in coveted sleep, and the three littlest ones animated from all of the attention.[lxx]

Bobby was not yet a year old, but likely able to pull himself upright at the low set windowsills in the kitchen, to scan the rocky terrain outside, standing alongside his two-year old brother Johnny, with whom he held unintelligible, but very important conversations, an inseparable twosome from that point onward. Tillie was only four, at a *cunnin'* age, sparkling eyes and a mass of curly black hair—at an age of adulation for her big sister, at an age in which she would naturally solicit Jo's attention. Though attentive, the older girl was understandably drawn to the company of Marie Peary, though their time together was rationed between Marie's invited social set and Josephine's chores. They managed nicely. Jo digested every social grace and bit of sophistication to which she was exposed—applying it wherever it fit. Unfortunately, when the Pearys left, there was not much of a proving ground on which to test her newfound graces— excepting on her mother, who was always a very willing sounding board.

Island life had a way of cementing an interest in the welfare of another with whom one bided a fragment of one's childhood. Aunt Jo delighted in the correspondence she and Marie kept alive through their adult years, a lasting bond, which was graciously sustained by two women who appreciated whatever they culled from their shared childhood experiences on Eagle Island.

More invitees arrived. Eagle began to stir socially. A newspaper reported: *"Antonio Gomez who is caretaker at the Peary estate on Eagle Island since the Commander and his faithful Captain Percy left last summer has a record for life saving. He has saved eight persons from drowning in Casco Bay, Boston Harbor, and Long Island Sound. He is a Spaniard by birth but speaks English and has served fourteen months in the Spanish Navy as a non-commissioned officer. Mr. Gomez comes to South Harpswell in a motorboat everyday for Mrs. Peary and gets mail and supplies for Eagle."* [lxxi]

Although some of those events actually took place, since the last interview with a reporter, there appears to be a shift in the amount of time he spent in the Spanish Navy, from six years to fourteen months. In another newspaper interview it was said that he spoke many languages, a true statement. The reporter neglected the fact that he spoke all of those languages—at once.

"Chawed the rag awhile with some Chebeaguers the other day. Hadn't seen those ole snots in a dog's age. I told 'em, at this pace, next time we see one another, one of us be in a pine box. Well, Ole Deah—it's true!

They sez Jimmy Hamilton, Clinton's son, found a good sized pearl in a "*mussel*." As many as they go through for bait, they wuz bound to trip ovah one eventu'ly. Never heard of mussels cultivatin' pearls. Have you? [lxxii]

Nope! Nope! They can't sell a single bushel of clams out of state—unless the clams have been canned, packed, or barreled between September 15th and June 1st. That particular law—not allowin' summer's harvest to be sold, has been on the books since 1850 when the industry started. Even sold 'em off to the European fishermen fishin' the Grand Banks. Ya know—they didn't start sellin' 'em for consumption at hotel dining rooms and at clambakes until thirty years ago when most inshore fisherman stopped usin' 'em for bait. Imagine, six, seven years back, they was gettin' sixty-nine cents a bushel, averagin' a thousand bushel a man—per season. Back breaking work. Tough ole birds. Indians usta dig clams for winta supply. Supposibly now, tourist ovah on Chebeague are all gabblin' over the Indian campers—think they're a *picturesque feetcha*. First Indian baby born on the island in recent years belongs to George Frances. Ayeh, he's full blooded, they say.

Down the *Eastend,* they's buildin' fancy cottages all around an old Indian burial ground. You didn't know they's one there? Well there is! Ask the Horr boys. They know where it is. If they don't get time to show ya, I'll take you down someday. Be good for the horse. Wonder if any of those fancy cottages hangin' over the burial ground are haunted? If they ain't, they should be.

Gettin' right up in the world ovah there ain't they? Mid-June they come-by some mail collection boxes, n' now, mail's delivered right ta the front door. No-no-no! Not just summah. Permanent—winta too. 'Fore I go home I'll run inside and ask

Marston if he's got us on the list for collection boxes yet. He always has the pa'ticulars.

Yep, gettin' up in the world all right. Tuesday, a few brave souls lifted off in six, newfangled rigs they call fire balloons.[57] Plunked myself on the ledges looking towards and Cliff, and followed the flight from there. Breathtakin'! Abs'lutely breathtakin'! They sailed from Chebeague to South Harpswell. Six-miles without a hitch. Every neck within the radius was craned skyward—jaws slacked open. Thot some would start droolin' any minute.

Harpswell sent over an invite to anyone with a motor boat to join in on the first annual boat race—no entrance fee. Those damn stay-up-all-nighters want to do it every year now. Best talk with 'em so's we won't be settin' over each other—grapplin' to hold it the same day, same spot.

Didn't I tell you them newfangled combustion rigs would catch on? Newspaper sez here that a Mrs. Hunt arrived in Portland last Friday in their *auto*. The roads were fine, she sez, *"except from Saco to Portland."* Marshes prubly gave her truble—awful low to he water there. Nawthin' but a cow path anyway.

High society is arrivin' every which way but Sunday. First of the month, Cornelius Vanderbilt's yacht, *North Star* arrived in Portland. Ayah, they sashayed aboard the *Sebascodegan* and paid us a visit heah on the island. Well, mister-man, I guess you did miss all the flurry. Lately—just like my dog—you're always on the wrong side of the door.

Well suh! Got some kerosene to wash the windows with. Afta—got some boards to nail up. Bees is tryin' to nest up under the eaves. Don't that woman keep me hard at it. Am busier than a cat covering his own crap in the flower garden. Heah! Minister passed out Henrietta's scratchins' at church. Saved one for ya. I take it to the outhouse. Awful good readin'."

---

[57] Fire Balloon - Hot air balloons

May 6th   First Sunday boat on Harpswell Line

_May 15th Mr. Horace Doughty had a finger taken off at
        Eye and Ear Hospital_

_   First late and early boat Casco Bay Line_

_   Mr. Ansel Bickford is building a popcorn stand
        at West End._

The previous year, Warren Woodbury contracted typhoid, was taken to the Maine Eye & Ear hospital where he succumbed to it. The highly contagious virus was an element of 1906, its transmissible behavior not yet understood. Five people died on the island in the same year, but it is not known if typhoid caught on, or if, in fact, the mortality rate was the norm.

To this point of discovery, the medical field did not know that well people were capable of carrying the virus. _"Typhoid Mary,"_ the infamous typhoid-carrying cook deposited the illness everywhere that she was employed. Because she showed no symptoms and was not sick, she strongly resisted the theory, but tests proved her wrong. She continued to resist, break quarantine, flee, and seek work as a cook. Investigators worked equally hard to isolate her. From that point, a person who changed jobs frequently was labeled a _"Typhoid Mary."_ [lxxiii]

Ole Deah & Ole Chum

"Doin' nicely old stock. Good o' you ta ask. Daow! Just puttyin' around t'day? What brings you back down heah t'night? Eyah, eyah, I see Cap'n Floyd take a party out to Cod ledge fishin' the other day in that one-lunger Hampton he bought, the _Lucy A._ Come in with two hundred fifty pounds of cod 'n haddock. Healthy pile to gut and fillet. Got himself a nice little business there to start out the '06 season. They'll all be out there soon. Mackerel's runnin'. Fish market's sellin' 'em three for five cents. Nah, don't care for 'em—little oily for me.

Ain't them women all in a lather ovah there? Look at 'em. Been blatherin', and complainin' that the weeds is grown so high on Ocean Street that it's turned into a pile of puckerbushes, impassible for them to sashay through in them big skirts. I thought they were whistlin' in the wind, but by gory, the bellyachin' worked. Surveyors already showed up to make plans for a five-foot wide, four-hundred foot long boardwalk startin' at the corner of Island and Garfield. Goin' all the way to the *Eastend* along the front of the island with it, they are. Horrs and Wallaces have had it damn quiet down there on that corner all these years, but all that sashaying down the boardwalk will put the kibosh to that. [58]

Them ladies swung on their heels, turned their wrath—bore down pretty hard on old Rohr to build bathhouses on Andrew's Beach for his summer visitors to use. Don't they know bushes don't hide much—or, don't they care? A bit gallin', if you ask me—too much skin for this puritanical bunch. If the poison ivy don't get 'em the cussed brown tail moths will. Cocoons are knitted into every tree and thicket all ovah the Bay, and right plump full of them little caterpillar larvae. Damn things will fall right out of nowhere on ya. A few of Rhor's people prubly left with rashes where the sun don't shine. A scourge, ain't they? Makin' waste of a whole damn season's foliage. Be lucky if we get any pears or apples. Gonna torch the nahsty buggers over to my place, 'n now the grass is turned dry am goin' to do some burnin'.[59] Enjoy the smell of burnin' grass, don't you? Don't worry yourself—got my broom and a couple pails of water handyby in case it gets away from me. Bothers you that much—come on ovah, give me a hand." [lxxiv]

🐟 🐟

---

[58] The boardwalk started Downfront on the Westend, ran the entire length of Island Avenue, to its end (where it intersects with Fern). It was where the Horr and Wallace families once lived. For an evening's constitutional, people walked its entire length each night.

[59] Burning - Annual fall burning of lawns and fields.

Alfred

The Gomez children coveted summers, relished the carefree time of freedom, as most school-aged children do, and the warm season of '06 started out laid back and lackadaisical. Johnny and Bobby were too young to be troublesome and the girls shrugged off the three older boy's boisterousness, though as the oldest, it was a forgone conclusion that Josephine was delegated as an overseer to the most animated of the brood. Complacency was easily borne within the petite community of her family. She could never have envisioned that the boys would take their rough and tumbles to an irreversible result and was horrified when frantically summons to the island's craggy edge. Eight-year old Alfred laid motionless down on the rocks. The rough and tumble had gone awry. The wooden barrel in which he was playfully rolling pitched off a cliff and landed on the rocks. He was obviously severely injured about the head. Jo was utterly beside herself and laden with guilt. Alfred incurred brain damage, but because he was cognizant they entertained some hope that he would live—and live he did. The tide of events went on as usual on the other islands, but it was far from usual for the family in the months that followed, a period that was wrought with anxiety and laden with a chronic sadness. A symptom of his particular brain damage affected his ability to retain fluids. In his frail state he struggled to guide the heavy glass water pitcher to his mouth in an attempt to quench an insatiable thirst. [60] There was not much that the medical field could do for him, but to put him in his mother's loving-hands, the very thing that probably kept him alive.

Winter gripped the bay. Temperatures were in the teens, dipping to below zero, with a mix of rain and snow. Antonio lowered the Union Jack in front of the big cottage, a signal for help, kept the flag down all day, but no one saw it. Alfred's condition began to deteriorate. His brain was swelling, and he was in much too fragile a condition to move. When no one responded to the signal, Antonio took Peary's motorboat to fetch a Portland doctor, but it stalled and rolled into the waves, him

---

[60] Ann Marie is the custodian of the pitcher.

100

with it. The dory was his only recourse and with two dry flannel shirts to replace the wet coat, he set off on the fourteen-mile row to Portland. A Harpswell fisherman finally picked up on the Eagle Island signal, responded, only to find that shortly after Antonio made way, Alfred succumbed.[61]

Left drained by the months of care, by the futility of trying to keep Alfred alive as his condition deteriorated, Maria understandably turned away from Eagle Island. The following night Antonio asked someone to pen a postal card addressed to Mrs. Peary, who was in New York attending a dinner with the Commodore, one in which he told her, in nine brief words that Alfred had gone to *"heven"*, then them bid them good-bye. The decision to leave Eagle Island and return to the Long Island community was instantaneous. He told the Portland Evening Express reporter that he wanted the boy to be where there were some people, that the *"de poor little feller"* would be lonesome when they left, for good. [lxxv]

Acute meningitis was the determined cause of the child's death. Five days later in the wintry-scape of Long Island they buried Alfred over in the left corner of the Westend cemetery. Ed Alexander stood off to the side waiting for the family to leave before he shoveled the dirt in over the small coffin.[62] *An ancient belief sets forth that the soul was created in the ocean and returns to it. In the fine arts and some psychiatric circles the psyche is considered the soul and its symbol is deep water. A part of Maria's own faith held a belief that holy water petitions Divine intervention. Innately, there was much spiritual good in being surrounded by the waters of Casco Bay. Innately she was right to seek the companionship of a community.*

The newspaper report was disconcerting, because the reporter spent so many words lauding Antonio's quest for a doctor. There was not a hint of the bravery, which was shown by a dying child, and not a single word about the person who selflessly invested

---

[61] Alfred died December 9, 1906 at 8 years, 7 months of age.

[62] The unmarked grave is located in the far, left rear of the Westend cemetery. The stone that was originally set there now lays in three pieces in the family plot over against Maria's gravestone.

the most in Alfred's well being—his mother. If there was one to tell, that was the story.

Antonio worked out his obligation as caretaker, until the Commodore returned with Captain Percy, but Maria and the children made the move to Long Island a permanent one.[63] Tony and Louie hooked up with their close pals Charlie and Walter Cushing, Jo with Harriet, the youngest Isusi girl. Maria set about re-establishing a semblance of normalcy and sent them off to join their friends at the Westend School.[64] At the school picnic, which was held on the last day of school in June 1907, Geneva Bickford won the first prize in the bean game and Charlie Cushing won the booby prize.[lxxvi]

***

Peary's 1905-06 attempt to reach the North Pole was not successful, an endeavor wrought with adverse weather, furious winds, ice conditions, seventy-two degree below zero temperatures, and a thwarted sledging season. Exertion beyond the limits wracked his body, and only sixteen of the one hundred-twenty dogs remained. In the spring he was forced to abandon his goal, to turn back at 87 degrees 06 minutes north and return to the States, but not without hope. His backers, the Peary Arctic Club remained confident and began raising money for yet another attempt. [lxxvii]

Henrietta's Long Island Church notes continue... 1906
~Seven houses were built and builder Albert Woodbury built one for himself at the Westend
~18 babies were born and of these, to the wife of Mark Stuart twins, boy and girl - both have died since June. To the wife of Peter Christianson - a daughter. It died at time of birth

---

[63] The Historian of Eagle Island is of the opinion that Antonio remained the caretaker of Eagle until Capt. Percy returned from the expedition.

[64] Portland's North School does not record any of the children in their records until Josephine's attendance in the 1908-09 session, which is the year the family first wintered at 143 Washington Avenue in Portland.

~The Reverend married 6 couples, including Mr. Frederick Keniston and Miss Susie Johnson and baptized 4 residents, and buried 8, including the only child of Benjamin MacVane, a five year old.
There was no specific mention of Alfred's death in the church notes.

Eagle Island Tour
Present Day

Absorbed in the nuances of the old house, and anticipating more, Ann Marie and I stepped deeper into the bygone era of the Peary cottage—amused that lowered tones and whispered dialogue were needed. Who in heavens name did we think would be disturbed if we spoke aloud? We were there to drink in the historical importance of the old cottage, but naturally it took on greater meaning knowing that Maria had sifted from room to room in the course of her daily routine.

A unique, free standing, three-sided hearth fireplace was built in the center of the living room, possibly the only one of its kind in the country, a creation of Admiral Peary's. Each face was made of different types of stone, some pulled from the island's shoreline, but the upper back mantle was set with quartz crystal brought back from Cape Sheridan where the *Roosevelt* wintered twice. Biographers never highlighted the artistic side of the explorer, but it was obvious, by this brainchild, that he had a creative bent—a contemplative and quaint one at that. He put me in mind of Thomas Jefferson—always challenging the status quo.[lxxviii]

The place seemed cleaned out—not what I expected. I was looking for the flag Matt Henson made for the *Roosevelt's* mainmast on their triumphant return after the discovery. Where were the carved ivory ornaments, the narwhal horn, ivory walrus tusks, the heads of polar bears, musk ox, and the stuffed birds? China from the Greeley headquarters at Fort Conger in Greenland should have been around somewhere. Peary was the first to enter Conger, fifteen years after Greeley abandoned the station on his march to Cape Sabine—the place where he was to meet a relief ship. The ship never arrived. Nearly all of Greeley's party starved to death as the result. It must have been a sobering and grim moment for Peary, even after fifteen years.

Part of the era and Peary's reality was to have stuffed animals and artifacts scattered about the cottage, and they were kept as decor up until the thirties. The climate of today wouldn't go for stuffed anything—that's for certain. The mission of the museum is to preserve a place for nature, not a place to warehouse the preserved. Obviously, much had been taken to another place for safekeeping. I didn't ask. It didn't matter.

Drawn to the light from a window in the dusky time worn kitchen, I nonchalantly sidled up, with my nose practically pressed to the glass—and instinctively took a half step backwards. The view on the other side of the windowpane must have made me a tad uncomfortable—the high cliffs, the sharp drop to the water's edge. Out beyond—right out there on Mark Island, mariners kept dry stores in the base of the stone monument.[65] Some dramatic event gave rise to the stowage of food in that crucial spot, likely a schooner that fetched up in zero visibility. Someone obviously experienced a desperate hunger; someone saw to it that no one else would.

When fog deftly hid one sailing vessel from another, the sound of the boat cutting through water reached out ahead of itself to the ears of the *sounder,* the crewman who stood in the bow of the other vessel. Usually, it was bellows from a hand-cranked foghorn that cut into the murmuring silence. Crews signaled one blast for a port tack, two for a starboard tack—three if the wind was abaft the beam, then listened for echoes of the foghorn's deep resonance to bounce off Eagle and back at them. Nothing completely prevented collisions and near swipes, at which time the verbal exchanges between two vessels rendered the air full of *sailor's blessings*, blessings a tinge bluer than the norm—which is not the same blue as a *blue dungeon,* the definitive *thick-a-fog* condition.

---

[65] Admiral Peary's daughter used the monument on Mark Island as a model for the monument erected in her father's name at Cape York in Greenland in 1932.

I lingered at that window longer than any other spot in the entire day's visit. Since Peary's carpenter set the small window in its casing nearly one hundred years ago, it has witnessed untold, eventful, and stirring phases. For me they were but fleeting moments of mental reflection on the speed of light, a *fogscape* of a by gone day. This rush of mental engrossment, which was generated by way of the scene on the other side of a dusty old pane of glass, was alone worth the trip—on the speed-of-light.

Ann Marie's and my mission was to seek out the familiar; something that spoke to our family's presence, and with our interest barely whetted we climbed the narrow, winding, stairs to the second floor—stealthily, cautiously, as though we wished not to wake anyone. They creaked and groaned beneath each careful footstep. The elevated view out to sea from the upstairs back room was absolutely captivating and because we were surrounded by antiquity, it was not difficult to envision scenes as they saw them, schooners under full sail on the long stretch of horizon.

The Admiral's dark and somber room, a very manly room in comparison to the feminine one from which we'd just stepped, not only resembled a chartroom on a ship, it felt and smelled like one from the leather covered books that sat on his huge desk. True to the character of the house, a trundle bed set in the corner of a boy's room, reminiscent of a bunk in a ship's cabin.

Needlework and tatted-lace edges on the pillowcases gave an airy and feminine quality to another room, doilies crocheted in a pineapple design—to us, a familiar decorative handiwork. We knew that Maria actually created voluminous amounts of needlework, a subject that spawned another whispered debate. It was decided that we would be presumptuous to assume any of this work was our grandmother's; after all, Mrs. Peary and her mother were most assuredly so inclined. I took the last glance backwards. As though I actually had the last word on the matter, with the common consent of one—I awarded the output of the pineapple crocheted handiwork to Maria, a veiled gesture, to give her a trifle—for her trouble.

It was easy to discern that the cottage was a refuge built with maritime amenities, a place in which a sailor would have much less longing for the sea—well, maybe for two weeks—three on the outside. That was dependent on how weary he was, and how strong the pull of the sea—or the north—magnetic or true! Outside, at the base of the front porch steps I assessed the size of the front lawn, basically because there was hardly any. Standing at the property's edge, I peered down onto the ledges below, and instantly thought of the child, Alfred.

A mother seagull scooted over near to me on the promontory on which I stood, a place, where in all probability the Gomez children hailed a few of the last stone sloops and tern schooners with a bellow and a hoot. Inches away, the mother gull solicited food that I didn't have. A fledgling, as big as she, chased her, squawking incessantly as she tried her level best to outrun its unrelenting entreaties. Their behavior was out of keeping for birds—not humanized, but obviously *people-ized* by the many tourists.

Wherever I looked, history permeated Eagle Island's preserve,

Alfred

and a historical giant became authentic, human. I'd accomplished what I'd come for—had gleaned a hint of my family's actuality—an exacting experience for them, one that came at great cost.

A perennial eight-year old boy shares the sanctuary with the wildlife, holds sway over the miniature strand—still hoots and bellows from the northern bluff. The hushed public estate is a perfect size on which to hold a youthful sovereignty, and Alfred does—in my mind's eye.

Chapter

5

...Palavering & Perambulating

Somewhere out beyond Casco Bay, Einstein had a general theory which, in 1907, he titled diminutively, E=mc2, and the International Signal symbol, SOS, was coined. Its poignant connotation translated into *Save Our Souls*—the denotation to the less lofty—*Save Our Ship*. The second Sunday in May was established as the first Mother's Day, and an '07 advertisement took the position that pure white lead was the *natural* paint pigment—s'*pose* to keep the water out of the wood. It did.

Henrietta's Long Island Church notes continue...1907
March 31 - first Sunday boat on Casco Bay - Easter Sunday.
April 8th 9th 10th and 18th - Snow storms.
The new Harpswell Line boat, the Machigonne that has been building at Philadelphia arrived at Portland
May 12th. Captain Long in command. It is a very fine boat. The best one of the size in Portland. It has all of the modern equipment.

Excursionist departing the passenger boats now had several wharves available to step onto, built so as to alleviate the long walk home. The Cushing's pier was the first, constructed at a time when a sparse number of houses occupied the island. A few hundred feet away, Ponce built one before the turn of the century to accommodate his hotel at its heyday. A bit further east, Mariner's Wharf, owned by the Harpswell Line was falling into disrepair. August of '07 Casco Bay Lines built Doughty's Landing just to the other side of Mariner's, which served the middle of the island. At the most Eastern end, Cleaves Landing accommodated the Eastenders. Once an island native stepped off the boat, they rarely traveled to the other areas of the island. One would think that the island, as a whole, was cloistered enough without tightening ones parameters even more so. Yet segregation between the *Westend,* Central, and *Eastend* parts of the island maintained a brand of requisite space, an indispensable radius that each third afforded the other two-thirds, a determining factor to successful living in the small, tightly populated society. Congregate meeting places, such as beaches, general stores, post offices, church, and hotel tearooms offered chances to pass pleasantries, to palaver, and perambulate.

Black coal-smoke belched from the stacks of Casco Bay Line's steamers, trailing hundreds of feet behind the vessel on their way to the island. On a particular pristine day, the *Machigonne* bulged at the seams with 600 tightly packed passengers, excited and expectant throngs that trod up over the hill, along boardwalks lined with gaslights—all the way up to the big hotels, beaches, and summer cottages. She eased into the dock and emptied of her day-trippers, and reappearing groups, such as the umpteenth reunion of the 7th, 13th, 14th, and 17th, Civil War Regiments who began rehashing Brandy Station, Gettysburg, Antietam, and Cedar Creek back before the boat left Portland. Was the 13th's Colonel, Neal Dow amongst them? He wasn't, if they had any intention of sharing some *spirits*—not the infamous Colonel who made all of his men *take the pledge*, which is why so many mothers wanted their sons in his regiment. The Confederates weren't spared either, not for a moment. They captured and imprisoned Dow—and really wished they hadn't— a wish shared by captives who were starving and parched. He was unrelenting in his war against demon rum, or Southern bourbon, as the case may be, and when he was exchanged for a Confederate prisoner of some fame, the Blue, the Grey, and the hooch-hounds breathed a collective sigh of relief. Stories of this flavor made the rounds amongst the reunited and made them laugh about a time in our history that was past bearing.[lxxix]

As though the blast of the boat's steam-whistle was a signal to step up the pace, hotel staff bustled, raced against time, fussed and mussed to ready everything that would meet their guest's needs. Meals were better than most. Lobster-clam bakes, on the beach, were established gastronomic productions, each lobster adding all of twenty-nine cents to the overhead costs. Eggs lay just beneath the surface of the steaming mountain of seaweed; then beneath those, in alternating layers—seaweed, clams, seaweed, lobsters, seaweed, corn, seaweed, potatoes, and lastly, deep at the base, seaweed atop a hot bed of rocks. When the eggs were done at the top, it was the sure signal that all else in between was cooked perfectly, the layers of seaweed then peeled away to unearth bushels of food, an operation that was as much entertainment as was the feast.

In this chapter of the island's development, the ends of the island were treeless from the harvest of wood for fireplaces, stoves, and clambakes, replaced with over a hundred cottages that peppered its rocky edges, awaiting the families that reappeared each summer. Captain Carl Morrell scanned the *Maquoit's* decks as they emptied of the families that sifted onto the wharves—where they awaited horse and buggies, or struck out on the long trudge down the road to their summer homes.[lxxx]

The domestics aired out the cottages and unpacked the summer apparel, then swept up all the dead flies. A delivery of ice was ordered to chill down the iceboxes that were packed with food. After which, the family wrote a few postcards, and strolled about to renew acquaintances with friends they had not seen for an entire year, dropping by Ansel Bickford's[66] new popcorn stand to partake. A big red sun sowed its warmth into the west and northwest side of the island, hovering above Cow Island in the late afternoon. There was no better spot in the world in which to bide one's time than in a big wicker chair on the piazza while they sipped on a freshly made raspberry shrub.[67]

Albeit a different generation, today the relatives of these same families file off the Maquoit II, step onto the single wharf at the Town of Long Island, loaded down with provisions, which they carry in a famous brand of canvas bag. All of it is piled into a car and they drive up tarred roads, talking to New York and

---

[66] Ansel Bickford – Brother to Geneva (Bickford) Rogers. Geneva eventually became owner of the *Spa*.

[67] Raspberry shrub was a bottled, strong, non-alcoholic drink made from crushed raspberries, vinegar and sugar…best served poured over ice and diluted with water.

Massachusetts on a cellular phone, drive up to the very same old refurbished cottages in which their grand and great grandparents summered. Much the same ritual takes place. First they air out the rooms, vacuum up the dead flies, plug in the refrigerators, fill them with food, and then renew acquaintances. In two minutes, and fifty seconds they are munching on a bag of micro-wave popcorn, basking in the afternoon sun on their decks—writing E-mails on a lap-top computer, and sipping on—raspberry flavored bottled water. From century to century, human nature has remained the constant. Only the tools have changed.

On second thought, a couple elements have been lost to time: the wrap-around piazza has been replaced by pressure treated (with arsenic) decks, which should last forever. Then there are the dirt roads that were once splattered with horse pucky—which we've exchanged for a less visible-type of energy, a splattering of known and unknown substances invisibly issued out through the car's exhaust pipe. At least we don't have to worry about stepping into it anymore, nevertheless, one might reason that pucky, by any other name—is still pucky.

Daylight brought on a game of tag between a flock of gulls and a flock of crows—resulting in a gentle awakening for the few vacationers who were early risers, those who enjoyed gossiping with the iceman. Far more agricultural than today, the island was pastoral, and too awoke to the racket made by the gulls and crows, but with fields of hay to reap, cows to milk, horses to shoe, pigs, oxen, and chickens to maintain.

Although the Model T was now on the market, horses and buggies were normal conveyances, the roads—little more than wide, hard packed gravel paths. Year 'rounders awoke to another day of working out the rudiments of subsistence while their summer counterparts planned their social fare. Sam Rogers dug clams, ate them every which-way imaginable at one point in his life. They didn't cost—but for his time—and managed to fill the hole in his stomach.

Antonio caught wind that the Cushing family slaughtered a pig, strung it up in the evergreen tree behind the barn to bleed out. Not much got by him, and he was on hand—just the same as in the old country. He worked with a tradition that had gone to seed on these shores, but was a yearly occurrence in Estepona where nothing went to waste when an animal was slaughtered, where everyone in the village came out to help in the process. The Cushings did not have a proclivity to use the blood of the animal, but Antonio did—and carried it home in a pail for a Spanish soup recipe—*another recipe that didn't make it through my osmotic curtain.*

Henrietta's Long Island Church notes continued... 1907
~During the year:
~4 houses were built.
~Seven babies were born: a daughter to the Reverend and the Mrs., two of which were twins of Henry Woodbury.
~Three residents died, one of which was a baby.
~The Reverend baptized two residents, married six couples, the last of which was Frank Littlejohn and Queenie Apleby before the Reverend and his family relocated in Berlin, NH

Clusters of summer children swarmed down over the white sand beaches at nine o'clock every morning with their mothers, who dutifully watched while they splashed around the water's edge. Women caught up on the exchange of news, on all of the grapevine whispers, polished their tarnished silver bracelets with the fine, white, pumice-like sand, and, basked—until afternoon arrived. They then bowed out, sunburned, and waterlogged, with half the sand on the beach wedged inside the children's bathing suits. Ornate castles, which the children worked so hard to create, stood sentinel—left to the mercy of the incoming tide. Twice a day the weight of the ocean bulldozed the architecture flat, obliterated any vestige of their creativity. July's mystical fog banks never deterred loyalists, although at the end of the day they were inevitably bewildered as to how much more sunburn they were than on the sunny days, snookered by Mother Nature's veiled mist.

Along about twilight, Ed Alexander wended the island, casting light into the dark nooks before he returned to his Harbor DeGrace home. The lamplighter likely took pleasure in the nightly greetings he received from those lounging on their piazzas in the sweet, balmy evening air. They were not yet ready to abdicate to the darkness. His go-by was taken as a signal to light an oil lamp inside the cottage, so as to have some illumination inside when, at last, the mosquitoes finally drove them into the house.

A lovely little circular island, shaped exactly like a basket, one situated just across from Long Island had long been a favored habitat for Sunday picnickers. Word was out that the uninhabited Basket Island passed into the possession of Commodore Peary's wife, but everyone doubted that she minded the Sunday cookouts, probably oblivious at this point. The Commodore had returned to Eagle.

Wind and hailstones battered the islands in August, the most violent thunder squall in years. Fallen trees severely damaged Larrabee's new cottage fell smack-dab across the recently built structure. The Harriman's second story completely blew down. A decade of past summers appears marred by high winds, yet none of this seemed to squash the social ambitions of the many vacationing teenagers.

Competition reigned as to the most innovative theme each could dream up for the whirlwind they created with their awkward-age turnouts. At Alice Eaton's cottage a Lemon Party caught the interest of at least twenty-five of her friends. Yellow decorations were easily harvested from the fields of goldenrod. Lemon ice, lemon drops, and lemon cake sufficiently sugared everyone's sweet tooth, followed by a lemon race in which Lillian Ford won the booby prize. Not to be undone, another young socialite, somewhat preoccupied by a theme of snaring and entanglement, first shrouded her piazza with masses of strings hung in a tangle. She hosted a Cobweb Party. Amidst the tangles of strings, her guests had to follow down a single string to a favor that was tied to the end. So as not to repeat the previous week's booby winnings, Lillian Ford aced the Penny Guessing Game, but at the next foray, Ruth Ford prevailed as top goober at the Peanut Party, and won the first prize for carrying the most peanuts on a knife. Ford girls, be they big winners or losers, seemed never to miss a party. Simplistic themes, games, and an entire era underscored the naiveté of the generation. It served them well. In November, long after the echoes of those soirées had faded Maria gave birth to Frances. She called her *"my Francie."* [lxxxi]

Ole Deah & Ole Chum
Walkin' the Cow Fence

"Wun't that Fourth of July a corker! Gotta say, '08 was the best, thus far. Were you there when they started at sunrise? Something happenin' every hour thereafta—boat races, parachute jumpin', clambakes, music. That balloon they sent up is said to be the biggest in the country. Largest throng of people in one day—a record, they say. A wonder the island didn't pop her cork and sink under all the weight.

Thot I'd nevah get that hawse settl'd last night. Wun't the only one! Hawses on both *Eastend* and *Westend* were right in a-rile. Ayup, first one of its kind down heah. Automobile—that's what they're callin' it—that confounded blattin' contraption. I didn't know what was comin'. Scared the bejezzus out of us. Ole-man Rohr—who else? Toured the entire island—big as Billy-Be-Damn. Wun't that somethin though'! S'pose now the place will be overrun with 'em. Aw-w-w, it's goin' to hell-in-a-bandbox anyway.

Been uncommonly low levels of water all ovah the bay. Figured I was gonna have ta dig another well 'fore that rain came. Glad when that cloud dumpt on us. Decent amount. Ayup! Filled the wells back to the brim. Good ta drop the oaken bucket and not have ta use a mile of rope. Makes ya wonder if them big hotels, roomin' houses, and the new pile of cottages are drawin' hard on the island's spring water supply. And there's Ponce buildin' more onto his place.

Newspaper editorial's askin' for an extension of the school vacation to September 15th sez here, 'cause the children *"are not in robust health."* Sittin' in a schoolroom all day, with a coal-stove puffin' away won't help either. Is it the health of the children, or the empty hotel rooms they're worried over once school starts?" [lxxxii]   🐟 🐟

"Find a Way or Make One"
Robert E. Peary July 7, 1908 [lxxxiii]

Commodore Peary's interviews in newspaper reports evolved around his intentions to conquer the Pole, articles that reached into the nooks and crannies of the Casco Bay population, to the faithful followers of his adventurous life. President Theodore Roosevelt, another faithful follower, was aboard the *Roosevelt* as a guest of the Arctic Club when the Navy tug, *Powhatan,* towed her out past Coney Island, New York. Photographers snapped away during the reception, which was held aboard while the ship readied to clear New York Harbor. Eking out every minute that they could before the clock began to mark another long-drawn out separation, Mrs. Peary and Marie finally disembarked onto the Navy tug and returned to shore.

The ship sailed for North Sidney where a large part of the Arctic crew would be taken aboard along with 250 dogs and 25 *Esquimau* drivers and hunters. Three years worth of provisions were to be taken-on there. Three years worth! The ship didn't look big enough. The list read: 30,000 pounds Pemmican, (a concentrated dried lean meat pounded into a paste with fat, then formed into cakes), 16,000 pounds of flour, 1,000 pounds of coffee, 800 pounds of tea, 10,000 pounds of sugar, 7,000 pounds of bacon, 10,000 pounds of biscuits, 100 cases of condensed milk, 50 cases of roast beef hash, 3,000 pounds dried fish-salted, 800 cases of kerosene oil, and 1,000 pounds smoking tobacco. *That should have staved off the hungry horrors—but their blood vessels must have caught hell.* [lxxxiv]

To keep from being separated from food supplies, the plans were to fully load the sledges, and cross the Big Lead. Two support parties were then to establish a base of supplies well up on the north coast of Greenland, a second detachment west along the northern coast of Grantland. Not until February did he plan to leave the *Roosevelt* and begin sledging, using Inuit Indians for the sledging party. It would be a year before anyone knew how the plans meshed.

To this point, I've not come across anything that would establish that Antonio was involved, even on a single leg of Peary's third expedition to the North Pole in '08, other than the picture of Antonio, which was included in an old article about the expedition. It is that particular expedition in which Antonio continuously touted that he was involved. The Admiral's grandson forwarded his opinion that Antonio did not go.

❧ Ole Deah & Ole Chum ❧
1908

"Look heah! Paper's reported the Army's target practice at Fort Williams shook windows and dishes in cottages. Well, la-ti-da! Implies the year 'round houses wun't affected. Why sho-ah! Last I looked I had windows and dishes. All them rumbles and shocks—felt like they hauled out and brushed off them twelve-inch cannons. Better hang onto all your parts mister-man—somethin's abrew! They ain't doin' it for their health ya know. Anyone interview you? Nope, me neither. Snotty upstarts!

Didn't see ya at the meetin' last night. Ayeh, 'bout sixty showed up. They made Cap'n McDonough, of the Portland Police, head squish of the squash team, then proceeded to wailed over what they term chaotic conditions at Ponce's Landin.' Prublem is—they's no one 'round to fix the prublem. The way I see it, too many hawses with carts budgin' to get close to the boat's plank. Store's delivery wagon's is takin' up too much space, freight all over the place. Dogs is fightin' midst the passengers, and now fancy-dancy automobiles. Thems earmarks of too many people if someone was to ask me, which they wun't a'course. Harry Clarke, Dr. Demarast, Dr. MacVane, and a few others jumpt in feet first and formed the Improvement Society. It'll improve all right—but not until the sum and total of them tourist 'n summer complaints dwindles.

Chebeague had people there—askin' us to hook up with them to make a strong appeal to the Telephone Company for a cable— immediately! Ain't they feisty when they got a bee in their bonnet! Ha'd' ya feel 'bout that? Oh—might prove interestin'— can't hurt. They's talkin' about party lines, ten, twelve houses on one line. With all that listenin' handy-by, won't need Henrietta's church notes anymore. Sounds more appealin' ev'ry minute. We'd best take in the next meetin'

Heard about it? Lord God, is there no food for the Master's dog? What next! Why, ev'ry time I turned around someone's bendin' my ear. Whats-his-name, ole Puckerfoot, built a place up on the Ridge Road. Unconventional! That's an understatement. Last I heard he assembled an inordinate number of rooms in the house—each one built with a sink in the corner. Intentions can't be any clearer than that. Well suh, way he seen it, the island was in dire need of some undomesticated ladies, and by gory, went and established himself a brothel. Tryin' his damnedest to citify this place. Heard a few of the island women whisperin'. If he don't watch it, they'll burn it down on him. Daow! He don't care what they say. Keeps flauntin', 'n paradin' them ladies around the island in an opened Tin Lizzie like he's King Tut. That, mister-man, was his undoin'—some imprudent move on his part. The hue n' cry of the Methodist membership fulminated up out of that church. Ayup, a'fore too long, them undomesticated ladies were summarily escorted off the island. Give anythin' to have been a fly on the wall when it happened. He might just as well give it up. Well—he asked for it. That house? It'll prubly stand a good long time as the vestige of a failed experiment— with a sink in every room. Bet you won't find one mention of this is Henrietta's notes.

Can you see up past them trees? Peaks Islanders got a boat every fifteen minutes now. Must have a humdinger of an Improvement Society workin' for 'em over there."

Average fisher folk were not often the subject of the socially driven summer newspaper—that is, until something extraordinary took place. A thirty-five foot shark caught everyone's collective attention—a fish story like none other—an urban myth in the making. Not a single soul, on hand, had arms with a span long enough to illustrate the inconceivable measurements of the mammoth find. As reported—a local fisherman discovered all 8,000 pounds-worth tightly bound up in his nets off Ragged Island, quite mangled, but non-the-less, identifiable. They slowly towed the dead shark into Harpswell before the disbelieving eyes of a group of locals on the dock. The breath of the tail measured 6 feet, the girth 15 feet, and the width of each vertebra, 6-8 inches. Not much was salvageable except the liver from which they extracted oil, a liver, which they said, *"was a large dory load unto itself."*

Sharks in these waters! I've never sighted one from shore, which can make one complaisant about sharks, especially on a late afternoon on Fowler's Beach in the gentle warmth of the late sun—long after everyone else had left for the day. I did that once—tarried a bit longer with my two young children, my niece Mary Susan, and a gaggle of their peers—toasting hot dogs over a little fire dug in the sand. A very high tide had gorged into the inlet submersing the beach area beneath the deep, ice cold waters of the Atlantic, reclaiming all but a strip of warm white sand into its green tinged expanse. The balmy air was to-die-for.

The surface at water's edge began to quiver and then boil like a cauldron. Upon encountering the extraordinary phenomenon, the children laid chase after an enormous school of minnow. Through their excitement and laughter, I watched as a lobster boat moved slowly in towards us—in closer than usual because of the spring tide. The lobsterman bellowed at me from the boat, wanted to make me aware that the "blues"[68] were running. Aah-ha! That's what was driving the small fish right up to the water's edge. Not finished with his message—he added, "and right behind the 'blues' I spotted a shark—and you'd best get the kids out of the water." The minnow sensation was memory making

---

[68] Blues - Bluefish

unto itself, but I recall thinking at the moment that the lobsterman's vigilance was of higher significance, one of the reasons that the community had justification for feeling more protected than most.

North School

Leaving the protection of the island community and their school friends behind, the Gomez family tramped from Casco Bay Lines to their new rental on 159 Washington Avenue in Portland, October of '08, a fair hike for them with bags and boxes to carry. Once settled, four of the children, including six-year old Tillie, were enrolled in North School on the 19th of October. Other island classmates, Ben and Reta Stewart moved practically next door at 149 Washington Avenue, and Clarence and Stella Clarke, Edwin's children were also enrolled, which lent the Gomez children a few familiar faces in and amongst the throngs of city children.

North School was made up of a large population of Jewish and Irish families, many who emigrated that year from Russia and Ireland. This meant that the teachers were working with a high ratio of children who were just learning the language. Italian families were barely represented, as of yet, but in that year ten year old Rosa Dipietro and eight-year old Vincenza Russo arrived from Italy, in what appears to be the initial influx of Italian families that would fill Munjoy Hill to the brim in just a few years time.

Five hundred twenty-six *new* enrollments must have been mind boggling for the teaching staff, an army of new kids on the block, including the Gomez clan, who perceivably experience the usual politics that came with having to work into groups of city children who'd lived and schooled together since Hector was a pup. The four children were assigned to different rooms and different teachers, wherein rules were laid down and all were expected to toe the mark. Records indicate that they were pretty good at it, and were not late, absent, truant, or written up. That means that they were never made to sit facing a corner, or to wear a dunce hat for infractions, such as; neglect of work, disorderly conduct, writing to and harassing girls, and mischief in a fire drill. Teachers did not have an ounce of tolerance for profanity, stealing, harassing notes, running away, laziness, sauciness, and the all time biggie—eating and passing peanuts. By February, five older students were discharged: one to work, another *"took himself away in flight,"* one to care for an ill mother, and one because she was put down from eighth grade. The last quit to *"loaf on the street."*

Should disobedience be a child's fortè, the student was tagged one of the fearsome foursome: willful disobedience, repeated disobedience, impertinent disobedience, or ugly disobedience. Then there was the king of infractions—truancy. For that, whomever the willful soul who dared, received *"reasonable"* use of the strap, and was sent home with a note, *where probably they were again dressed down by their parents.* Somewhere in this entire environment, they learned, but each day must have been exacting, for both teacher and student, a whole different *can of worms* for the island children.

In the one year that Josephine attended North school,[69] before going onto high school, she made the honor roll for excellent attendance. School was called off for only three and one-half days for weather: in November for a fifty-eight mile an hour wind that blew through, and one each in January and February, for the usual heavy snows, rain, and high winds. Winter sickness screwed up, an otherwise perfect record for Tony Junior in February. He was fortunate that it was not the infectious diphtheria that made the rounds at North School. Several students were fatally affected. They learned to beware of the *Ides of March* with its high winds *and hail*—stayed home, but only for half a day this time around. Spring couldn't come quickly

---

[69] All attended North School in Portland, usually from fall to spring, starting out and ending the school year on the island. This began in 1908 until the last child, Margie, graduated from grammar school in 1922. Jo, Tillie, Johnny, Bobby, Frances, and Margie were mentioned on the honor rolls in the several years they attended. Jo, Frances and Margie completed high school; the others attended only until they acquired full-time work. Having read many pieces of correspondence written by my father, the eleven years of schooling he received gave him an excellent base for English. North School Records MS88-106-3 Me. Historical Soc.

enough, and by the end of May they packed up and trouped down over India Street, again loaded down with boxes and suitcases, back to their familiar stomping grounds on Long Island. [lxxxv]

Northern Lights

Inuit Indians believed that when Northern lights danced in waves across the dark skies, their ancestors were guiding lost souls to rest. Although the news would not reach the States for months, on April 6, 1909 the unstoppable Peary and his crew made it to the North Pole: the Commodore's quest realized after years of chasing the elusive coordinates beneath the wavering lights on top of the earth. He was not lost; but in fact, found to history's archives, ad infinitum. The experience had wrested years from him, probably shortened his life. He could now rest on his oars. [lxxxvi]

▲ Ole Deah & Ole Chum ▲
June 24 - September 02, 1909

"Well, they stopped that cluster buildin' of cottages some slick. Alst they needed to do was set down a few fire laws. Yup crowdin' 'em in pretty tight over on the *Westend* somethin' awful. 'Bout time—'bout time!

Hotel owners' been askin' around for some of us to grow peas, beans, corn, and cucumbers so's to sell wholesale to them. Pete MacVane's the man they want for that—got a corker of garden. So good they wrote him up in the newspaper a few years back. Them MacVanes is on the move. That little Westend school marm's gone. Went and married George MacVane. Moved way out to East Podunk—Naples I believe. Them kids'll miss her— wicked bad.

Say! Eva Clarke's startid at the post office at Marston's stoah, 'cross from the Granite Hotel Monday last—as an assistant. Not too many days thereafta, ole Sam Marston took his last breath. Prubly saw it comin.' He was a good ole duff, wun't he? Gonna be missed—yes suh. Next to Marston's, Littlejohn's stoah is hangin' on. Them Littlejohn's been around since dirt was

120

invented, ain't they? Now ole Ponce is got somethin' serious wrong with him, too. They say things happen in threes. Best watch your back, Ole Deah.

You'da laughed—was on the upper deck of the *Aucocisco*. Heard these crones complainin' because no tea is served on the boat. *'At the least,* they sez, *the engineer could draw hot water off the engine and the deckhands serve it up,'* Last I looked there was nawthin' in an engineer's license that covers servin' high tea. Where do they get these highfalutin ideas? Always causin' a tempest in a teapot! Serve 'em right if one of them engineers came up out of the engine room lookin' like the dirty end of a mop, carryin' a teapot in his hand—then stick them stubs for fingers that's been chopped off, right in front of their noses. Hah! That would fetch 'em up—prubly give 'em the vapors. Laughed so hard thinkin' 'bout it, I got teary-eyed. Them women would be best served to get home and watch their own teacups. The 5th and 49th companies are at it again. Heavy rumblin's and shocks at Ft. Williams emanatin' from them ten and twelve inch cannons. Hang on to the riggin's. Mark my word—they're gettin' us into a war.

Now we got some birdbrain in Washin'ton out to get the dogfish, a Mass'chusetts legislator. Yesuh, he went and offered up a Dogfish Bounty Bill. Wants to exterminate 'em all. Law forbids canned dog fish ya know, but the law would accept 'em as fertilizer. Our guys didn't buy it—let it die on the vine. One of 'em musta lumped fish[70] when he was a kid.

Lord, look another blaze—hit over there at Shelter Island, another one Peary owns. Some numb-ass went off and left a clambake burnin'. Healthy conflagration—charred the trees right to the ground. When I was out in the skiff, noticed the flag's been flying at Eagle Island since June. The Commodore's Mrs must be there.

Here's one for ya. Remember Dr. Cook, one of them Arctic explorers that went with Peary '91-'92—you know who I mean?

---

[70] To lump fish: Shovel fish out of the boat's hole into containers that are hoisted onto the wharf.

Well, his wife landed out there on Harpswell at the Hamilton cottage with her two kids. Caterwauling all over 'bout the success of her husband's race to the Pole. Evident'ly she got it from a message Cook sent dated April 21, 1908 that claimed he reached the Pole b'fore Peary. She sez she's awaitin' official confirmation. Bridge will be built to these islands b'fore that happens—and you know how much of a pipe dream that is. Now—of all the places in this entire country that Cook's wife had to make these claims public, she chose to plunk herself within two miles of Mrs. Peary. What's she doin' in these parts? Does she belong to any Harpswell family? I'm just tryin' to work this out in my head. Didn't Mrs. Cook have a whole year to speak out on her husband's claim? Then why did she choose to do so just four days b'fore word arrived on Eagle from Peary? I find that awful intriguin'.

Well, best motivate myself up over Clarke's Hill, Ole Deah. The ole lady has some spawn stew on the stove. Come on ovah if you're interested. Nah—she won't mind." 🐟 🐠

Long Island 1909-10

On their way down Garfield Street, headed for the base of Ponce's landing, Tony Jr. tagged, begged, and whined to go along with his father in the boat to whatever the destination that day. His old man was not of the same mind, was not gladdened to have a pesky child in tow, yet allowed the twelve-year-old to climb aboard the dory. Moreover it is apparent that before the second oar was in the water Antonio knew exactly how he was going to resolve the situation. Halfway into the excursion he dropped his son off onto a bell buoy and rowed away, giving Tony no choice but to hang on to the bobbing buoy amidst the incessant gongs of the clappers, not certain if his father was going to retrieve him. Some eight hours later, pickled to the gills, Antonio plucked his son off the buoy. *By the way that he told the story in later years, it was apparent that the boy never forgave his father for the shear meanness shown to him on that day.*

Long Island School held onto the children for two months before transferring them for the winter-hold-over in Portland in the fall of '09, at least until Maria and the new baby could travel. Margaret Isabella was born in October, and they named the spunky little dickens after Isabella ll, Queen of Spain when Maria was a child. Margie was their last child, the tenth born in a fifteen-year span of time, and it took but three winks for her brothers and sisters to lift the heavy mantle from her little shoulders and call her Margie. By mid November, she was a month old when they moved into a different rent at 143 Washington Avenue, a few doors closer to North School than the previous year. A slew of older Long Island children arrived at North School in November, Alice Mae and Elsie Clarke on the first, and at the last of the month Estella, Edwin Clarke's daughter, Geneva Bickford, and cousin Doris Bickford. Most hung tough until mid March and then beat track for the island. The Gomez kids had to suffer it out until mid June.

***

Newspapers teemed with anticipation of the dramatic flash across the sky created by Haley's comet on its seventy-six year cycle around the galaxy in 1910. The last time that it held the earth's population spellbound happened on the very night that Mark Twain was born in 1834. Storyteller that he was, Twain predicted that on Haley's return in 1910 he would exit this earth. One would not take that type of prediction seriously, but true to his word, he waited exactly seventy-five years and died—from a simple case of old age!

This was the year government census-takers knocked at every door in the city, a sweeping count of the country's population taken every ten years. Census taker, Althea Fickett drew the short straw in April, had to traipse down over Custom House Wharf, jump a passenger boat to Long Island and trudge the dirt roads for her question and answer sessions. She could bank on a community quite densely populated with fishermen and lobstermen, father and son teams from the seafarers that were listed decades back when the census was inaugurated.

Island Avenue was a good place to start, because it ran the entire front of the island. A good plan was to then cut down Lovett Street. There they were—all those fishermen from the

Horr, Wallace, Rich, and Morton families. Over there was another cluster in the Doughty, Burgess, Doggett, and Fowler compounds. Just as with the previously visited households, Althea may have found the men out fishing in the McLeod, Stuart, Bickford, and York households, wouldn't be home until the late afternoon, or next Tuesday, as the case may be; therefore, the women would have to fill out the information with Althea. Woodbury, Johnson, MacVane, Cushing, and Ross; was there no end to the fisher folk in the settlement?

However, as she wended her way on Island and Lovett Streets, she found a surprising gamut of other livelihoods within the same core families. Ruben, and John Woodbury, Albion MacVane, Stephen Dorsey, and Ruben Johnson must have preferred a weekly check, which they received from the Portland police department. Though they did not have to weather the waters, as did the majority of their relatives, they did have to weather the tide of human frailties and scurrilous behavior in the city of Portland. Game warden, Joseph Wallace walked a fine line amidst his relatives and fishermen neighbors, but he probably didn't lose any sleep over handing out fines to them when he caught any with short lobsters. Master mariner, Asa Littlejohn considered his place on Island Avenue home, but one can assume his wife Martha saw little of him until his forty years at sea began to tell on him.

Farmer and milkman Winfield Horr and his seventeen-year old son Frank maintained a dairy herd, and were up and about before the sun—and before everybody else. Dawn to dusk, a farmer was married to his work. *In the sequel of Winfield's life-story, while in the precarious process of off loading a calf from his dory, Winfield lost his grip at the top of the ladder, and with the calf in his arms fell backwards down onto the dory, calf atop him. The internal injuries that he sustained proved fatal.*

Grocery store owners and salesmen, Henry Clarke, George and Benjamin Griffin, Peter Littlejohn, Peter Christianson, and George Woodbury were part of the group of merchants who maintained their year 'round business, kept everybody in comestibles and staples, and provided a hospitable nook in which to gather. Gathering was important, in the middle of the winter.

Another store owner, the old-widow Rich, was *hanging-to* at seventy-five years old. Mary had ten children in her lifetime, yet only two survived, there with her to help keep the wolves from the door.

As like as not, along about lunchtime some genial homemaker on Island Avenue probably took pity on Althea, the census taker, and invited her in for a cup of coffee, to break bread, or use the facilities. Because she had a sizable job to complete, island protocol would never allow a stranger with a mission to go without amenities.

Picking up where she left off, she found one of the Woodburys had been hired as a teamster, William Johnson, an expressman for the city, and the two teenage Griffin boys worked for a skating rink. Althea listed those who were a shoemaker, bookkeeper, dressmaker, one steamfitter, and a cook on a vessel. A bustling housing boom supported several carpenters, house painters, and a cabinetmaker, and there were, at least, two homes in which servants were a part of the household.

Lamplighter-undertaker, Ed Alexander, his wife Lidia and two children were fairing well on the street. Clergyman Frank Baldwin lived a short walk from Ed and the church, close enough to watch over the well digging, especially when they set explosives off in the ledge in front of the church to make way for the well.

Did Althea find it remarkable to discover that the Latham sisters were schoolteachers? Why, at ages seventeen and nineteen, the girls had hardly been away from the schoolroom for very long, themselves. Although, young island teachers were known to keep a school afloat until a seasoned educator was found. On Whaleboat Island, in the year 1888, fourteen-year old Gerty Grady *"performed a good work,"* so reported the Town of Harpswell. She probably read a *mean* rendition of *The Lady of the Lake,* and *Black Beauty,* preferred schoolbook reading at the time.

Vincent Mountfort ran a restaurant. Mr. Jenks and Mr. Cushing ran hotels on Long Island, though logically, it was not a thriving business in April. Every one of these people on Island Avenue and Lovett Street were in their twenties, thirties, and forties, very few were in their seventies; none were in their eighties or nineties. Althea, the census taker, had a ways to go, had just scratched the surface. She still had to search out the *Westend*, the far *Eastend* and, of course, Mount Hunger and the good-widow Gould. Long Island, it could be said, was in robust condition in April of nineteen and ten. [lxxxvii]

Chapter

6   ...Snow In the Woodbox

July 1911 delivered searing temperatures, a heat record of over 105 degrees in some of the mainland towns, but because the islands were surrounded by water they could rely on being a *whole* five degrees cooler. The Gomez children found the heat of discord equally stifling and snuck out of the house when their mother was otherwise distracted, when their father arrived on the scene, sullen, and ill tempered. Young as he was, Bobby dragged an inner tube down onto the front beach in front of Cushing's Hotel, a makeshift bed in which to sleep, a way to remove himself from the heat and fray. Lulled by the sound of the waves at the water's edge, cradled by the old rubber inner-tube, the child forgot to take into consideration the rising tide and awoke with a start, fully afloat, a fair distance from the shore—the quintessential rude awakening. Though certainly taken unawares, he had presence of mind to make his way back ashore and bunked down again, this time, just above the mean waterline. *It's fair to assume, because he and Johnny were so intensely close to one another, and so very young, that Johnny was also there on the beach, though probably sound asleep.*

Old age claimed the old, faded Pettengill homestead that sat *Downfront* overlooking the Granite Springs, the one out behind Peter Littlejohn's store, the one in which ninety-year old Ann Eliza Cushing was born in the year 1820. The dilapidated place may well have been one of the original four homes built on the island, and since few homes were ever razed, the demolition in August drew sidewalk superintendents from all points—the old, the young, and the ever present old codgers like *Ole Deah* and *Ole Chum*. Once the original building-block of the community was rendered a pile of rubble, imaginably, it spawned exchanges between the old-timers—folktales that harkened to the days

127

when the Longs, Cushings, and Pettengills cleared and farmed the land, fished from the rocks—of how they beat small paths to each other's homes, and hung strong until a fourth, a fifth, and a sixth family arrived. What would old Ignatius Cushing make of steam engines, automobiles, and the ever popular secession from England? When he walked the island, settlers were said to have utilized birch twigs with which to whisk food, George II was sitting high on the English throne, still in charge, somewhat…and another George (Washington) was barely out of knickers, just eight years old, learning to size up cherry trees. *I wonder…if Ignatius was "for or a' gin" secession from England?* Someone in the crowd that was assembled around Pettengill's demolished home knew the answer to that question.

After all of the excitement, an ice cream *was* in order, over at the recently opened Day's Spa. Actually, Day's merely opened the front door and everyone wandered in to take a look-see at what was new and interesting. Men, as always, dressed in suit and vest, greeted one another with a handshake and a nod. Husbands, upon seeing their wives, courteously took their hats off in a proper greeting, a sign of the gentility of the era, for those who were into gentility. Most were.[lxxxviii]

The Eastenders headed for home. They had their own brand-new store to patronize—thank you very much, and Peter Christiansen not only had ice cream and candy, he had *"superior table food."* The newly opened Long Island Market, located at the head of Doughty's Landing, was advertising;
"Are you with us?" [lxxxix]

Reemergence into the Washington Avenue community took the Gomez family beyond the normal boundaries during the 1911 turn-around school year, which as usual, started on the island, then continued in Portland in late October. Nothing else about it was the least bit usual. They did not return to the 143 address where their father lived, but to 83 Washington Ave with their mother. Her name was listed as sole parent when they signed in for the school year.

Divorces were rare—an understatement indeed, for it was unheard of in 1911. Maria was no longer able to withstand or abide her husband's dark side. A small column appeared in the Portland paper to announce Justice King's decision to all that Antonio was: *"found to have gross and confirmed habits of intoxication and exhibited extreme cruelty."* She most certainly endured embarrassment and the social stigma that accompanies divorce, but whatever she perceived to be the worst of worst on the horizon, it was, evidently, far better than whatever she and the children faced on a daily basis. Maria and the children were in for a siege. They faced it together. [xc]

Washington Avenue brimmed, to overflowing, with North School students, and the flow all headed towards the big brick building on Bobby's first morning at school. The six-year old trooped along with Tony, Louie, Tillie, and Johnny for his first day, leaving four-year old Frances, and two year-old Margie, behind with their mother. Johnny, just one year ahead of Bobby, was a perfect guide, in that the previous year he'd tested the terrain during his own initiation into the educational milieu. Bobby was a quick study. A child with five older siblings, and two younger, would already have the politics down pat.

With papa living down the street, uninvited, unpleasant domestic discord continued to invade the house, and what better place to escape the unsavory atmosphere than the corner of Washington Avenue and Congress Street where they encountered a flurry of traffic and neighbor children. Their questing little minds were otherwise engaged by an entirely different brand of noise and haste—nearby at the fire station on India Street. Powerful horses pulling fire apparatus, the vitality and brawn of the uniformed men ringing bells to clear the way as they charged to a fire up on Munjoy Hill was just the type of commotion that transfixed the children and garnered their attention—actually—most everyone's attention.

Transition from horse to the internal combustion engine was gradually making way. A creative man by the name of C. F. McCann,[71] along with the Portland Company, developed a three-wheel tractor designed and built to haul existing fire equipment

---

[71] C. F. McCann -For more insight into the life of this superfluous man, go to www.mccannfiretrucks.com.

the City owned, a concept that would, if accepted, replace the horses. Down around the corner from where the Gomez family lived, McCann paid a visit to the old firehouse on India Street; drove his three-wheel tractor up to a prearranged appointment with the fire chief to convince him that the City of Portland should replace their horses with these tractors. The chief was waiting with the best horses in the City, all in harness, and attached to the fire equipment. The idea was to ring the fire alarm, at which time the horses would dash out of the barn. McCann's role was to attempt to race them to the Portland Observatory in the tractor. After a nice chat, the chief walked away, and without warning, rang the bell, calling out, *"Fire at the Portland Observatory!"* He charged out of the barn, lashing at the animals as he careened up Munjoy Hill, shades of the *Hare and the Tortoise* story. McCann, in his pathetic 1910 tractor, chugged along and in due time, made it to the top of the hill. Waiting at the observatory, the chief had a big laugh on him, stating that those contraptions would never replace horses such as the likes of those hooked to the fire equipment. [xci]

They then journeyed down the hill, the chief jocular and triumphant. He unbridled the lathered horses and put them out in back of the fire barn to munch on some well-deserved hay. When the chief had finally accomplished all of those tasks, McCann walked over, hit the fire bell and called out, *"Fire at the Portland Observatory,"* then took off, leaving the chief in the dust, just as he'd been left behind the first time around. McCann made his point—won the battle, and proved the machine, but lost the war of words—the Chief having the last one on the matter.

Portland geared up for the Christmas season, but none in the family had a red cent to expend for the most minimal of holiday gifts or decorations. Their skills at improvising were put through a bitter test, and improvise they did for the little ones, who at that point ranged in ages from two to seven years old. It saddened Jo and Tillie to be in such dire striates. To shield Johnny, Bobby, Frances, and Margie from the harsh reality, they searched about the place for materials to fashion something—anything that said it was Christmas. Imagination and brown paper bags merged to fabricate decorations. Scraps were concocted into gifts. The girls felt it a gesture that, at least, afforded the spirit of the holiday. Three days after Christmas, in 1911, Maria received a bill for the balance of the divorce from the lawyer for fourteen dollars and ninety-seven cents.

She labored as the family tottered between basic poverty and abject poverty. The older children helped support in whatever way they could. If they made fifty-cents it went into the family coffer. Though it was not in her to beg, she was finally forced to approach the Cathedral of the Immaculate Conception for help; there was no food. Possibly because of the divorce, the Church denied any form of assistance, which left their welfare depressingly bleak. The minister, from the Preble Street Methodist Church, was told of her plight and immediately intervened, provided food, and gave her the foot up that she needed in the way of work. It was the family's watershed, the turning point to recovery. It also was a turning point in their spiritual base. From that day forth, although the oldest were left to make their choice, the four younger children were baptized and raised in the Methodist religion.

Until this present day, I did not know that my father was immersed in the North School's student body, or that he had this solid tie to Portland's warp and weft from such an early age. The news was an eye-opener for me and handily explained why, as an adult, he exhibited a familiar attitude towards the many Portland business owners—his old classmates. I wish I'd known of this because, when I arrived at Portland High School in '56, my school roster read as though it was his North School in 1911, albeit a new generation of Aceto, Gribben, DiFilippo, Napolitano, Russo, Cirillo, and Cavanaugh children, to name a few of the many. I might not have felt as unconnected had I been aware of the link, a handy piece of knowledge to have possessed when the city's educational system was thrust upon all of us.

***

The miserable reality of the *Titanic's* dramatic and sorrowful misfortune in April of 1912 captivated Portland's attention. The

Carpathia[72] was too far away to see the flares, but received her SOS calls and steamed full bore to rescue the passengers and crew. Over the years, the story was made into a romanticized passage in maritime history. However, in this port, where countless *sinkings* are a stark reality, none will ever deny the poetic and idealized memory bestowed to the twelve hundred terrified souls lost to the sea that night. *We are practiced at idealizing the memories of those we lose to the sea. It is the least we can do for them.*

During this month, young Tony made the decision to leave school in lieu of a permanent job, with a twofold base for his decision. Though he advanced to the next grade each year that he attended North School, sometime before he entered there in '08, he was held back a grade or two, possibly during the period that Alfred died, a time when he may have missed too much school. When he was younger, it didn't matter as much, but now at age fifteen, he was too old for the sixth grade, though it appears that each grade did have its fair share of older students. Obviously, if a student didn't make the grade, they weren't arbitrarily handed the brass ring. Though his education was on the back burner, it would not be forgotten there. For the time being, the family's income was paramount. At that moment, he likely did not lose any sleep over it.

***

Over at the base of Rhor's Hill at the beginning of summer, the McCanns of Portland returned to their Comfort Cottage—the Bates of Boston vacationed at Idyllhurst—and the Fords opened Fordette. A state representative of Cambridge, Massachusetts, E. Long arrived in August to stay at the Longwood cottage on the Eastend. Tagging a name onto one's summer home characterized the cottage, labeled it for a century, despite attrition and change of ownership over the years.

Winter homes, owned by those who for one or more generation bore up under all four seasons, were naturally tagged with the family name, a name which indelibly stuck as the source of reference—even after they, too, became dearly departed. It

---

[72] During World War I, the *Carpathia* was sunk off Ireland

mattered not who bought the house thereafter... *"Head down the road towards Fowlers* (beach). *It's the one just up from Bickford's old house—the one next door to the old Thompson place,"* [73] (an empty lot for forty years). New owners wrestled with the fact that the previous owners were part of the package— came with the deed—a co-tenancy of sorts—not with their ghosts, but with a tenor of the original owners. The island was too interlaced to let go, because in a broad sense, to do so would be to cast away part of one's self.

It should be added that a small number of select homeowners might dispute my notion that they have inherited the" tenor" of previous owners and may feel it understates their particular situation. Decades worth of narratives gives credence that a few select homes have had spirited co-tenancies with active supernatural visitants, that came with the deed—at no extra cost.

Mrs. MacVane and the island ladies saw it necessary to pool their pantry supplies—to offer baskets of comestibles to Maria when she and the children returned to the island at the end of May. It makes one to wonder if Antonio was making good the alimony that was laid down by the divorce settlement for support of the children. The ladies good intention was a restorative act of kindness, solace for a sagging spirit that needed only that, an act that tightly bonded the family to the community from that day forward. For all of their lives, the family worked to pay it back, one dividend at a time.

Maria busily developed ways to make a dollar, literally—a penny at a time. The island, it would seem, had a voracious sweet tooth and several women on Garfield Street had a whip-snap recipe for needhams, a chocolate covered coconut morsel that used mashed potato as its base, and added paraffin wax to the chocolate to make it more solid and shiny. Maria's chickens laid an abundance of eggs that gave her an easy base for her brand of candy. Egg white, plus sugar, nuts, a whisk, and an innate sense of confectionery know-how whipped the concoction into melt-in-the-mouth nougats. Her Johnny *loved* nougats, the ones covered in dark, rich chocolate. In Spain, nougats were

---

[73] Adeline (Thompson) Cushing's family

made only at Christmastime. Candy was the means of income for the Catholic nuns when Maria was a child, as was educating children in the craft a part of the orderly process. Does it follow that it was in that sphere that Maria learned the craft—for when she decided to produce candy in quantity, it did not take much of a stretch. She threw her long bib-apron into the ring, threw up the summer kitchen window, and opened for business on a street that somehow sustained an inordinate number of households that sold candy, a street that drew children from as *far away* as the *Eastend*.

🐟 Ole Deah & Ole Chum 🐟
1912

"Finest kind! Finest kind old dear—and you? Since that dredgin's started up it's provided a pile of entertainment for the island. Look at them pip-squeaks over on Cushin's wharf. Right into the thick of it, ain't they? Kids love that stuff. Quite an ole steam fired rig. Clamshell bucket seems to dig a decent pile of mud. You say they're dredgin' Ponce's too? Told'ja that *Machigonne* had too much draught to her—too impractical—too damn big for this bay. 'Course, no one evah wants to hear my opinion. Look at all them pilin's she's loosened and stove-up since she's been on the run. Costly? I wouldn't want the bill. While back, Harpswell wanted to blast around Pottses.[74] Too tight makin' the turn there. She has to make that big long swing around Haskell to keep from groundin' out. Adds forty-five minutes to the run. Must be hard to keep a schedule. Why don't they just sell the damn thing? [xcii]

Dredgin' shut down for that gale that scudded on through. Some ole blowy day, wun't it? George Morton and Charlie Floyd were smack out in the middle of it on the *Kate L. Palmer*. Dories and gear got swept ovah, and wind drove 'em for sixty hours and one hundred miles b'fore it abated. Bet that was a hairy ride. Look at 'em, they don't look none-the-worse for the wear. Tough little buggers, ain't they?

---

[74] Pottses – Pott's Point

Iceman's on short notice. Emery Waterhouse is advertisin' refrigerators. Must mean 'lectricity's on its way—prubly 'bout the same time as them phones. 'Bout 400 of them phone people showed up at Cushin's for their first annual outin'. Phone company's already chastisin' its mainland customers for wrong numbers, admonished them to look up the numbers in the *catalogue and pronounce them distinctly* to the operator; after all, they have four hundred and twenty thousand telephones in Maine, Mass'chusetts, New Hampsha, and V'mont.

Glanced ovah this paper. Editorial in heah by some Cliff Island summer complaint—whinin' 'bout awful noises them motor boats is makin'. He's askin' they put mufflers on 'em. He sez heah, *'His comfort is entirely destroyed by the clatter.'* Well-suh! My comfort is being destroyed by the clatter that comes out of them summer cottage association meetin's. Enough to give ya triple dyspepsia.

Pile of guests over at Frank Chase's house on Island Ave the other day. Ayup, he and the Mrs entertained the Metropolitan Club, 'bout twenty-four. First the ladies arrived in the mornin' all gussied-up, 'course. Spent the day sewin'. Five o'clock, the men arrived for suppah—'scuse me—dinnah. Buggy eatin' underneath them trees. Lanterns draw 'em. Noticed everybody's decoratin' with Japanese lanterns these days.

Now, if you don't spend all your money on Japanese lanterns, for a price, there's a fella givin' demonstrations of a Wright Brother's plane on pontoons. Forty-one foot wingspan they say. Anyone notice if he snarled up any of our gear? More 'round heah be satisfied with a docile game of whist. At least ya come out of it with a fancy Irish lace handkerchief for a prize. Well— it's prissy, but it's better than a sharp stick in the eye. 'Course, the real competition is that Chebeague amateur show. You gotta go some mister to get by Gerald Doughty and Herbie Ross and their clever clog dance. Ain't they a caution! Yesuh, they did— won first prize. Ain't quite as shy as they'd like you to think. Not much moss is gatherin' on anyone over there. Got a cocker of a golf course, some bowlin' alleys, a shootin' gallery, baseball park 'n movin' pictures. If ya have any pooch left they's a double tennis court and dancin' three nights a week. Attractin' too many city-folk, I say.

Chebeaguers are snittin' too, ya know. Ayup, it's the garbage the tourists 'n summer people are throwin' all over their roads. Next thing you know, they'll have ta hire someone full time to clean up, or put barrels all ovah. Changin' the flavor of the island, ain't they? Lord! That editorial person is become irritatin'—gettin' awful pushy. Started plaguin' us lubstermen 'bout *our* noisy mufflers. She sez heah, *'do this—don't do that—fix your lawn—give a party—get the shotgun—sandpeepers are out.'* For such an educated person, she ain't learned that it's better to be thought a fool, than for her to open her mouth, and remove all doubt. I got more important things brewin' than to be wastin' time givin' parties and target shootin' sandpeepers for sport. She needs to get out there and toil for a livin'.

Commodore Peary is sellin' off things they say. Last year he sold some property on Cliff Island—two hundred fifty-foot of Island Ave—sold it back to the islanders for a libary. Here it sez his ship, the *Roosevelt*, was put on auction in New York. Originally cost a hundred thousand to build. This McDermott fella bought it for $35,000. Damn decent buy. What he's gonna do with it? What kinda condition ya s'pose she was in afta runnin around in the ice?

Hafta pick up a few things at Clarke's. Looks like the Shaw's family-run grocery store *Uptown*, is gonna give Clarke & Griffin's a run for their money. Now they got one on Congress and a second on Preble Street. They's advertisin' as purveyors of Delicatessen Dainties, and are willin' to ship to the Bay Lines. Now, they's two ways of lookin' at it. Gonna cost freight either way. If we don't patronize Clarke's, we'll lose the stoah, and in the middle of the winta, mister-man, we'll be wishin' we had 'em. 'Course, I'm not that keen on canned foods yet. Don't like the looks of that black stuff 'round the seams inside the cans. I'll stick to the food in those canning jars the ole lady puts to use.

Clarke's become a purveyor too, ya know. Wicked pile of new things on their shelves—pencils—a brand new invention. Be able to carry 'em in your pocket. Has tooth powder on the shelves too. Don't have to swish with whisky anymore. Too late comin' for me! Damn! Am always forgettin' my uppers. Been wantin' to try them popcorn fritters at the Days Spa. Someone told me that theys sellin' caramel corn in a box with a little prize down inside the corn. Kids is buyin' 'em up left and right, just for the prize. Let me borry five cents for a loaf of bread. Was too hot to bake bread yesterday. Think I'll take a squint Downfront 'n see what boats are in. Take care—you ole hayrack. Don't do anything I wouldn't do!"

🐟 🐠

Ponce went back to Spain before 1912, so say some. A serious illness befell him back in '08, and now his holdings were sold off under the aegis of his estate. The original architects of the Granite Springs bought back the hotel. In a catalog of his Long Island properties, notes were scribbled all over his map, put there to guide the person who had charge of the sales and stated that some people were not to be considered because of very questionable credit. By April of 1912 the estate of Ernesto Ponce sold the house on Garfield Street to Maria for six hundred dollars, the exact amount of dollars it was priced-at fourteen years earlier. Maria must not have been a risk.[75]

The wording on the mortgage is noteworthy, "In witness whereof, I the said Maria A. Gomez, and being unmarried..." On a twenty-year mortgage, and in her unmarried state, it took her less than ten years to pay it off. She did it with washtubs of laundry, a little midwifery, upper crust dinner party fare, and a few pieces of candy at a time.

To bring the sweet tasting water up from the deep springs that ran through the ledges, water pipes and a hand pump by the kitchen sink were the first improvements made. That did away with the accumulation of wooden pails beside the sink and the chore of hauling water from the well. Rainwater that came off the roof was captured in wooden barrels, an extra supply for the regular scrub board washes that she did for summer residents.

---

[75] A map shows the house and an outbuilding on the property in 1904.

Clothes were softer when washed and rinsed in rainwater, and hair is never as soft as when washed at the rain barrel.

Between the flurry of impulsive and impetuous Gomez children on the down side of the street, and the cow pasture that nudged up next to them on the upside, there was no rest for Hulda and Frank Mountfort who, along with their rooming house, were tightly sandwiched between the two. To add insult to injury, Beach Avenue foot traffic, looking for a shortcut to Garfield, cut a path along the lower end of the cow fence. So steady was the traffic beneath Mountfort's windows, that it eventually created what everyone thought was an overgrown street.

To lay bare the mysterious patterns of why some things are the way they are on the island, ninety years after the cows were gone, ninety years after any knowledge of a cattle fence remained in anyone's memory—the shortcut remained well traveled. All of those years it was assumed to be a right away, or a paper street. Recently, while digging for a foundation for his home, (on what was the lower end of the cow pasture) a present heir and assign got snarled up in bales of wire fencing, and piles of huge bones. Per his recollection the wire and bones had no place being in an area of residential house lots. The "find" left him scratching his head.

An old 1913 Long Island street plan held the key, and he studied the many changes on the street, asked questions, and after a fashion, looked up from the documents and blurted, "That's it! There it is!" He'd found the origin for the bales of wire nestled in a drafter's neatly drawn rendition of the fencing and the cow pasture that none knew existed. He deduced that the bones were remnants of a slaughtering area. The lower boundary of the fence, which ran from Beach Avenue across to Garfield, was of particular interest to him, the very spot on which he built his house. Islanders continued to walk through his yard, around the house, then skirted around a large vegetable garden that ran the back of the lot, just to cut on through. Why did they continue to do that? He found the reason in the natural path of the fence line. It's biological osmosis, I say. Obviously, even shortcuts on an island are governed by a biological osmosis—if not that—then what governs an Elephant walk?

Frank Mountfort took care of Casco Bay Line's business on Ponce's Landing—whatever that entailed. He elected to live next to a family of Spaniards, a strange lot to draw for a veteran of the Spanish-American war. He and Hulda had no children of their own, though the rooming house and its tenants held their undivided attention and harnessed all of their energies. Hulda, an immigrant too, tested her Swedish recipes on their visiting guests, planted rock gardens and rambling roses, an old fashioned variety that climbed all over her piazza, the type that dripped with big clumps of tiny, deep pink flowers in July, thirty miniature roses to a clump. *I know it was exactly thirty to a clump, because on one of my slow days, I took the time to count them.*

Cats teetered all over the porch railings, sat in the windows, and held sovereignty over a domain of their own making. Most every house was filled with cats, for company, and to rat the general area. They teemed all over the property, even though Frank methodically drowned the newborns in a pail of water as soon as they were born—the accepted way of population control in those days. He, like everyone, put some adult cats in a tightly tied burlap sack weighted with big rocks and flung them off the wharf, another accepted approach to overpopulation. Once in nine lifetimes a cat fought its way out of the sack and returned, found waiting, of all places—at the back door of its *cattusidal keeper*, sopping wet, ears pinned back to reflect its frame of mind. Survivorship inoculated a Lazarus cat from ever again being consigned to the bag of rocks. Actually, it was allowed to reach antiquity for having tenaciously held to life, allowed to live—that is—if the dogs didn't pack up on it. Packs of dogs were problematic. Sheep had to keep watch over their shoulders, too.[xciii]

North School's graduating class of 1913 arrived on the island for a class picnic, and since it was Louie's class, Tillie, Johnny, and Bobby were probably on the wharf to show the way, a quasi-hospitality team for the fifty city kids and their teachers. A threatening windstorm greeted the start of the summer season, blew-over bathhouses, beached boats, and uprooted trees. The island never missed a beat—but the winds of war were full and by. [xciv]

❧ Ole Deah & Ole Chum ❧
1913

"I know I'm late. Made the mistake of sittin' in the parlor afta dinnah and slipped into one of those digestive comas. God, she served up the *best* corned-hake t'night—slathered all atop potatoes, with a sprinklin' of crispy pork scraps and onions. Enough to tear out every taste bud I have in my mouth.

Say, you hear there's a woman runnin' Ponce's place 'til the new owners take ovah? She's opened a Japanese tearoom and is havin' Dutch lunches. I've heard of Dutch Elms, a Dutch oven, Dutch uncles, and being in-Dutch. What the hell's a Dutch lunch? If she didn't get drove out by that windstorm—maybe she'll last. [xcv]

Got that Jonah off our back. Nahant Line in Boston bought the *Machigonne* this spring. Not long afta she was put on schedule, she rammed the fishin' schooner *Priscilla* off Commonwealth Pier, scatterin' the fisherman for the lifeboats. The schooner sank quicker than an over-loaded stone sloop—right to the tops'il.

Take a gander over there. Nope, nope—that's Diamond Island b'God! Fierce fire billowin' into the sky. Jiminy—even got the fireboat hauled out. Early Fourth of Julyers prubly set it off. Dry spell's helpin' to fan it. Looks like Fort McKinley has some apparatus there too. Gimmie my spyglass[76] 'Bout twenty-five men just went ashore with axes. Hoard of people come tearin' up from the *Eastend*. Told me they thot it was this end of this island goin' up in smoke. Can't fault 'em. That's one menacing black cloud. Be a while snuffin' it out.

Arthur Demmons cut his foot awful bad. Been livin' out there on Marsh Island. Had ta wait 'til low tide' til the bar was exposed to come acrost at mid point off Andrew's Beach. Don't know how he lives out there. Just one humongous mass of poison ivy. Prubly is runnin' all through his system b'now.

---

[76] Spyglass - telescope

Ole man Cushin's havin' dances every Wednesday night and then opened the Pavilion to the Catholics for church on Sunday. Ain't it just like Charlie to wear down a pile of soles dancin' on Wednesday night, then turn around and help save a soul or two on Sunday mornin'. Priest come ovah from Peaks for the first service[77] ever held on the island. Listened outside—can't understand a word of his preachin'. I know its Latin! My mother didn't raise no fool ya know. Chebeaguers and Cliff Islanders came over too. Then there's Reverend Leigh, revving up his flock with square and round dancin' hoe-downs he's been puttin' on. 'Fore long my wife will be blattin' at me to take her out to one of 'em. I'll feign a gimp. Usually works.

Glendenning's prubly not too happy that Henry Clarke has taken over the postal job. Say the service will be improved with him in charge—mail twice a day, handy to the hotels, other stores, and wharves. We'll see. Give it time.

Readin' the paper 'bout the game over at Cliff Island—sez heah: *"Whale's, pitcher for Long Island's baseball team pitched a fine game against Cliff Island and easily won, 6-2. Not a run was made off his delivery until the ninth innin'. This was due to a two banger by Devine Griffin, and an error and wild throw by Long's fielders. Although at times LI fielding was ragged, the team played a good game and something out of the ordinary was absent—Cliff's 'kicking' and continuous wrangling over the umpire's decisions."* Caan't you see Devine right up in that umpire's face? What a rig!

Keerise! Look down there at that mess of jellyfish that's come in on the tide. Best fetch a blat at them summer kids—get 'em out of the water. Prubly don't know the diff''rence between the white ones and them cussid red ones. They'll be lucky if they don't come out of it plastered with rashes.

Been entertained the whole month with mine explosions. Just like the Fourth of July all over. Mine Plantin' Department, at Ft. McKinley on Diamond, set-up that practice operation. Quite a spectacle! Water was thrown hundreds of feet into the air. A few industrious souls rowed over and gathered them stunned fish,

---

[77] First Catholic Mass - June 1913

netted the dead ones too. One of 'em hauled in three hundred pounds. Sold 'em for ten dollars. How come you didn't get in on that?

Personally, I'da like ta gotten in on young Fred Bickford's haul. Brought in eighty-three swordfish on his schooner. Took the load to the Boston fish market n' by gorry, he pocketed $153 for nine days work. A hundred-fifty-three-dollars! Ayuh, now that I think on it, he *is* the youngest captain we got on Long Island.

Dasst stay much longa. Look at that sky blackenin' up in the west—good size squall's makin' its way ovah. Pile of 'lectricity in them clouds. *Eastenders* ain't gonna be any too happy. Likes to strike down there. Ayup! Before we go, let's pull Jake's punt up above the high water mark."

Buffalo Bill Cody's famous Wild-West Show & Pawnee Bill's Far-East Show came roaring into Portland. Cody was unhappily aligned with what was, by all intense purposes, a watered down version of his exhibition that traveled Europe and throughout the States. Lamentably it had little resemblance to the spectacular show he owned for thirty years with stars like Annie Oakley and Sitting Bull. He had great respect for the Chief, thought him to be a native intellect, and he was. From the list of awe-inspiring feats performed by Cody, the one that made a lasting impression on one eight-year old were the enormous cakes that Buffalo Bill Cody baked. Whatever the deal was with the cakes could have been part of why the consummate showman was said to be so unhappy. But on that day little Bobby Gomez met an actual, dyed-in-the-wool, national hero who started his career with the Pony Express at age twelve, a business that never hired anyone under eighteen, preferred orphans, and surprisingly lasted only eighteen months.

The end of Cody's career seemed long and drawn out; the farewell tour took three years alone until it went stone broke in 1913. He was sixty-eight and for the last four years of his life he did a circus outfit's bidding.

Now—because history never seems up close, I looked straight into Dad's eyes with total disbelief when he told me that he actually met Buffalo Bill and then gave him my best, squinty eyed, seedy look when he handed me the cake story. We could tell when he was joshing. His mouth always turned up at the corners and his eyes sparkled. I didn't read a josh in this one. Maybe Cody was one of those men who liked to bake. This piece of Americana is one that must be further pursued. [xcvi]

***

Gloves were an indispensable item to the fashion conscious and Jo now had full time work at the Eastman Brother's department store in their glove department. Sixteen-year-old Tony, with his inclination for mechanics, had been working at the Southworth Machine Co. on Preble Street. Tillie picked up work at a restaurant at Prouts Neck, Louie as an apprentice at Banks Motor Car Co. Even Johnny, at eleven, and by all intents and purposes, handicapped with paralyses of both hands from birth, found work at a laundry. The disability that he worked around normally rendered individuals born with this condition with either, both hands paralyzed closed, or—both hands paralyzed opened. The saving grace, which gave him the ability to grasp items between both hands, was that one of his hands was frozen opened and one closed tightly. *None that I knew ever considered Uncle Johnny disable—including Uncle Johnny.*

Politely displaying their social graces, the two older girls inquired as to the nature of Johnny's workload at the laundry, to which he gleefully responded, *"I shake farts out of the sheets."* They *knew* better than to ask. *They knew better!* Much to their chagrin it would not be the last time that he buried their social graces in the aftermath of his incorrigible, but amiable behavior. He, in turn, earned a lengthy comeuppance for his coarse and vulgar language, although it was every bit to his delight, because he owned the animated moment and cackled about it for a week.

Ah yes! The boys were feeling their oats, setting Jo and Tillie's indignation meter to new heights. Tony's compulsion to work off a pile of energy with a climb to the top of the partially built *Million Dollar Bridge* was the crowning touch. He perched

143

atop a girder, as though surveying a domain, while down at its base, a Portland policeman bellowed at him to come down—but to no avail. Tony stayed put until he was damn ready to make his descent. He was King of the Hill, untouchable, with a sense of regency, and a bird's eye view of Casco Bay. Obviously he eventually tired of his minute of fame, slithered down the girder and into the strong arm of the law, and a reprimand delivered in a strong Irish brogue. Delivered he was, right to their Washington Avenue door, and into the burning glares of his sisters.

The world took a giant leap into World War I in 1914, and subsequently began to trip all over each other for dominance. Austria and Hungary declared war on Serbia—Serbia and Montenegro on Germany—Germany on Russia—Russia on Turkey—France and Britain on Germany—France on Austria—Britain on Austria—Austria on Russia—Austria on Belgium—and France and Britain on Turkey. *Wasn't anybody getting along over there?* [xcvii]

The island's young men were fitted out in the brown Doeboy uniforms and left for the war, mustard gas, and the Great Influenza epidemic. For many, the call to service was the first time in their lives that they'd traveled any further than Portland's waterfront, a stark awareness that there existed hostile environments in the world—like none they had ever experienced. Antonio[78] took his snarly attitude, went off with the U.S. Transport Service, and stayed out of his family's lives for a few years.

---

[78] 1915 Portland City Directory lists Antonio as: removed to South Carolina.

Chapter

7

...Scorched Strand

What Comes Around, Goes Around

Exactly two o'clock every summer afternoon, ladies in long dresses, fanciful hats, gloves, and with parasols perched on their shoulders promenaded down the boardwalk to attend a high tea at the Dirigo Hotel.[79] Margie, too, skipped down the boardwalk with penny clenched in hand, destination—the Spa's candy-counter, the *boughten* variety. Isn't that just like a five-year old child to want the store variety when the homemade candy was readily available? Traversing in the same direction towards a high tea, a very stoic lady sallied onto the boardwalk. Pompous and unkind that day, she pushed the child off the boardwalk to make way for herself. More because she lost her penny down the crack of the boardwalk than for the insult, Margie scampered back up the street with a plaintive wail and choked up enough of the facts to send the ordinarily passive Maria hell-bent down over the hill—frothing mad. She did not go to the front door but stood on the boardwalk and in her best and worst broken English utterly scandalized the woman.

As adages are wont to do, the *"What comes around, goes around"*—came 'round, and Margie had the good fortune to have front seat tickets to the show between the selfsame lady and an aged couple who lived directly across the street. The old woman and her elderly, bed-ridden husband had endured just about enough priggish and self-righteous manners to last for more time than they had left. Once and for all, she would bring it to an end. On the day of reckoning she laid wait in her husband's second story sickroom behind the lace curtains, waited for the

---

[79] The Dirigo Hotel was the first hotel on the island, followed by Cushing's Casco Bay House, then Ponce's Granite Springs.

two o'clock tea drinker to traverse directly beneath the second floor window. When the moment was precise the old lady let loose the ripe contents of her husband's chamber pot, showering it down upon the startled and mortified woman, sending her home humiliated, furious, and incensed by the crass retaliation directed upon her person.

Peals of laughter emanated from the second story window, a rejoicing, a settle-the-score laughing jag that broadcast all over the Downfront—forever sealing any interaction between the neighbors—ever, ever again. Maria's scathing rebuke had made its mark, too. So much so that several years later when called to minister at the deathbed of the ailing socialite she found her emptied of the self-importance, and absolutely filled with fright, certain that Maria would entertain retaliation on her for the once upon a time affront. That time was long past. The moments needed to be purposefully spent.

Fire Downfront

Fire hit Downfront Long Island on a Sunday night in June 1914, ignited by sparks thrown off from the huge open fireplace at the Granite Springs Hotel, a spectacular inferno that occurred not long after the original architects bought it back from the Ponce estate. The looming structure became a tinderbox from which twenty employees fled in their nightclothes.

Sam Rogers, then a purser on one of the late running passenger boats, was first to spot the fire and reported it. A high northeast wind fanned the flames throughout the hotel, its barbershop, spreading to the bakery across the street; all buildings were consumed by the inferno. The wind bridged the flames to many west-end businesses including the Day's Spa, Clarke & Griffin's grocery store and post office, John Bickford's cottage, and a building owned by Dr. MacVane,[80] in which Nick Tilley ran a pool room and store. Fortuitously, Day's Spa had just taken an insurance policy out on the place the previous Tuesday. Wind

---

[80] Doctor MacVane was a dentist.

driven sparks then set Ponce's landing afire, destroying a large section at the head of the dock.[xcviii]

One by one, the Gomez children climbed out of a bedroom window onto the front porch roof and sat huddled together in their nightclothes, front row to the drama before them, watching wide-eyed as the fire advanced towards their house—with every expectation that theirs would be fully involved. A severe thunderstorm came tearing through behind the high winds, and the skies opened up, dumping torrents of rain that forced them back into the house. In the morning, those who spent two cents for the newspaper found a small article, way down at the bottom of the front page, which reported that point four zero inches of rain fell in twelve minutes, at two in the morning—two inches an hour. Once again, Divine Superintendence came riding in on the wind and took charge. The driving winds and torrents of rain were indicators that an intense front had moved through, one that may have initially set the fire by blowing down the fireplace's chimney, blowing the sparks into the lobby. Portentously, it was also a storm that extinguished it—eventually!

Sprinting on past the charred remains of the *Downfront* stores, out on an errand for their mother, Johnny and Bobby kept going, past Cushing's Hotel, up the hill to Cushing's Pavilion where Clarke and Griffin had temporarily set up shop. In a month's time, all of the destroyed grounds had been cleared of burned buildings, foundations laid, and framework started on several places. They all buzzed over a bevy of what ifs: what if the Perry cottage, which set just below Maria's home—and Littlejohn's, which set across the way from the Granite Springs had burned? Had that happened, there would have been nothing in the way to save the entire *Westend*—straight across to Andrew Beach. Thankfully, neighbors helped to save the Perry cottage.

Not yet on the road to recovery from the fire, another severe storm hit on July 30th. This one was big enough to take down trees, flagpoles, and orchards. It played freakish tricks, picking up an outhouse, carrying it away, to be later discovered in a neighbor's garden. Despite the fire and the second storm, eight weeks, almost to the day, on August 13th Clarke and Griffin opened their new store. Now the island could get back to the normal, over the counter, palaver, where they learned that meat prices had soared. Whale meat was touted as a fair substitute, nutty tasting, they said. The islanders, for some reason, never quite cottoned to the idea.

Captain Toothaker of South Harpswell put into Union Wharf and tied her up, thought it time to give up sword-fishing for the season due to scarcity of fish and low prices—just playing out the age old game. He said that fifty miles southwest of Cape Elizabeth he spotted, what he thought was a warship hove-to—a British cruiser in wait of foreign craft. That little tidbit of news made the distant war a mite intimate.

The island, itself, went to war, over unexpected ruts, stones, and roots growing across roads, and the need for better streets and streetlights. They asserted, *"It's almost like taking one's life in one's hands to venture on a walk at night where the only source of illumination is the moon."*

Oblivious to war, whale meat, and low fish prices Maria had made it through the rueful years that preceded and followed the dissolve of her marriage and managed to heal her own fretted heart. With that, her hearty laugh and good humor returned. The simple motivation throughout each thorny problem was to keep her family safe and together. In doing so she advanced them a step further than the spot to which she was relegated, by her own choices, and by life's circumstances. She earned and carved out a place in the community—which is different than owning a place on the island—very different. Her children were required to earn this spot on their own merit, and to a greater degree, all did so. *The third generation, my peers, inherited it outright, and I doubt any of us knew what we were gifted at the time. We do now!*

Papa in Absentia

Marjorie answered a knock on the back door. Strangers knocking at the door were a rarity. Most people just walked into the house, but this one greeted the seven-year old knowingly from behind the screen door. Her mother peered out into the summer kitchen to see for herself and said to Margie, *"Thata is no stranger baby; thata is you Papa."* The last time he saw the child, she was tiny, just two years old. Antonio had returned after a five-year absence, there on the island for a visit. On his return from Europe in 1916 he filled them with wild adventurous stories. The US Transport Service employed him—said he was torpedoed off England—said he was captured by the Germans and set adrift in a lifeboat with others—said he hid a compass and saved everybody, including the captain—said he went to the North Pole on Peary's third expedition—said he fell out of an air plane and broke his leg. That is what he said!

A Minus Thirty Degrees, Flatarse Calm

Buckling and grinding ice added an eerie sound to the frigid quiet nights throughout the bay; thick sheets of ice moved together with the ebb and flow of the tides, a new batch of problems mounting during the winter of 1918 when the bay froze over. The stories that we were told were straight and to the point. The generation simply stated, *"We walked to Portland when Casco Bay froze over in 1918"*—end of story!

What they did not elaborate on—was that in mid December, Sebago Lake froze over, one of the earliest dates ever for that to happen. They never hinted that the freezing line dipped far south into Georgia, or mentioned that by the first of January, the town of Hiram registered forty below zero; Portland rested at thirty below, with winds less than ten miles per hour—a sure-fire recipe for freezing salt water. In New Bedford, Massachusetts, tugs hesitated to plow out into an ice floe to attempt the rescue of five schooners that had become locked in, for fear of getting caught in the floe too.

Long lines of urchins with sleds trailing behind them begged for nuggets of coal over at the Randall & McAllister coal pocket in Portland. Having spent most winters in Portland, Bobby and Johnny, as like as not, were amongst them. Neighbors created vigilance committees to inform the authorities as to who exactly, in their neighborhood, was hoarding coal in their cellar. It mattered not that the *hoarders* might be those who thought ahead and stocked up in the summer months when the supply was available and the price low. They, too, were reported. The crucial part of the big story was that New York to the Maritimes was in the middle of a critically severe coal shortage. Tugs and barges simply couldn't get here—from there.

The passenger boat *Aucocisco* was two and a-half-hours behind schedule making its way down the bay, and back to Custom House Wharf on the turn-a-round trip. The area around Deer Point on Chebeague was buttoned in; the hardest stretch of buckling ice through which she had to smash. Her sister ship, the *Merryconeag* was normally called out to break ice for the other vessels, but the problem was overwhelming, leaving the *Auco* to fend for herself. Ice extended well out and away from the wharves leaving the passengers to embark onto the ice for a walk to shore.

If queen of the bay was how the *Merryconeag* was perceived, her sister, the *Auco* was the princess. Islanders bonded strongly with these two, particular passenger boats, their following—a devoted lot. The vessels had enormous character, were beautiful to look at, had handsome lines, and were comfortable vessels on which to ride. Crews took enormous pride in their work. Harry Ricker,[81] who hailed from Chebeague, was engineer on the *Auco*, made the crew polish the brass twice a day on the steam engine, kept it so polished that it would blind you. Grouchy cuss that he was, anyone who dared step across the doorsill, muss it up, or lay a smudge on anything that hinted of brass got a cussing-out. His ploy worked. People steered clear. They didn't pay him for having a cuddly personality, but rather to maintain the steam engine so well that her pitch could gently lull the tension out of Lucifer, himself, and that he did.

By the third of January, ice around any anchorage became a menace to the moored boats, placed pressure on the hulls, put them in peril of being swept- away in ice floes. Clam-flats were solidly covered and eight to ten-inches of thick ice locked-in the channel between Chebeague and Cousins, strong enough to hold the weight of teams of horses and men in their crossings. Northeast storm warnings were out; fishing was at a standstill.

---

[81] Family Connection - Harry Ricker of Chebeague, first cousin to fisherman Robert.

Had they made an attempt to go outside, the makeup of ice on vessels would have been fierce—had they been able to move at all.

With no end in sight, out-of-work fishermen walked the ice to the mainland to find work. To the *Souther'd,* the sixty-mile an hour gale sent tugs and coal-laden barges scurrying for cover, delaying them for days in great fields of ice. No coal would make it to Boston for another week.

❧ Ole Deah & Ole Chum ❧
Warmin' Up Aside the Potbelly

"What a mess! WHAT-A-MESS! Near three-weeks now. Normally, ya know, them areas down fringin' the shoreline slushes over with a skim of slob ice, loose stuff—just rises and falls 'top the water. What done us in, Ole Deah, was that early stretch without wind—all them subzero days and nights. You're right! Snowfall was the clincher. Yup! All that fresh water, dumped 'top the slob by the storm locked us in tighter than zip's you-know-what. Gawd, any worse and we'll all be down with the chilblains. Just can't seem to warm up.

See how them tides drove all that mess up between the islands; locked us all together. *Simular* to those two cows I read about—ones up North a farmer found one mornin' in his barn—with their breath froze t'gether. Lookin' for what little warmth they could find, sounds like. He was lucky—whole cows is freezin' to death—let alone their breath.

High-pressure 'n low temperatures, are stretchin' from Hudson Bay to Key West. I heah Narragansett Bay is froze right over. Ships is ice bound as far as Baltimore, sez heah in the papers. Ain't seen nawthin' like it. Forecast don't look promisin' either.

No choice! Ain't no way to get to Portland but to walk the ice! 'Course, we'll save on a boat ticket, ya know. Could save enough to buy a ticket to one of them six-reelers at the Elm Theater featurin' William S. Hart. I could go for one of them silent westerns myself. Comin' back—when we get to the Diamonds, let's traverse to Cow, then the longest stretch to circumvent to get back heah will be the weak areas 'cross the mouth of

Hussys.[82] Bring a sled along to haul some coal home—if theys any to be found.

Saw young Tony Gawmez walkin' the ice from Portland on the weekend. What's he now—twenty-one? Been workin' as a machinist since he was knee-high. Them kids can't stay away from the island. Prubly checkin' on the place. He signed up for the war, ya know. Was refused 'cause of his eyes, and I think, 'cause he was too short. Don't quote me on that. He turned, just as he was leavin' and told the recruitin' officers, *"It's your loss."* He was prubly right.

Let me borry your paper again. Worry sick 'bout our boys. Some's comin' back from the war awful messed up. If they ain't wounded, they's shell shocked, gassed, or sick-a-bed in the woodbox with that scary influenza. Don't hardly seem right.

Well—ole stock—I've been procrastinatin' long enough—gotta go shovel six inches of partly-cloudy off my doorstoop. If you need me, you know where I'll be."

In the middle of it all, a *Meatless & Wheat-less Meals* conservation pitch was weighing heavily on every household—for the war effort. Recipes handed out at a Patriotic Food show asked people to substitute whale meat for beef and pork. Leaflets fluttered down upon Portland, dropped from planes, war bond savings posters that solicited a little *dough* from the good folk of Portland for the Doughboys. Somewhere in upstate Maine, a dear lady knitted forty-five pairs of stockings for soldiers in the trenches—doing her part for the war. And to top it off—had the area not been in a deep freeze, the number of casualties from the Great Influenza, which was killing millions around the world, would have been out of sight. Signs were all over telling all to *"Secure fresh air day or night—avoid overcrowded stuffy cars and theaters—not to use common articles such as roller towels and drinking cups."* They got tough on spitters, with anti-spitting laws.

---

[82] Hussys - Hussy's Sound, an area surrounded on three sides by land and one side by open seas…located between Long Island and Peaks Island.

Congress, Middle, and St. John Streets had light usage cut fifty percent, and it stayed that way. Four weeks into it, all of the New England States were made to adopt *lightless nights*. A second gale came scudding up the coast at fifty-miles an hour, with more cold weather following, the forecasters said. Was any one listening by this time?

Old Orchard's nine miles of high water mark became an eerie arctic terrain lined with cavernous drifts that were encased in ice, hollowed out twelve-foot drifts, in which a person could have easily stood. Maine Central had only two days of coal supply left as the gale dumped nine and a half more inches of snow, but where there is snowfall, temperatures rise. The cycle was broken. But for a month, the islanders were absolutely taken with the fact that they could bridge this enormous expanse of water on foot.
xcix

The following November, the *Aucocisco* raced from Portland to Orrs Island after the crew was notified that the *Merryconeag* was ablaze. They arrived in the middle of the night, though there was nothing that could be done but to stand vigil as the sister ship fiercely burned out of control, burned completely down to the waterline.

Egress & Ingress

Daylight savings-time was introduced throughout the country in 1919; a new concept that extended the work day, provided one more hour of daylight in the latter part of the day during mid-winter. The phrase, *"spring ahead, fall behind,"* was coined to help the citizenry remember just which way to set their clocks, an hour ahead in the spring, an hour behind in the fall, an addled concept for the more rural communities, enough to flummox the best. Prohibition was enacted to prohibit the sale of liquor, and the influenza epidemic raged on, the number of deaths, world wide, tallied at twenty-two million. No one in the family was affected—by the influenza that is.

Weddings galvanized the family. Jo was the first to marry in 1919, then Tillie in 1920 after which she moved to Boston. Tony Jr. left too, for New York City. Louie plugged away at a clerk's job, and Johnny retained the one at the Greeley Laundry. Bobby had been on the honor role, not only for never being absent, but also for never being late, or dismissed. Setting that aside, he quit in lieu of full time work in February 1920, during his first year at Portland High School, at the age fourteen—just as his three older brothers had done before—just as a great many impoverished teenagers did in those days.

Since their father's return from Europe, Jo and Tillie

Back row (l to r): Bobby, Tony Jr., Josephine, Tillie, Louie, Johnny. *Front row (l to r)* Margie, Maria, Antonio, Frances

adamantly pressed Maria for reconciliation. When he returned from Hoboken, NJ, Maria succumbed to the girls' pressure. He was fifty-three and she fifty when they remarried before A. C. Pettengill in January of 1921, sealing the accord with a photograph of the family's all-togetherness that was taken in an ice cold-freezing studio in Portland. The old man had a smile on his face and an enormous wad of chewing gum in his mouth. Jo and Tillie stood behind their parents in a pose of satisfaction and appeasement. Maria reflected the cold temperature of the room, the suspicious air of skepticism, and appeared as though she would have preferred being someplace else. She looked worn.

She would have bode well had she followed her initial instincts. The boys were less enthusiastic about their father's restored bearings in the household, than were the girls. It took little time for discord to descend upon the house once again, and Maria threw him out—for good. He managed to sneak back in when she was occupied, to raid the single bottle of brandy that she kept in the pantry, the one on hand when her sugars dropped to unsafe levels. She caught on—filled the bottle with vinegar, and regretted only that she was not there to see his face when he tipped the bottle to take the first big swig.

A newspaper article arrived at the house in '22. Antonio, while at the Seamen's Institute in NY, wished the family to know that he was revered in certain circles—a legend. There it was—the formal family-picture, right smack dab on the front page. By the sounds of that headline, one would get the distinct impression that he was Peary's best pal. Together they read the same sagas that he'd depicted again and again around the dinner table...saved some girls from an oncoming car...saved Lillian Sawyer from a fire...Mrs Hamilton...Frank Andrews. *Through it all, it would seem that he forgot to find room to save his wife and children.* He gave the reporter the story about going to the North Pole with Admiral Peary...third trip. Then the one about being stranded on Little Whaleboat Island...used a fallen tree for a mast...used his shirt as a flag. His children heard his shouts...sent someone to save him. *They were living on Long Island in 1909, and the distance from Little Whaleboat to Long was four and one half miles—give or take.* There *were* some new people that he saved, two in shark infested waters, but now the stories involved French ports, being shipwrecked seven times...torpedoed twice...two days and two nights adrift...flying in a plane...a bullet in the leg. *Last time he told the story to the family, didn't he say he fell out of the plane?* He would get miles and miles and miles out of those war stories. One of his statements was one hundred percent on the mark. Looking at the family photograph, he told the reporter that his sons were fine boys. At least he did not take the credit for himself for raising them, but then, neither did he pass on any praise to their mother. Twenty years later he would walk back through those very same doors of the Seaman's Institute.

***

Tillie presented the family with the first grandchild, Phyllis, in '23, and the first member of the third generation wanted for nothing. She was a source of enormous pride, the family's initiation into what it was like to dote, and as she grew, they poured it all into the little dark-eyed beauty. They went so far as to drive to Massachusetts to scoop her up for the summer season, lest she miss out on an island summer with her grandmother— and with them. Now her aunts had an excuse to go on shopping sprees for fine clothes, a coat trimmed with ermine, beautifully made dresses, all in her size. *Can you just hear Jo, Margie and*

Frances? ...I can! "Sit up straight dear!" "Don't slouch!" "Did you wash your hands?" "Where are you going—for how long?"

Maria and her cherished grandchild spent hours thumbing through the red velvet photo album, the one Maria brought from Spain, a vicarious visit with a family that she would never, ever meet, but through the heart and mind of her grandmother. She thought the Campos family to be dignified and stately—nothing like she had envisioned. Summer people arrived from New York, Boston, and all points, and on seeing the little one and her grandmother on the porch, made certain to register their arrival with the venerated woman, to glean a warm welcome as though it validated the beginning of their vacation. Not many passed by without doing so.

They traveled to Portland together to shop at the grocery store on Congress Street, the one owned by the Shaw family. Maria, still dressed in long dresses, a fashion quite out of vogue, at that point, clutched a long, written list in her hand of items that Clarke's did not carry. Sometimes there was a bit of confusion over the product. Maria wanted some *"Showtime"* coffee. Between the name and the accent, the clerk didn't have a clue, but Maria kept repeating, in broken English, *"Showtime" coffee, "Showtime,"*—until somebody caught the connection between one of the famous brands and its catchy advertisement on the radio program, *"Show Time."*

Winter travel and a visit to her grandmother, on Christmas Eve, was a standing course of action, but this time of the year she traveled with her entire family. A late start, slow travel, whatever the hang up, the last boat left without them, and Tillie, with her ingrained island mind-set in high gear, managed to snag a lobsterman heading in the right direction. Every single star showed in the sky that cold, crisp night, the bay, quiet as a pond as they headed down the bay for Ponce's. It was a new and altogether awesome perspective for the child, who otherwise would have made the trip up inside a passenger cabin, would never have met with the stirring experience.

Up on Garfield Street an electric Santa shown brightly on the chimney, a personal welcome broadcast to the little apple of their collective eye. Uncle Bobby had been exceedingly busy—heart and soul into the spirit of Christmas. Hugs at the door, a house filled with home cooked aromas, food prepared with tradition and love set the scene. Not to be missed, heightening the fervency of the season, awaiting her *under* the tree, there stood a four-foot tall, hand crafted, electrified doll-house—with furniture fashioned out of cigar boxes—tenderly made by Bobby. Heightening the fervency of the season was becoming one of his long suits.

Although her immigrant grandmother spoke in hesitant words and broken English, the child came to understand that Maria was far from uneducated, untutored, or unlearned.[83] On the contrary! Her penchant ran heavily to the classical side of the compass. Once radio hit the scene, which it did in '24, one restriction was levied on the child, actually, a restriction that was levied on *everyone* in the house. When Maria sat in her wicker chair on Saturday afternoons, with the *new-fangled* radio tuned into the NY Metropolitan Opera, she was not to be disturbed. No one did.

***

Bobby and Johnny probably did not aspire to the heavy mantle of responsibilities discarded by their father, but they certainly did assume it, took care of everything. Frances and Margie seemed oblivious and roared into the teenage years with their best friend Adeline Thompson[84], and a tribe of *Westend* adolescents.

For the five years following her mother's death, Adeline was as much a part of the household as was Maria's own children. Long after Adeline's grandmother had finished raising ten of her own, she inherited the girl and her brothers, and Maria helped fill some part of the void, a maternal essence that was most assuredly missed. Preschool children, birthing mothers, frail elders, the terminally ill, all those within Maria's purview found a gentle and knowledgeable caregiver. Life was full, arduous, but had leveled.

---

[83] The 1900 and 1910 census lists that Maria could read and write; though it sounds as though it was minimal. Antonio could not.

[84] Family connection - Adeline (Thompson) Cushing wife of Walter Cushing. Walter descended from early settlers, Ignatius and Ezekiel Cushing. Adeline was mother to Susan (Cushing) Longanecker.

Though Americanized, fragments of the old country flitted into Maria's day-to-day from out of nowhere. In her youth, Maria swept easily into the gypsy Flamenco dance, absolutely delighted in it, and thought it an enlivening piece of her former self to pass onto Frances and Margie. The inseparable teenage twosome was a strong-willed handful, but they loved their mother dearly, and indulged her this resurgence. Garbed in the complete Andalusian gypsy costumes they tried their best to learn the foot stomping, hand clapping, and castanets routine, but each time they made the attempt, they fell into gales of side-splitting laughter—to the point of collapse. They were perfectly awful at it—although the formal pictures did turn out rather nicely.

Margie & Frances

Maria, now in her late fifties, permanently settled into the island house in '25, along with Bobby, Johnny, Frances and Margie. The family turned a corner; wintering in the city was part of the past. Bobby, now a foreman for Simmons & Ham Mfg. Company, an ice cream and candy manufacturer, earned enough to help support the household. Johnny strongly pulled his end of it as part of the infrastructure of the island. Maria, not one to rest on her laurels, garnered work as before, and the girls waited tables at the Cushing Hotel in the summers. Frances spent much, too much, time table-hopping, simply gabbing with the patrons. It was obvious to the Cushings, to the guest, and probably to Frances, that the maidservant stint was not her fortè.

A small fish shack appeared on the rocks where the Granite Springs Hotel once stood, a build-as-you-go type structure. It had a loft, some bedding—a space no bigger than what a ship had to offer. To his family's dismay, Antonio had settled, not very far away, in the shack. He used the hull of a small wooden sailboat, moored beneath the wharf, as a makeshift icebox. When filled with cold, ocean water, the butter, milk, and whatever needed chilling stayed that way. Lobstering, odd jobs pruning trees for the Portland Park department, hanging off the front grid of the Portland trolleys to shoo cows off the tracks kept him afloat, financially. Passengers found him at the base of Ponce's Landing, hawking bowls of fish chowder he'd cooked in the shack. The City Directory lost him ten years before, never again to be recorded in the yearly census, though he was there—then absent—most times thereabouts—some periods out of sight, up-staked, but mostly somewhere around the corner.

Maria took Frances and Margie to work at Mrs. Rigo's elegant summer home over on the Ridge Road overlooking the ocean, a lovely place where the elite met. It was in her home that both girls learned the finer points of entertaining—points that would serve them well in adulthood. Mrs Rigo's posh dinner parties, afternoon luncheons, and elegant silver teas were fodder for the grapevine, essentially, because she did them so well. Following her formal dinners, the gentlemen would retire to the large wrap-around piazza with a pony of brandy, and the ladies, with glasses of Benedictine, out onto the piazza where they continued the art of savoring...on an ocean vista to die for. A conservative game of croquet rounded out the balmy evenings.

Her oversized cottage was wrapped in what I consider the most definitive piazza one could ever want, but not without work—a great deal of repair—replacement—and paint. Did I mention paint—gallons, and gallons worth of paint? Last summer, I looked in on my perennial, summer friend, Marylou, the person who now owns Mrs Rigo's cottage, whose husband, luckily, has become a master in the art of maintaining wrap-around piazzas. We sat atop the wide, steep set of stairs that lead to a rolling two-tiered lawn—where croquet balls, wickets, and mallets once set ready, in a by-gone day. Where at that very moment—just at the edge of the wall of bayberry bushes, a mother fox was teaching her three kits the fine art of the romp. For fifty weeks out of the year it was the fox's dominion, and the animal glanced up at us frequently, wondering, I suppose, when we would take leave. I thought of Mrs. Rigo, and reflected on how a free roaming fox would have fit into her silver tea parties.

For fifty years Marylou and I have been able to pick-up where we left-off the year before, have actually made an art out of swapping twelve months worth of gab in one or two sittings. Marylou makes it the more rich with a droll, straight from the hip, clear and crisp storytelling talent. I laud her that ability, cherish her friendship, and have such appreciation that she didn't slip off into the ether, back when she deliberated her life's path, thankful that her husband took-to-us. Spouses don't always take to the island—or to a lifetime commitment in the renovation of piazzas.

Chapter

8 ...Devil's Fiddle

Chebeague Island's Ricker Family 1927

In the company of their cohorts Calvin, and Eben Doughty, the Ricker brothers, Will and Ray, [85] could not really be characterized as hellers, but they were crowding it some. Darkness had just settled over the island and they were idly puttyin' around, feeling their oats, itchy—bored. They needed to kick-start the night, to liven things up and chose to serenade George Higgins, a neighbor, and his tiny old-lady housekeeper who wore old-fashioned, long, black dresses and dusted all-purpose flour on her face—so much of it that she appeared white as a ghost. The boys weren't carrying a hoedown fiddle with them, with which to strike up a ditty. Oh nooooo! Not that bunch. In the pitch black of the night, they went to all the trouble to string up a devil's fiddle. They so relished plaguing George.

Stealthily they tied one end of a fine wire to the back of the old man's house, snuck out into the trees in the back yard, and then pulled the other end taunt. Once away from the lights, hidden by the darkness, they rode a stick back and forth over the tight wire until it commenced to throw out a piercing, high pitched, eerie racket that resonated off the side of the house. 'Course, they persisted until the old man was wound up tighter than a drum, until he burst out through his back door, bellowing into the darkness, *"Will Ricker, I know that's you, you little baastid. Yes suh, your father is going to hear of this mister-man. Now, you put that in your book."*

---

[85] Family Connection - Robert William Junior (Will) and Raymond Ricker, teenage sons of fisherman Robert and Anniebelle. Grandsons to Stone sloop captain Stephen.

They were halfway home in a shot, breathless from the sprint, but more so from the fit of laughter that overtook them, and was just warming up when Goldie Doughty's outhouse caught their collective interests. The devil's fiddle and moving outhouses were signature Chebeague Island pranks, always good for a hoot. The four quickly positioned themselves on the four-corners of the small building, and in *herniated* grunts, picked the building up at its base, and was launching it towards a hiding place—when a hollow shriek came forth from inside the structure. It was Goldie, seated on the throne, seething mad, so bent out of shape that she was ready to throttle them. She blatted, *"Will Ricker and Eben Doughty, I know that's you. I'll get you sons-of-bitches."*

Well, on that night it was two for two. Neither the old man nor Goldie had laid an eye on Will, yet he had been unmasked. The boys dropped the outhouse, Goldie in it—totally discombobulated at this point. As fast as their legs would take them, and far as the second round of hysterics would allow, they sprinted for home, quite satisfied with their endeavors, and slept peaceful as a babe-in-arms the minute each head hit the pillow. There obviously wasn't an ounce of conscience in any of them, on that night of their lives anyway.

With morning cobwebs shrouding his sleepy brain, Will had difficulty making sense of what he saw from the front door. Then it dawned on him—Goldie was good for her word. While he slept, she and her brother ever so neatly removed the entire length of a stone wall that ran the front of the Ricker property line, rock by rock, and deposited them—in like fashion—*acrost* the street!

Families saw to it that few ever died alone. Some homes were built with birthing rooms that doubled as a dying room too, a separate room in the corner of the house. Everyone took turns sitting beside the deathbed, including teenagers. The onus was placed upon young Will to sit with his grandfather, Stephen, who had but a few breaths left to him in his eighty-fourth year.[86]

The old-timer had been given ample time to saunter the island in retirement, time to inspect how Wentworth's old oak was

---

[86] Stephen died in 1928.

managing out on *The Hook*—then ramble over to gander out beyond the profusion of wild beach-roses—out at the disintegrating bones of the sloop *Newcomb* as she, by that time, lay in ruination off Rose's beach. It probably tugged at him to envision the seventy-five year old sloop in her prime, with him on it—tugged another quarter turn when her remains washed out with the ice in 1916.

Will found out that being involved with the mystery of mortality to be a straightforward encounter. There was nothing sugar-coated about the struggle the old man experienced in shedding his earthly shell, and no bigger feeling of inadequacy for the young man, who would have much preferred the *Grim Reaper* be kept at bay. Nevertheless, the vigil gave him pause to reflect on the importance of the unassuming man, who, with a small fraternity of *stone-sloopers*, left his hand print up and down the coast in magnificent buildings—structures that would stand for centuries; no small legacy to leave behind—for an unassuming man.

Civil engineer, Dana Savage arrived in Portland to view the new Million Dollar Bridge. He and his family had returned to the States, in 1930, after a long period of time in Cuba and Puerto Rico where he had engineered the building of bridges. Hailed as an innovative span and a valuable study, the *Million Dollar* tweaked his sensibilities. He and his wife, Ruth, snatched up a summer rental on Chebeague Island, the old brick cottage over by the church. Like so many others, they became enamored with Casco Bay, and shortly joined the annual throng of summer inhabitants. Young Will Ricker found delivering ice not as much of a drudge once the Savages became summer regulars. He, too, eventually became enamored—with Savage's youngest daughter, Fran.[87] The rest is history.

Will's mother, Anniebelle, died from a ruptured appendix in March of 1931—much too early, at the age of fifty-two. From a window overlooking the shore, Will watched, as his father stood out on the rocks in Coleman Cove—raging with grief, defiant

---

[87] Family Connection – Fran Savage married Will Ricker (Robert William Junior) Oct 1936.

fists raised to the heavens for the senselessness of his wife's death. They had nine children together, the youngest only eleven years old. Some Chebeague Islanders thought that Robert's blasphemous confrontation surely tested the fates, and it was thought that in his ranting a bolt of lightening would come out of the clear sky to strike him for such impiety. It didn't. Perhaps God thought that her death and the Depression were enough agony for any one man.

Robert, like his father, Stephen, embraced seamanship as naturally as he breathed air, was in his element—doing the work to which he was innately suited. At one point in time, there were so many Rickers on Chebeague that if one of them put his fingers to his mouth and whistled, he'd have had you surrounded in less than a minute. The only Ricker men who remain on Chebeague today are listed on the tombstones in the church cemetery.

Robert never quite popped back from his wife's death and was afforded another ten years after Anniebelle died—more years than he wanted. In 1945 he died in his sleep aboard the PW boat, "Joy," on which he'd been taxiing naval dignitaries, ...working the bay until the very end.

***

Few stories circulate on Chebeague or Long Island about the Depression, none that depicted the hardships, soup kitchens, and dust bowl images that come at us through faded newspapers and grainy, black and white film. The lack of any tales, in itself, said much, indicating that if an individual didn't have much to begin with—then the crash of '29 was a moot point. By and large, island natives had a lifetime of practice, were masterful at working within little to no income, their food harvested from the sea, from farm animals, and summer gardens that women transformed into neat rows of canned jars on the household's pantry shelves. Or was it that they basically put the hardships handed to them by political and economic winds behind them—then closed the door? They were masterful at that, too.

Summer residents faired less well in the Crash. With fortunes forfeited to Wall Street, their summer homes took the same route. In the aftermath, sadly some lost the will to live. Stories of suicide were a reality for a few. Dispossessed of an easily, or hard-won fortune, summer homes passed hands through bank foreclosures. Live-in housekeepers, maids, nannies and festive guests were less likely to be milling about. Those who did not lose the island real estate to liquidation licked their wounds of mediocrity and began to cook their own meals, empty the trash, and work to maintain their place in the sun—but they did it with such class. Just as the steamboats created a pivotal change for the islands, by transforming isolated communities into unique resorts, so, too, did the Crash of '29—only in reverse.

***

In spite of the country's economy having gone down the tubes in '29, the careers of the Gomez children went well. All sought their way in areas to which each was best suited.

Josephine, serious and matronly, married a South Portland Policeman in the 20s, continued her job as a clerk with Eastman Brothers in the glove department and poured her artistic bent into photography and a floral club.

Tony Jr., a smiling dandy, moved to Long Island, New York, picked up where he left off, and received a high school diploma. He was briefly married, studied tool and die at the Pratt Institute and worked for the American Safety Razor Company until retirement.

Louie, the quiet one, moved in '25 to Camp Ellis, Maine, a small coastal community and ran a boat repair service. He married, twice, and had one child, "Junior." When the spirit moved Louie, he'd take a boat on a test run, zip up the coast the few nautical miles, to visit the family on the island, an inclination all came to expect of him for the next thirty years.

Tillie married, moved to Massachusetts, and raised two children, Phyllis and Lloyd. Her abilities as a competent businesswoman would not be realized until the children were grown. She bought the Beach Avenue House from brother Johnny and ran a successful rooming house. Cooking was certainly her fortè.

Johnny became the island's affable iceman and milkman, stayed close to home and was his mother's right hand. He bought the Beach Avenue House, ran a taxi, hauled the mail and freight, ran the school bus, did janitorial work for the school, then married, and grew the most beautiful begonias on the island.

Frances, a socialite to the end, thanks to the financial support of her brothers, graduated from Gorham Normal School in '28 with an accreditation to teach. She taught in South Portland, on Peaks and Cliff Islands for a time, then landed one of the two teaching positions at Long Island School and became its principal. She married Charles Barrett, bought Glendenning's old post office on Garfield Street for her home. In the forties, their only daughter,

Suzanne, arrived. Frances lived her career, and relished the island's social scene.

Bobby, the genial breadwinner, the toiler, was his mother's left hand. He made the transition along with the ice cream company when it became the Cumberland Cold Storage Company on Commercial Street in Portland, a wholesale food distribution company, where he worked up to the position of president/general manager. In an era of soup kitchens, a career in wholesale foods was a logical choice. He married and had five children, gave up city work in 1950 to become a part of the island's inner works.

Marjorie, the baby, headstrong, bold, and spicy, sabotaged any concerted effort made by her older siblings to guide her through nursing school in New York, and was a chameleon for every changing fashion statement that came along. She was a stunner—married for a short time then moved back to New York where she jumped feet first into work at the New York World's Fair, hit the fancy-dancy night clubs, kicked up her heels, and in general, enjoyed herself. She married a sailor in the forties, a solid and lasting marriage, moved to Florida and lived amidst the orange groves. Left widowed she married, once again, to a retired Navy chief.

Bob's Gift to the Island 1931
Lillian (LeBlanc) Gomez

Bobby Gomez had not yet found anyone, at all, with whom he wanted as his life's partner in 1931—that is, until he saw a young woman arrive on the island with the Long family from Massachusetts, a domestic, Lillian LeBlanc. She was a personable, unassuming, learned young woman, who had an incredible musical talent, but to crown all of those virtues that drew his interest—she was your basic eyeful, which conjecturally is the reason he noticed her in the first place. Smitten is not the word; Bob was struck!

Lillian embarked from the small town of Sheridan, Maine to live with her Aunt Eugenie in Reading Massachusetts, to help her aunt with a new baby. For the young people of Northern Maine, relatives, who settled in the industrial areas of New England, were the typical ticket into the job market. That led her to work as a domestic for the Long family in Reading, people who valued her, as well as her musical talent at dinner parties and church activities. Summer's arrival created a nuance to Lillian's routine. The Longs packed their travel bags to over-flowing, covered the furniture with sheets, and with Lillian in tow, wended their way to their Eastend cottage on Long Island, Maine.

Lil, a farm girl who was landlocked all of her life, needed to learn the rudiments of boat travel, and often faced travel on the Casco Bay Line boats with errands to run for her employers. It was no short or easy hike from the foot of Ponce's landing to the Longwood cottage at the *Eastend* with arms filled with packages, although, Island protocol was graciously vigilant. People were never left stranded on the wharf with a heavy load. Just *by happenstance*, Bob Gomez delegated himself as a purveyor of island protocol and assisted Lil, who looked a bit adrift and laden with bags. He offered a ride, then another, and after several of these *happenstance* meetings on the dock, the relationship took very little time to develop into a courtship. She was always amazed that he just *happened* to be on the wharf when she needed a ride. Despite the fact that Bob lived on the  opposite end of the island, this *Westender* was, by island convention, possibly out of his territory—but obviously not out of his pervious. Summer romances are notoriously short lived, cooled by the months of seasonal absences; nevertheless, for three summers she returned to the island and likewise, Bob visited her in Reading.

Obviously, she was not in a hurry to marry, as another suitor from Reading unhappily discovered when, after a few brief dates, he took her for a visit to his parent's home. To Lillian's astonishment, on the spot, the emboldened blond lad presumptuously proposed marriage in front of his whole family—and just as quickly—Lil declined. Rebuffed, and with ring still in hand, his sweet demeanor turned to anger and indignation. She never heard from *him* again.

In view of the quick turn of his temper, as one of her children, I am personally thankful that she did not choose him—for us. But then, we would not have been "us." We would have been blond,

with blue eyes—and a presumptuous and indignant personality.
We would not have been islanders! Perish the thought!

In a timely fashion Bob proposed marriage in 1934. In the proverbial manly fashion, he drove ten hours up the winding Haynesville Road in his brand new Pontiac Coup, way up into the County to meet Lil's parents, and to ask for her hand in marriage. His best friend, McGowan went along, to read the map, but mostly to shore-up his resolve. The big sticking point, that could well have posed a stumbling block, was that he was not raised a Catholic. But he offered *something* not too many suitors could—a Catholic Church squarely located in his back yard on the island. It was not hard for Annie and Willy LeBlanc to determine that this was a man who adored their daughter. *Although they had no way to look into the future, he would be kind and indulgent for all of their married life.*

Sealed by Bob's promise to the Church that he and Lillian would raise their children Catholic, the priest on Peaks Island performed the marriage ceremony. Everyone had handfuls of rice to throw at the Casco Bay Line boat as it pulled away from the Forest City Landing with the newlyweds aboard. Brother Johnny threw a pair of old fishermen's hip boots on the deck, a bit of horseplay that drew laughter from the on looking passengers, who were caught up in the fervor of the new bride and groom. [88]

Niagara Falls was the first leg of their honeymoon, which extended up through Canada to see five babies that had captured the world, the Dionne quintuplets. The five small girls, with hair neatly braided, all dressed prettily in alike dresses, were brought into an amphitheater playground by nurses—to be viewed by the public—who stood behind darkened windows.

Their first-born, Ann Marie, looked so much like the Dionne quintuplets that *"they could have been sisters,"* Mother said. With the enormous sized families and relatives living in both Canada and the northern areas of Maine, though not likely, they

---

[88] Forest City Landing – Peaks Island dock. Although the Catholic Church built a church on the island in 1924, Bob and Lil were married on Peaks Island because Long Island's summer church was closed in October for the season.

conceivably could have been related—three-thousand-seven-hundred-twenty-six times removed. Somewhere a cabby in New York identified it correctly—as a facial stamp.

LeBlanc Family
Northern Maine 1888 – 1911

Acadia existed as a French colony in the sixteen hundreds, an area that encompassed huge parts of Northeastern Maine and Canada before wars with England, and before borders were set between the two countries. A remote, abstracted view lays bare England's deportation of the Acadian Frenchmen to the southern States, most specifically Louisiana where they settled and grew into a lively piece of Americana known as the Louisiana Cajuns.

Farming families were exceedingly large; ten to fifteen babies per family, but in the late 1800s railroads were being built from one coast to the other and for those who followed the construction work, babies could well be born most anywhere—with wilderness, desolation, and howling wolves as a backdrop. That was exactly the beginnings of Lillian's father, Willie LeBlanc, who was born in a caboose, en route from Lachine Canada, the family in transit to Mattawamkeg, Maine in pursuit of the migrating railroad work. They resettled in Sheridan, a hamlet and teeming mill town, so busy that on one side of the lumber mill railroad box cars steadily lined up to take on loads of building materials destined for the lower States. On the other side, huge log runs barreled down the Aroostook River delivering raw material to the mill. Silas Noble's newly invented toothpick machine ran full bore, churning out four hundred thousand toothpicks for every white birch tree they threw onto the conveyor belt.[c]

The area, with its harsh weather and short-season farming was a rather unforgiving terrain on which to settle. Winters were early, were severe, and stayed late. Willie's mother, Azilda,[89] said to be a member of a Northeast American Indian tribe, died in the spring of '98, giving birth to their eighth child—only four

---

[89] Azilda Boulanger

of which survived birth. Within the year, his father, Moise [90] married again; with his second wife, Clarisse produced nine more children, and built a relatively successful hotel that housed several shops and a novel movie house. As one of the four older children, Willie was involved with the business and ran the movie projector at the movie house, while one of the town's musically talented ladies was enlisted to play the piano during

the running of the silent films. The income from the businesses provided Willie with two years at a business college. Once finished with the education, he was satisfied to work the mill, and kept tight inventory of the finished product, which was stuffed inside railroad cars and made ready for delivery to the southern States. More hours were filled delivering food and mail for his uncle's grocery store, and after his marriage, to Annie Chasse, a pious young schoolteacher, he became an American citizen in 1911.

Wedding day for Annie & Willie LeBlanc

Marie Lilian,[91] as was written in long hand on Lillian's baptismal papers, was the first born in a succession of ten babies to Willie and Annie. To aid in the survival of the smaller babies they utilized a prototype of the modern incubator; a small crib made of warmed bricks lined with cotton batting. Lilian was delivered in 1912 by the family doctor, at home, in the first finished bedroom of the house that her father built, and without the need for cotton batting and warmed bricks. The LeBlanc house seemed to have most of the modern conveniences: electricity, a telephone, a wringer washer, a big hand pump (outdoors) for well water, and a woodshed—more than most in the community. An old man in the center of town had a single cow from which they bought raw cow's milk for the babies while

---

[90] Family Connection – Moise LeBlanc - father of William (Willy) – grandfather to Lillian. Moise is the French derivation of Moses.

[91] Lillian's name was Americanized from the French derivation, Marie Lilian, pronounced Lili-anne

they weaned from the breast. The other children drank only sweet, delicious, very cold water from the well, but no milk from a very young age. Life was prudent because of the mindset—not because of the income. They managed well with what he provided.

At age five, Lilian was sent for an extended education, to the Notre Dame de la Sargesse Convent up near the Canadian boarder in Saint Agathe, the town in which her mother, Annie was raised. Private education was costly and only two other children from Sheridan were sent to the convent at the same time, as was Lilian. An education in a convent was the norm for the devout Catholic mother, and after all, her family was close by. But if given the choice, living fifty miles from home was not what the five-year old would have preferred.

Separation from her family was not borne well by one so young; the visits from the Chasse family were sparse. Other children's nightmares caused her to pull the sheets up over her head, to shut out her fears until sleep cordoned off the longing for home. The nuns learned to look for her sitting, with feet not yet able to reach the pedals of an old pump organ, waiting for someone to play. Music furnished easement, was the balm, filled the void. Through that she developed an aptitude for music that advanced far beyond the base education. If each of us comes from a center, Lilian's was music.

Education under the tutelage of the nuns was quite thorough, where she excelled in spelling, both in French and English. At the Notre Dame de la Sargesse she learned to speak a second language, perfect English, without a hint of an accent. But in contrast to her modest demeanor, smoldering beneath the child's demure reserve was the competitive nature of a seasoned crapshooter, a part of her character that was out to win every spelling bee and its sought after prize—the highly coveted, exquisitely decorated, empty, chocolate box.

The same Great Influenza outbreak that killed more troops than did bullets in the trenches of World War I, swept through Northern Maine, and sifted into the convent where Lilian contracted the infectious disease. Though in a delirium she was conscious that the nuns lifted her from her bed with a sheet, as though it was a hammock, she thought because her nosebleed was messing up the bed. All stricken children were carried to the infirmary up on the top floor. One boy quickly succumbed. Lilian remained unaware that she was nearly lost to the contagious virus and thought little of it until years later, when she better understood the ramifications and scope of the illness.

1917-1926

Throughout the five years of schooling, summer vacation was spent back at home, a carefree time acquainting herself with the newest of the brood, a new one almost every year—reconnecting with her younger siblings, doing chores, enjoying the town's summer fling. Lilian and the other children burst with pride when their dad marched down the street with the town's band, she listening intently, able to cull the sound of his coronet from

Lil and brother Ed

the musical blend of the other instruments. She was honing her own musical ear. [ci]

Portland's Henry Wadsworth Longfellow immortalized the Acadian plight of their ancestors in his romantic poem, *Evangeline*. Sheridan, Maine celebrated the poet's story annually with a festival and a huge parade in which Septimus Bearce guided his ox cart down the middle of town, the very one on which he traveled during the early days.

Roscoe Hewes fired up the tiny *"potato bug"* that he used in the fields, a miniature gasoline driven rig that set low to the ground, and was equipped with two seed potato bags hanging from the driver's side. Another townsman loaded an old spinning wheel and large loom on a horse-driven cart to show everybody what the early settlers used to weave their own clothes. They had pride in their beginnings.

To feed the multitude, cooking began the day before with big pots of beans that were buried in the ground atop hot rocks to cook all night, served to the crowds the next day along with a hefty chicken stew and dumplings. Households churned butter and made bread to slather it on, and apple pies, tables upon tables of apple pies. Several years later, in the 1930 pageant, teenagers Lilian and brother, Ed wore the Acadian costumes, and gave the reading from Longfellow's *Evangeline* and Gabriel. The news reported the two as descendants of those who fled from Acadia to the Northern Maine County.

Early Sunday mornings, a booming, rise and shine call from their father enticed the young children downstairs for breakfast, a meal that he blithely enjoyed cooking. Single file, they tiptoed their way down over the stairs, amidst giggles, for a meal that was assembled not merely for sustenance, but for the awe-inspiring demonstrations of flapjack flipping, those cooked directly on the top of the wood cook-stove, a memory that remains one of her sweetest.

They were invited a mile up the road to her grandfather Moise's farm, to spend entire days plucking small wild strawberries from the field, accumulating a *whole* quart by day's end. It was less a chore for Lilian and more the stage for a social turnout and capers devised by her teen cousins. Their grandfather's massive size and looming figure was the brunt of a favorite caper, which was to confiscate a pair of his mammoth work pants off the clothesline. Not one, but two teens climbed into a single pant leg, then captured the silly pose on camera. He truly was strapping.[92]

An exception to the season of lightness and freedom occupied a summer when her eight-month old baby brother, Arthur, died from cholera, they theorized from drinking the raw cow's milk. The family quietly treaded the long road that led directly from the front of their home uphill to a dense, wooded area where they gathered at the Catholic cemetery site for the somber rites. Willy carried the small wooden coffin, and he buried the child, as all in attendance offered up prayers to accompany his soul out of Limbo, then scolded Lilian for smiling too much. She was all of seven, and didn't have a single clue as how to deal with this

---

[92] Family Connection – Children of William and Annie (Chassie) LeBlanc: Marie Lilian (Lillian), Azilda, (Hazel), René, Edward, Emil, Grace, Roland, and Juanita. Two other baby boys died before age one.

terrible day—nor, evidently, did any adult have the presence of thought to comfort and show her.

Mother Superior and her underlings were in for a true test when Hazel, Lilian's gregarious, and younger sister, was enrolled. Lilian adored her. No one took her gargantuan strong will into account. The child dug her heels in, and at the onset, adamantly refused to stay at the convent. She'd have none of that appalling food, or any of the tight constraints placed on her strong will. Lilian ran to offer her protection, but the nuns thwarted any vestige of sisterly patronage. Lilian needed not to worry. Hazel's will was triumphant; the tenure short lived.

Lilian's five-year cultivation went the mile and ultimately ended just before her tenth birthday. She returned to her family, very happy to do so. The convent had accomplished its educational mission. In the Sheridan school, Lilian found herself immediately advanced to the next grade, by ten she could read music masterfully, and at thirteen she was asked to play the organ for the church. Proud and willing, she accepted. *Almost every Sunday since, she has been so inclined for the past seventy-eight years.*

In contrast to Lilian's quiet beauty and demeanor, Hazel was a strikingly beautiful, spicy, and vivacious child, who took little guff from anyone growing up, especially from the boys. In all probability she wore-out more than one string of rosary beds at the behest of her mother. Hazel displayed little need to open a book, was very bright, in fact, helped the teacher give lessons to the other students—in Latin, no less! By the twelfth grade she was chosen as the valedictorian of her graduating class.

So, too, behest was each of the four sons who became altar boys in the Catholic parish. That particular Sabbath day chore was a forgone conclusion. No discussion! End of conversation! Under the watchful eye of their mother, they all awoke to prayer, and offered up another round of the nightly rosary as they knelt by their beds. Religious holidays were exactly that—religious. Saint Nicholaus, though benevolent, left very little, though on one perfect Christmas morning Lil found the most wonderful tiny, working sewing machine beneath the tree, one that her father brought back from a business trip.

Saint Nicholaus' successor, Santa Claus, was not yet a part of the American-way, not for at least, another twenty years—when a visionary working for a famous cola company created the whimsical, red suited, bearded, portly patron as a part of an advertising campaign.

Winter's blanketed terrain brought out horse drawn sleighs, several of which lined up outside of the house—some rigs as ornate as those depicted in a Currier and Ives print. Upon sighting Moise's second wife, Clarisse, skimming down over the hill in her rig towards them, the children scrambled out to meet her in a flurry of animated excitement. Unintentionally they spooked the horse, which took-off in an out-of-control gallop, capsizing the sleigh, pitching step-grand Mèmère, tush over derrière into a snow bank. Was this cause for an extra round of devotional exercise? Probably!

Unplowed roads and rough trudging was par for the course when they struck out on the two-mile trek to high school at seven in the morning—remained unplowed for the two-mile tread back in the afternoon. The weather forecast mattered not. Consequently, they frequently chanced a short cut on the railroad tracks, that is until they faced down an engine, and boxcars headed towards them at full steam, forcing each to leap into the high snow bank and hug the incline until all the cars had passed. Was this encounter shared with Mèmère? Probably not!

In the years that followed, simplicity and devotions colored their lives although a big war would soon put devotions to a serious test. Lilian readied to leave for Aunt Eugènie's home in Reading to help with a new baby, but in fact, was on the brink of her life's path and devotion.

Sacrosanct Roses
1936 – 1940

Spain was in the middle of an ugly civil war—and in the span of one month Picasso completed an eleven-foot by twenty-five foot abstract depicting the horrors of the war, a mythological composition based on fact, and rooted in his fury. *"Guernica"* emerged as one of his most heralded and important paintings.

The frail Maria sadly learned that all of her brothers and sisters were killed in the uprising.

She became relegated to long days in bed due to serious bouts with diabetes. The boys revamped the front porch, a room that afforded her cross breezes and a wrap around view of the road leading past the house. From that vantage-point she hailed every passer-by, and each morning broadcast a quiet greeting of affection to Geneva Rogers[93] when she walk down over the hill to open the Roger's Spa for the day's business.

All of her children provided for her in these last days with attention, care and whatever was needed. Bob, Lill and their two babies lived in a camp that he built in the backyard. Their firstborn, Ann Marie, knew where to make herself as welcomed as a breath of fresh air. Unannounced, she pushed through the back door, dauntlessly toddled through the house and clambered up onto Maria's sickbed on the porch with *Puzzizie* the cat, imparting unconditional love and attention that only a toddler could offer—just what the old woman needed. Maria cooed endearingly, *"She lova me. She lova me."*

Peter Alfred arrived in '39, squeaked into the world, just in time for his grandmother to coo over him too—and his name? How nice! Bob and Lil named him after Alfred, the brother that Bobby never knew. What Bobby did know was that the link would bring warmth to his mother. Alfred would now be carried in someone's thoughts—at least for a while.

"I am ready any time to go," she dictated in a letter to Margie who was in New York with Tony Jr. Maria died in 1940, at age seventy. An over-riding theme defined her belief systems. Accumulated adventures, godsends, mistakes, and the dispirited experiences in her life were all cultivated in much the same way as she developed fragile propagated cuttings into mature flowering bushes. Those experiences were facets of a gradual evolution to the perennial development of her spirituality, and in the end it was the petals of her very own soul that opened to the light. She was dearly loved and tenderly borne to memory.

---

[93] Family Connection - Geneva Bickford married Sam Rogers.

Japanese quince, lilacs, and rose bushes that she planted remain a part of the character of the house today. A rose bush that Bob planted next to the front steps still stands sentinel at the entrance of the walkway, and for sixty summers Lillian has placed the pale pink roses on the Catholic Church altar, within inches of the consecration ceremony. Although a vicarious commemoration, in view of Maria's deep faith, it remains a befitting memorial.

Maria (Campos) Gomez
1871 - 1940

Chapter

9

...and the Thoughts of Youth Are Long, Long Thoughts

Henry W. Longfellow

World War II
Long Island, Maine 1941-1942

Europe was heating up. Strangers appeared on the island, vanished, then reappeared with completed designs to metamorphose the island from its sleepy state into—can you believe it—a strategic hub for America's military buildup? Earmarked as *the* refueling depot for the *entire* North Atlantic Fleet, the Annex on Long Island accommodated *every* large vessel in the armada, up through and to the end of the war in 1945. Once upon a time the waters, horizons, and skies that surrounded the island were known, predictable elements, but once transformed into a genuine government secret, anonymity and gravity traveled on, and beneath every wave. We were the last port, the final fuel-up, and oil change before they sailed back out through Hussys Sound and headed for Newfoundland, the European Theater, and to an eventual victory.

Liken to a fisherman casting a net upon the waters, in '42 the government cast its eminent domain from the northern shore, athwart the island, to within a few hundred yards of the southern shore, thus completely enveloping the entire mid section. Workmen tore down familiar homes, painted the few remaining structures brindled-green, blasted holes in ledges big enough to accommodate enormous oil storage tanks, and in their zeal, cut the source for the spring-fed wells located outside of the military base, including the well in front of the Gomez house. Water pipes, laid across the bay to the mainland, connected the Annex to the fresh waters of Sebago Lake.

The shoreline inside the chain-link fencing was filled to the brim with necessary berthing apparatus for large ships including a lea that was needed for the huge piers that were built to last a twenty-year span. A long granite breakwater sprung up where vacationer's boats once set at anchor in front of the Granite Springs Hotel. Because submarines were a part of the equation, a submarine net was created using old sailing vessels that were sunk off the far *Eastend* point. Where once faithful neighbors and a rural integrated way of life abode, just thirty-feet from the Gomez family's front porch, an astounding aberration took its first deep breath. The military was in for the long haul.

In the era when steam-powered vessels displaced commercial sailing ships, the last burnt offering made to the commercial sailing fleet in the United States was from Maine, the four-mast schooner "Zebedee E. Cliff". Becalmed just miles from its destination off California, on principle, it refused assistance from a near-by steam powered tug that offered help. Failing in the attempt to deliver its cargo, she lost the contract and returned to Casco Bay. Her fate sealed, she was scuttled in 1942 off the rocks of the eastern part of Long Island, Maine, and was made a part of the submarine nets of World War II.

Scuttlebutt had it, that when ships were built, the workmen placed a gold coin beneath the mainmast before it was set in place. One of the islanders, I know, crawled around the rotted timbers of the "Zebedee" at low tide, but if he found the coin, he stayed tight-lipped about it. I should make him fess-up—if only for history's sake.

Navy personnel came to the door one afternoon and handed Lillian a box in which she found a few pieces of old clothing, a pair of false teeth, and a boiled egg. Old Antonio, then seventy-five, struck a deal with the Navy, sold his shack at the base of Ponce's for a thousand dollars; to wit, they tore it down. Without so much as a how-do-you-do, the old man vacated—back to the homestead to live with Bob and Lillian.

With the *Eastend* now separated from the *Westend*, the road on the backside of the island was paved to link the two civilian ends together, the New Hill,[94] as it was dubbed, was a formidable

---

[94] More than a half a century later the island continues to refer to the steep incline as the *New Hill*.

incline that dropped sharply to its base at the fresh water marsh at Harbor De Grace. At the top of the New Hill the US Army made it presence know by building a Tower, put there to scan the open sea, and set gun turrets into the ledges on the seaward side of the island. The only other route, which the *Eastend* and *Westend* citizenry had to access each other, was through the restricted Navy base. Islanders could pass through the military's gate, but only if it was open and only if one identified oneself to the guard at one of the two checkpoints. They could not just wave and stroll on by; they had to go up to the window. The guard at the opposite end was notified that someone was coming through and reported back when the individual was no longer on the property.

Some youngsters thought nothing of jumping the fence in order to take a short cut, but only once, the day they heard the security guard shout, *"Halt,"* heard a frightful and disquieting response—a gun shot, one that was directly aimed over their heads. Islanders came to terms with the fact that every inch of the place was not theirs anymore for the asking—*that is—not for thirty more years.*

Looming on the crest of a hill near the Navy piers, large barracks were built for the single sailors. Way down at the other gate, enlisted men with families were housed in long row houses made up of two bedroom units. Existing single homes, scattered along the shoreline, were earmarked for the officers. It was a self-contained community with a generator and boiler house, fire-fighting equipment, hydrants, an independent source of water, and a garage.

Medical help for the Navy community came by way of pharmacist mates, and in the more serious situations, available to islanders. Entertainment was not to be denied; forthwith a bowling alley, movie-theater and tennis courts were nestled amidst the brindle green real estate. Islanders always felt that the Annex probably contained an equal amount of things of which we had absolutely no knowledge. A maelstrom of military activity—this realm unto itself, secured and housed inside the fence—now went about the business of war—and the island went about its way of working around it. Workmen hung a big sign up on the chain link fencing, to the left of the gate, to tell all that this was the Long Island Annex.

We did not refer to that place inside the fencing as The Annex, but gave it a more enigmatic title; we called it *The Area*. The name doesn't conger up the same mysterious association as does the name Roswell, New Mexico, but it did contain the same element of concealed secrecy.

Gargantuan, looming destroyers, landing crafts, and a small aircraft carrier created an ominous spectacle as they steamed in through Hussy Sound and docked at the piers. Picture taking was absolutely forbidden. The drastic change must have been difficult to put into perspective for the old-timers, though there was never picketing outside of the Naval Annex. There were pockets of descent in the country, but for the most, patriotism ran extraordinarily high. We, along with the majority, displayed a nationalistic fervor, were swept up by Roosevelt's powerful fireside addresses, and the monotone, oratorical excellence of Churchill, both voices, ones of comfort and strength. Radio personalities worked war bond sales into the programming as though part of the story line. Up to this point, sultry high-class models owned the colorful cosmetic magazine ads, but were replaced with stark black and white ads that highlighted the military's WAVES, and WACS[95] They left one hint of color in a lipstick ad, the ruby red lips. It was quite effective.

Islanders were required to install thick window shades for air raid blackouts, to save aluminum for ammunition production, and were required to use ration stamps, so as to make the supply of gasoline, cheese, meat, sugar, coffee, butter, and shoes, available for the troops. Civilians responded without a second thought. Everyone was told that no enemy submarines were plying the waters, but when the air-raid sirens blew after sundown in Portland, even those on the street were absolutely forbidden to light so much as a cigarette. The military wanted the coast as dark as a pocket. Not many living on the coast, if asked, believed the ocean was clear of menace.

***

---

[95] WAVES – Women's branch of the Navy. WACS – Women's Army Corp.

Will Ricker boarded the Casco Bay boat at Chebeague's Chandlers Cove, headed for Long Island to work on the Army boats and on Boston Sand & Gravel's, *John C.*, a towboat that hauled sand and gravel for the construction of the base in '42. Brothers, Ray and Pood, were ensconced at the Navy base, too, and paved the way with Commander Beady for Will as a stationary engineer in the Navy's generator plant, *a job that paid damn well, mister-man.* Now and forevermore, claming on a low tide in the middle of the night, with a flashlight tied to his head was relegated to youthful memories, put in the same depository as was tipping over outhouses and the devil's fiddle. From this maritime seasoning, he walked into his life's work with a brand-spanking new Chief engineer's license for vessels of 500 horsepower, propelled by gas, fluid naphtha, or electric motors, a license that served him for a lifetime.

"Shipmates in Company"

Each of Lillian's four handsome brothers departed from the Ashland train station to entered World War II early in '42 —all on the very same Easter day. One enlisted in the army, one entered the Air Force, and two joined the Navy. Emil and Eddy were only months apart in age, extraordinarily close, and elated to find that they had been assigned to the same ship.

Emil LeBlanc, Mother Annie and Ed LeBlanc

The boys were piped aboard the *Quincy*, a nine-thousand-ton heavy cruiser, and a vessel that saw immediate action in the Pacific. Guadalcanal, August 1942, Ed and Emil found themselves a part of a campaign off the Solomon Islands in support of the Marines on shore. Lines of communication were disrupted and the Japanese slipped through at midnight on August eighth.

In the disastrous Battle of Salvo the surprise attack destroyed four of the cruisers, including the *Quincy.* Ed saw his brother's gun turret hit and went in frantic search of Emil amidst decks awash with fuel. Wounded three times in the attempt, Ed waded through waves of explosions, fire, injured men and carnage. He knew what he had witnessed, but hoped against hope that Emil made it overboard and was picked up by another ship—hoped until he had to abandon ship himself. The *Quincy* went down, resting in three thousand feet of water in *Iron Bottom Sound*. Of the twelve hundred fifty-two men aboard, a mere twenty-five were rescued. Ed was one. After months of search from his hospital bed in New Zealand, Eddy finally rested that Emil's last moment was inside the explosion that he witnessed. The Purple Heart medal was awarded to Ed and posthumously to Emil, after which, Ed closed the door to an epochal period in our country's history, a chapter that he avoided revisiting—with anyone.

Months after Emil was declared killed in action, at the time when Ed was recovering from wounds, Congress passed the law that prohibited brothers from serving on the same ship. The single tragedy that prompted the enactment of the Sullivan law took place in November of 1942 when all six brothers of the Sullivan family, serving aboard the same vessel, died in battle.

Fifty-five years after the ordeal, Uncle Eddy (Ed) and my daughter Suzanne sat quietly in his home on Eagle Lake, a small town up near the Canadian border, both surrounded by a library of photo albums and books on the LeBlanc/Chasse family's genealogy. This fruit of his labor was a valiant effort; because the Chasse family of Saint Agathe was so large that a newspaper out of Madawaska, the St. John Valley Times, prints a quarterly who's who for the thousands of Chasse relatives. Outlasting the course of time, Ed's handsome, sunny face was animated by his and Suzy's joint quest. Not many young people in the family met his level of interest in the time-consuming study until he and his sister, Lillian's granddaughter connected—a marriage of two generations.

As his eyes rested on Emil's picture, he waited a moment then made a concerted effort to step back through the threshold, to acquiesce to that protected recess of his heart, mind, and soul, softly relating the story to Suzanne, and in a trice—his eyes welled with tears. The war commanded a great a price from him, and as was apparent, he held the balance of it tied up in sackcloth. The quiet hero had held his brother's spirit as close as a thought, having never let go. Then again—who is to say? It may well have been mutual.

I scanned photos on a US Navy Internet site, groups of war ships in New York, first studying the earliest pictures of the "Quincy." One came up titled "Taken from a Japanese ship" and there she was—afire, minutes before she sank, and then another with her fully engulfed. I sat inches from the screen, drawn into the moment as though I could find what Ed had not, knowing he, too, may well have been in those waters when the picture was taken, and in a trice...

One more photo lay beneath a click of the mouse. I wasn't ready for it. It took a moment to focus on an abstract of a rusting gun turret that stood out in the blue black curtain of water, pictures taken fifty-years after the war, beneath the three thousand feet of water where she settled. She lies upright in the deep water, with her bow broken off immediately in front of her forward eight-inch gun turrets, both of which are trained out to starboard. The ship's shell-riddled forward superstructure, shattered left gun of Turret #2, the destroyed aircraft hangar, and collapsed after-deck are indicators of the battering she received from Japanese weapons during her final moments on the surface, and from the crushing force of the deep sea after she sank. I know now why the raising of sunken ships bothers me.[cii]

***

Explosions in the Area became a part of the everyday-to-day experience for Lillian, some set-off to make way for water pipes, some to make way for the construction of the tanks that would hold the stored fuel. The process for building the tanks, which held bunker-C fuel, took awhile, because they built them from cement, and reinforcing rods—tons of reinforcing rods, more than they needed to use, just because they had them.

The purpose for the explosions mattered not to Lillian, pregnancy was difficult enough to deal with and the many blasts emanating from the Area didn't help the state of affairs in her corner of the world. Getting to the Maine General Hospital to give birth to their third child proved more complicated than for

Ann Marie and Peter Alfred. At two o'clock in the morning she knew something was amiss though she was unaware, at the moment, that the pregnancy had evolved into a placenta priva. Bobby's boat was inoperable. At two in the morning it was hard-won to find someone to take them to town, although he did managed to finally drag somebody out of bed.

Maine General's priest was called. A heated debate ensued. Should the delivery go any more awry than it had thus far, the priest's established position dictated that the child's life would be saved over the mother's. Bobby hit the ceiling. There was no room for debate as far as Lillian's welfare was concerned. What debate? End of discussion! At seven-thirty in the AM, the baby was born, healthy—a girl. Much to Dad's relief, Lillian was out of danger.

Sibling rivalry is a given in any family, the politics greet you at the front door, as it did in ours. My sibling noodged at me over what they perceived as parental favoritism—most specifically in their minds was Dad's towards me. It is true that I was so named after him, a decision in which I had no say. It is true that he was amused by some of the things I said and did, but even that was not a saving grace when I ran amuck of his dos and don'ts—no different response than what was directed at them. I didn't see it, but they perceived the favoritism, which made it a done deal. September of '42 at the Maine General Hospital required revisiting—from a wider perspective than that of my sibling's or mine, to grasp Dad's thorny decision regarding the welfare of his wife and unborn baby, a situation that was certainly exacerbated by the intervention from the priest. It was the first grave decision-making that affected his young family.

I was the infant born that night. My thought is that my presence from that point on was a reminder of the ramifications of what could have happened, and how exceedingly grateful Dad was that the worst didn't happen. That is what he saw in me— ergo the favoritism, if it can be called that. For the rough start, of which I have no recall, I turned out non-the worse for the wear, other than a chronic case of noodging, which crops up now and again at family gatherings.

Not many months later, in '43, Mother's sister Hazel was stricken with a life threatening illness. Mom left quickly to be with her in Massachusetts. The Army refused to contact Hazel's husband, who was a forward artillery observer, one of the big, bad, dangerous jobs. He was fair, square in the middle of heavy combat. Hazel died, at age twenty-seven, with her mother, father, and sisters around her, but pitifully, she left behind a five-year old boy. The situation could not have been more tragic.

The funeral was held in Sheridan, but Mother was called back to the island before they headed north. I had spiked a temperature of hundred-and-four while in Aunt Margie's care. Obviously Mother was torn. It was a trying period for her; a youthful brother and sister gone within the year, another recovering from war injuries, two toddlers to care for, an infant with a fever, and an excessively difficult, aging father-in-law to weather.

Lost & Found
LeBlanc Family Reunion
Present Day

In recent years, plans for a reunion on Mother's side of the family evolved through the efforts of several first cousins that live within a close radius of one another, all of them third generation LeBlancs. Predictably, an irresistible question popped up amongst us during the planning, a subject we invariably touched upon when we were all together, and a curiosity as to how Hazel's five-year-old son had faired in his life. He would be over sixty now. We should send him an invitation. Where is he? Do you suppose he can be found? Does he want to be found?

Our youngsters went in search on the Internet and found four names that matched. Ann Marie called the first on the list and to her great surprise his elderly father answered. From him she acquired the telephone number and dialed, introduced herself, and asked for Francis. He replied, "What are you selling?" He had not gone by that name for decades, and was well aware that only people from the family would address him by his proper name. Ann Marie was the one he remembered from a gathering in Sheridan back in the forties. They talked for hours. The reconnection bowled him over, as it did us.

He lived too far away to be expected to travel for the few hours that we'd be together, but on the day of the reunion I looked up and saw a tall, vibrant man come across the lawn accompanied by his lovely wife. In him I saw a more handsome version of Willy, our grandfather, and his personality was likewise more outgoing, worldly, and spicy. He carried himself as one would if a seasoned businessman, was extremely intelligent, happy at heart, and rather playful, exhibiting a clever wit that slipped out between the hundreds of questions. In another time, that could have been a description of his mother, Hazel. The apple had fallen pretty close to the tree.

I thought he was brave to face all of us after fifty years. How does one become accustomed to the concept of newly acquired relatives, aunts and an uncle, who knew and loved a mother he only vaguely remembered? And then there were all of his first and second cousins, all the once-removed faction, a hundred-fifty in all at the party. He had no clue that we were out here in the ether, and he said to me, "You have hair just like me!" Most importantly, he became reacquainted with his mother's memory. He could make a fair assessment of what she was like by taking an average amongst those who were present, though he'd be more close to the mark by looking into a mirror.

He'd never been given pictures of her, but on that day, a library of scrapbooks was spread before him and the seniors of the clan took him through each page and answered his questions. Ann Marie gave him a scrapbook of his own with copies of all the pictures we had of his mother, plus our families. This was the beginning, and although it started out as a reunion, it ended up being a welcome home party for our lost cousin, the perennial five-year-old.

"Hello, Mr.& Mrs. America and All the Ships at Sea!"
1944 – 1947

Nineteen forty-four, Mercy Hospital, two years later, two years old, tonsillectomy, trauma time, vivid bits and fits of recall, and scream—didn't I scream! Mom's had these blasted maternal instincts that reared up, and made it difficult for her to keep going down State Street towards Casco Bay Lines. Being able to hear the screaming—from outside of the hospital didn't help matters. The crib was big, made of cold metal piping that was painted white. My throat hurt. Moreover, these strangers put me on a total diet of ice cream—old fashioned vanilla. The screaming stopped.

Age did little to quell Antonio's difficult behavior. An old, black and white eight-millimeter film revealed a vacant look in his eyes, a sudden snap into a chilling dark glare. Tony Jr., Bob, and Johnny felt it more appropriate for their father to move into the Seaman's Home in Snug Harbor, New York, not far from Tony Junior's home on Sunnyside, Long Island. The old man lived out his days over-looking the busy Harbor, spun yarns to any listening ear available, built large model sailing ships, making fancy knot boards. He died in 1946 and was brought back to the island for burial. [ciii]

Amongst the tumult, my younger sister was born, but any memory of Carmen's arrival was trumped by other significant events—as they affected me, of course! Uncle René and his bride, Dotty, absconded with me on a long, rolling, rocking, overnight train ride upstate to Sheridan while Mother was in the hospital for a whole week after giving birth. René was the most handsome man in his Air Force uniform, Dotty looked like Veronica Lake, and their two-year old *abscondee* had motion sickness the whole trip. His uniform got the worst of it.

Like magic, Carmen appeared one Christmas day when she was two, there in amongst the tinsel, examining a beautiful baby doll identical to both Ann's and mine. The dolls were soft and smelled of sweet talcum powder—just like Carmen.

Servicemen were hellers, but of the throngs, most were behaved when outside of the Area. Throughout all of those years, only one wayward soul directly affected our home, figuratively and literally for only a flash. No one locked the doors at night, or at any other time of the day. The thought never occurred to them that a stranger would have the audacity to come in uninvited, but one individual did—in the dark of night. Mother awoke from a dead sleep in the darkened room to discover a man standing at the foot of the bed attempting to disrobe. She let out a scream, one that startled the hell out of him. All *twound-up* in one half of his divested clothing, the dark figure bolted, in not too graceful a manner, tripping, stumbling, hell-bent down over the stairs, Dad behind him with some implement in his hand that would do someone severe bodily harm. The bogyman lept out through the back door and melt into the darkness. During the commotion, the littlest awoke, with a fear that a big dog had made its way into the house. Dad told Carmen to go back to sleep—not to worry—everything was fine.

Mother's midnight apparition stood the test in the light of day. In her morning search, a pair of grass covered Army boots lay just outside of the back door, just where he'd left them in his hasty departure. They never did take up the practice of locking the door, and heard from Frank Mountfort that the interloper was out on a bender, had intended to stay at Mountfort's Inn, and only missed his destination by one door. *But why did he take his boots off before entering the house? Good manners, perhaps?*

Requiescat In Pacer
(Rest in Peace)
Present Day

In a recent time, twenty or so aging Veterans and their wives filed onto the deck at the newly renovated island restaurant, The Spar. Despite the polite smiles on the faces of the women, the festive quality that usually accompanies such a gathering was absent; actually, a somber tone prevailed. They spoke in low tones and rather than lending attention to each other, or looking out in the direction of a grand water scene, they directed their attention over to where half a century before, there stood piers, ships, and chain link fencing. Only a few vestiges of the Navy Annex remained for them to reference and point out because President Kennedy closed the base down forty years ago. Piers built to last for a twenty year period fell away, little by little, storm after storm, right, smack dab, within the twenty-year timeline, until there was little to nothing left but for the breakwater, which is a lea now used by the island lobstermen to protect their boats. Whatever the retired Navy men expected, they could readily see that the island had reclaimed itself.

All were just boys all full of piss and vinegar when they sailed into the island and stood amongst us for a minute during wartime. Their ship was filled with fuel, packed with stores—and they, infallible spirits all, sailed back out through Hussy's Sound and onto a war that consumed too much of the world. The island was the last American soil on which some would stand—ever.

Somber expressions on the aging faces made me wonder if the stopover had less to do with sight seeing, and more about being in the last place in which a crew, in its entirety, once stood together. If so, it was a befitting memorial service for shipmates on any level. They probably thought that none of us remembered. They most assuredly did not know that the affects of the war lingered in this small community, in each of us, and was threaded all through our outlook on life.

* * *

Navy PT boats ran at a pretty good clip past Ponce's Landing, roared by the front beach that stretched along the shore, down below the old, tired looking Cushing Hotel—the beach where mother always took the four of us to play. It was the same place where Cushing's wharf once stood, the same smooth rounded ledges that shored it up, the very ones we were scampering down over to get to the beach and water's edge. Nothing of Cushing's wharf remained, and the weathered hotel was now a shadow of its former resplendence and distinction.

Larger ships sailed by more slowly than did the PT types, and had a way of consuming the entire horizon, especially the grey battleships with their huge guns and multiple decks. We stood captivated at the water's edge and waved outward to the line of white uniformed figures that lined the railings of the ships. They waved back, enthusiastically circling their white hats in the air.

Mom passed us red hot dogs in a bun with green piccalilli, orange soda in a burnt orange-colored, *ripply* bottle, and worked to keep our skin from burning to a crisp. Although, some of us browned up nicely on our own—one of the benefits of being Spanish, in which half again as much French was blended, then suffused with a blush of American Indian. Dad was busy beneath the hull of his beached lobster boat, a long, sleek, pretty boat, which had no name. While he brushed on a coat of red lead primer, we otherwise occupied ourselves with childish undertakings, anything that caught our fancy, the older siblings in the advance position.

"A mess of black periwinkles, that's what we need! In a large can! Someone get a large can! While you're at it, get a little salt water in it! Someone start the fire! Put those white periwinkles down! They'll make you sick. You got potatoes in your ears? I *said*, just the black ones! Jeepers Creepers! I *said*...just a *little* salt water!"

Our huddled state around the fire caught our father's attention, interrupted his work, not that the periwinkles were a problem, but the empty can of dried, red, *lead* paint in which they were boiled was. He abruptly ended the shore dinner before we had a chance to savor a morsel, and we skulked away with furrows between our eyes, with our mouths turned down at the corners, grumbling little nothings.

Our eyes and attention diverted quickly towards the direction of the Navy piers where an engine was gearing up to a high pitch, the distinct sound of a PT boat pulling away from the piers—at full bore. Yeah! Be patient. It will clear from around the breakwater any moment. This is what we waited for on the front beach—boats that created a formidable wake and formidable waves that drew us to the water's edge. Fearlessly, we negotiated the humongous waves that rolled towards us—a very animated scene as we jumped over and dove through each one—a time when Mother became more vigilant.

One round of thunderous wave action caught me good, drew me under. I recall looking up to the surface through a tinge of green water, through the long tangle of my own hair. The muffled, gurgling noises of rocks and pebbles made it sound as though I was inside a drum as they rolled in and out with the wave action, and I felt no fear, probably too young to realize my plight. I saw Mom's hand reach in to pluck me out of the watery cauldron. None of us drowned—or were poisoned by lead paint that day. Sailors were not the only ones who earned medals of conduct and valor. Mother and Dad were unsung heroes every day of our little lives.

Though not always, we wore life preservers when swimming at the raft. Preservers came in one size—huge. They were canvas covered, eighteen-inch long slabs of cork sewn together, with a cord tied around the middle, a hazard, as well as a savior, as Ann Marie found out on a swim around the raft at the base of Ponces. Her straps became entangled on the raft's anchor chain during that frightening incident, and she began hearing bells before she finally freed up from the struggle. That was a close one, and as we crowded around listening intently, from her graphic description we now knew, first hand, what it sounded like when you go under, ringing bells—the sounds of drowning.

None of us feared the great expanse. What we had for it was an inherent respect, inherent to the marrow. We did know most of its dangers. It was just there, surrounding us, like the highways on the mainland, a way to get from here to there. City kids couldn't play on the highway, but we could—play in and over ours. When it turned ugly, we simply steered clear of it, always with one eye peeled in its direction.

It was a surprise to learn that so many of the lobstermen did not know how to swim. Although any that did drown did not do so from lack of a swimming ability, but because they forgot to carry a small knife in their pocket to cut the trap warp in which they became entangled as the traps were being set-off. Sight of a boat circling in the water struck a dread in the hearts of those who scrambled for the boats to go in search. Sadly, retrieval was simple. They needed only haul the closest stringer of traps located nearest the circling boat—which invariably belonged to the missing lobsterman.

Some birdbrain arrived one fine day with the mission to teach island children how to swim. Not a second after he stuck my head under water, and held it there, I pulled free, *harrumphed* up over Fowler's Beach, and beat it for home. The dog paddle was just fine for the moment, thank you very much!

Maria's unpainted, weather-beaten summer kitchen was transformed into a bright year 'round kitchen, with rows of windows, a porcelain sink, faucets, and, can you believe it—running water. They called it an artesian well, but doesn't water freely bubble up out of the ground of its own accord in a true artesian? Eighty feet later, after days of enduring the sound of the rig pounding through clay and into the bedrock, we finally had our water. The depth of a well was one of those island points of pride. Whereas, one well received a goodly volume of water into the well pipe per minute, after digging thirty feet, another might dig to two hundred feet, with only five gallons per minute. Every household prayed that they not tap a cursed saltwater vein. The only option remaining when that happened was to whittle out a new dowsing stick, drop back ten, and punt.

The four of us were herded into one bedroom over looking the well digging rig, shades down, room darkened, all of us terribly sick with a virulent case of German measles. Mother made a circle of our beds around a table where she put liquids to drink, a basin of cold water, and face cloths with which to sponge us down, her attempts to keep the high fevers in check. She had her work cut out for her. Carmen was particularly bad-off, barely moving in her crib, with her eyes swollen shut. Every time the drill hit ledge, it rattled our brains. I am still not certain if the headaches were from the measles, or from the infernal pounding outside of our window. The whole-of-us were lucky not to have come out of it with more than a peak-ed-look and a memory.

Whooping cough, chicken pox, mumps, and old-fashioned measles invaded our well being in the early days of our childhood. School was the breeding ground for all of those infectious bugs, including cooties that someone brought home for Mom to eradicate, with a foul smelling liquid, and a metal fine-toothed comb, the very reason that our long pig-tails eventually met with a pair of scissors.

Hail and hallelujah! Indoor bathroom facilities were completed. Mother was saved from escort duty when two or more or us, with the same urge—at the same time, sprinted out into the far corner of the back yard to an ominous, dark hovel that spiders loved to inhabit. Successful potty training was a confounded miracle, for it was such a spooky deal to anyone under two-feet tall, a test of bravery—that of overcoming the ever present fear of falling down through the big oval hole. Strong updrafts rushed up through one large and one small oval hole in the bench seat—on which sat a copy of the book, *Peter Rabbit*. Mother read, *"...the birds...they implored him to exert himself,"* a subliminal hint if ever there was one.

Maria's proper dining room was made over into the *piano room* and the old kitchen was transformed into a dining room with cupboards galore. They took the weight off a peculiar nook called the pantry, a deep closet with shelves that reached from the floor to the ceiling, a place where dry goods were stored and afforded a small counter on which to make piecrust or grind coffee. *It is regretful that pantries went out of vogue in the fifties, because they were handier than cupboards, a magical place where items appeared out of the blue as though by some alchemistic process that took place when the door was closed. I miss a pantry and keep trying to turn some part of my own home into one.*

Strong searching winds sifted under the rug in the living room causing it to undulate and flutter. Wood Baston made every floor in the downstairs air-tight with a particular issue of iron clad, inlaid linoleum, *which after sixty years and hard use is still going strong.* The same quality of workmanship went into the ceilings—*today as good as new.* The man took redecorating to a new height by building an ironing board unit into the wall, one made unobtrusive by using the same design as the cupboards—innovative for the times. He was a master at readying the house for a great deal of wear and tear, a heavy, second go-around—once again filled with a gaggle of feisty, active children.

By six in the morning, the early sun cast patches of lemony warmth into the kitchen. Mother stood at the stove stirring up a big pot of oatmeal, a mixture that bubbled like molten magma on the back of the oil stove. Dry milk was a new by-product of the war. It was in the same league as nylon stockings; but unfortunately, the tasteless brew took the place of the cream topped bottles of milk that were delivered to the house, up to that point, by Uncle Johnny.

***

I lay across the breadth of our round dining room table on my stomach, my ear into the cathedral shaped radio, making room for myself midst the shakers of salt, pepper, a bowl of oleo, and a sugar bowl. It was my singular duty to eat the light crust of sugar off the spoon that I found stuck in the sugar bowl, the one put back into the bowl after *somebody* had stirred *his* coffee.

Don McNeil's Breakfast Hour had a festive atmosphere to it, lots of clapping by the audience. He urged his listeners to march around the breakfast table; a summons that fit nicely into a four-year old mind-set. *The Arthur Godfrey Show* came across laid-back and mellow, both toastmasters my personal playmates, a part of the morning's imaginings.

Yappy talk shows melted into anguish-ridden, heart-wrenching, long-suffering soap operas, *Our Gal Sunday* and *Helen Trent,* a string of them—all of which were ushered in with signature classical music. Generally they chose music written in the minor key, *the sound of the black keys on the piano, a sound that was more melancholic and woeful than music written on the white keys, and a sound that a child reared in music obviously was able to pick out of the air.* An in-studio organist was busy running up and down the scales, emphasizing the drama that unfolded—perpetually unfolded. Each story was an open-ended love story that went on, and on, and on—mixed in with catchy commercials for *Oxydol* laundry soap, and a bevy of cleaning product jingles that were more entertainment than the actual programming. I lay on the table listening, memorizing the jingles, humming, and eating the crusted sugar off the spoon. The tatted lace tablecloth left fancy indentations in my cheeks.

196

No one was allowed to stretch out on the dining room table when set for the evening meal; therefore we all shifted our focal point to the tall floor radio in the living room in the late afternoon, and during nightly programs. Dad sat forward in the chair with both arms resting on his knees during the six-o'clock news, his hands clasped—shushing us. We needed constant shushing. He was intent on every word Lowell Thomas had to report on the war and cupped his ear towards the radio. He suspected that more lurked beneath the waves off the Casco Bay Islands than lobsters, cod, and haddock. Later in the evening, he again sat with both arms resting on his knees, with a squirming little boy child wrapped around his feet, and the both took in a boxing match through the backdrop of a frenzied crowd. So absorbed, was he, with the visual images described by the announcer, that he was not aware that both of his hands were clenched tightly into fists, moving in short jerks—as though he was one of the fighters in the ring.

***

Chester A. Riley, Throckmorten P. Gildersleeve and Digger O'Dell, characters of nighttime radio, luminaries of the entertainment world who gave us hours of amusement inside of their fictitious lives, and through their signature voices. *Fibber MaGee and Molly* hailed from 79 Wistful Vista and consistently lost their composure to fits of laughter right in the middle of a script. In every episode we were unable to prevent Fibber from opening the infamous bulging hall-closet, and squealed when he, at some point before every show's end, absent-mindedly opened the door, which unleashed the avalanche of crashing, clattering piles of squirreled away stuff. *MaGee's closet* is what we called any mess that needed straightening away—except Dad's workshop out back. That was all good stuff out there.

Ventriloquist Edgar Bergen—yes, a ventriloquist on radio, divvied his voice and his brain between two dummies. The most verbal, the smart-mouthed Charley McCarthy dressed in a top hat, tux, and wore a monocle. Mortimer Snerd, the cross-eyed, do-do, dressed in a straw hat, mismatched plaid outfits, and duhhhed and yukked his way through the evening. Charley was incorrigible, couldn't be verbally trusted whenever he flirted and chortled with glamorous guests, Lana Turner and Rita Hayworth.

We were carried on the wave of Gracie Allen's convoluted labyrinth of ditsy reasoning, afforded her patience along with her composed, unruffled husband, George Burns. Their scripts were simple, entertaining, and a panacea for the weighty period in our country's history. Whole segments of Fred Allen's show, and his conversations with old Tidus Moody, were relegated to the *whys and wherefores* of buying United States savings bonds. To that point, I never knew radio to be anything but a major conduit for national fervor.

Lux Radio Theater aired a program called *The Birds,* a story that should have had a disclaimer for little ears. Throughout the entire harrowing adaptation, I leaned against the big radio, sponging up every minute of the program, one that left me with a long series of nightmares, beginning that very night.

Alfred Hitchcock revived it in movie theaters twenty years later, a movie that I watched with interest so as to compare it with my own vivid recollections. By far, the rendition born in the arms of Morpheus, in which I adapted the house next door as the stage for the program, surpassed anything created by the special effects in the movie—in as much as I was the actor, director, and producer in my nightmare. By the way—because of the hammer, nails, and cedar shakes that I just happened to have on hand in the nightmare, the seagulls never made it through the barricaded windows on the upper floor in the little house next door— the window that looked down over Captain Percy Perry's cottage.

Now and again, my ear catches Bob Hope's closing song, "Thanks For the Memories" and Walter Winchell's opening bark, "Good evening Mr. and Mrs. America, and all the ships at sea." The quick-step in which they delivered their words is portage into a forgotten environment, a throw back to the magical aura of childhood. Likewise, whenever I hear the first bars from any of the particular classics used to open the soap opera programming, I am afforded immediate portage into that period, a jog to my auditory memory—melodies that invariably deliver me to that dining room in 1945. The smell of lilacs produces the same results. As I think on it, I can listen to Mozart for hours, but I've never listened to more than two to three minutes of any of those classics at any one sitting. It is the two to three minutes of melody used as the announcer asked, "Can a little girl from a mid-western town find love...."

The poignant line from the song "Toyland" reveals what I perceive to be a profound truth about early childhood. The lyric says, "Once you leave its boarders you may never return again." It speaks to the fanciful interpretations of that elfin world and the point at which a little-one ceases seeing things in mystical, fluid terms. Physiologists theorize that the magical perceptions of childhood seem to stop about the time a child begins to learn linearly, as in 1,2,3,4,5, A, B, C, D, E, everything all in a row, and they say that mentally, the period can never re-entered. How about that! Picasso said that it took years to learn to paint like Raphael, but it took a lifetime to paint like a child, which strongly indicates, that he caught the watershed moment too. On the average, we have seventy years of all of that linear thinking, therefore, those first pure years are a gift that we are all given until age five, seemingly, a one shot deal, and as brief as it is, a significant respite to preserve. I am left with a misty aura of that tabletop, radio, and sugar spoon moment, and do find it a lovely, lasting impression, though it is one that has always been a little out of focus. Thanks to songwriter, Victor Herbert, lyricist, Glen MacDonough, the physiologists, and Picasso, I just may have inkling as to why those recollections remained gauzy.

***

Waking up in the morning was not difficult, but getting out of the sunken, warm, pocket in my bed was, into nippy temperatures, cold enough to freeze the chamber pot under the bed. We wore three heavy quilts over us when we slept, ones that Grammy LeBlanc made from her discarded woolen clothes, colors dark and somber. Three of her quilts were heavy enough to pin us to the mattress, kept us warm, especially when I wrapped one over my head to capture the warmth of my breath, a strategy used to keep my nose warm.

The arrival of those quilts was a novelty. So much work went into them and she created them—just for us? Other than that, we never heard from her. She visited once, twice. I caught the feeling that she didn't approve of us, or was it that she was generally a disapproving person—or were we a bunch of rapscallions? Her accent was thick and she swung into French dialogue in a wink. She and Mom talked French all the time. I thought it rude. Because Mom didn't have the accent, I forgot that she was capable of speaking another language, actually, her primary language. Did her brain still think in French first, or not at all, anymore? Mom should talk to us in French, the thought having little to do with becoming bilingual, but more to satisfy our needle-nose tendencies.[96]

Six Degrees of Separation 1983

THEY say—if you stand in the middle of Times Square in NYC you will meet someone you know. Then, too, there is that concept that all of us are within six degrees of separation. Both theories caught up with me, in of all places, the Maine Medical Center— in a hospital cafeteria where I was gathering a bit of sustenance before heading back to stand vigil in my dad-in-law, Will's hospital room.

A woman of my age, looking as haggard as I felt at the moment, asked if she could share the table with me in the noisy, overcrowded room that was filled with a couple hundred people. Politely, I inquired as to how things were going for her and she, filled to overflowing with worry, poured forth her story, about her son, seriously injured, transferred from a hospital in northern Maine to the MMC. They hailed from a little place up in the County, she said, one that she was sure I'd not heard of, the town of Sheridan. Leaning into her, I took notice! Northern Maine seemed a figment of my imagination, viewed from a child's memory of train rides, snow, horses, wagons, strawberry milk in tall, glass milk-bottles, and a great deal of mud.

In her discourse she dropped the family's surname, Poitras. Astonished, I took double notice. When a space opened in her story I interjected the most definitive questions that I could

---

[96] To be a needle-nose is to be nosey—very, very nosey.

summon, ones that would substantiate a conclusion formed in my mind, by asking, "Did you live in the house across from Willie LeBlanc's store, and is your Shetland pony still alive?"

She looked at me—refocused, looked deeper into my eyes and with the most confounded expression on her face and answered, "Yes, and—no!" Her eyes widened when I described her home, mouth slacked open when describing my grandparent's store, one that Willie built onto the house after his children had grown. We talked of its rough wood interior, squeaking floorboards, pickle barrel, and huge ornate potbelly stove. The store had a distinct smell to it, not a bad one, a mixture of burning wood, root vegetables, and penny candy. The first activity, after hugs and kisses for our grandparents, was for us to dart across the street and visit the Poitras children and their wondrous Shetland pony. The woman I was talking with, of course, was one of the round faced, barefooted imps, the one with a thumb in her mouth, who greeted us at the shed door. What is the law-of-averages for a chance meeting of that ilk? Was this a coincidence? Really!

***

Uncle Johnny stopped in early in the morning, just as we sprinted down over the stairs to warm our backsides against the wood stove in the living room. He bided a moment, teased a bit, and waited for a kiss on the cheek before he left, never calling us by name, but simply tagging us with sister or brother. The camp out back was his home and he an integral part of our family circle, an important one at that. He brought a pure, gentle affection into the mix.

Advantageous as it was for Dad to be in the wholesale food business, it did have its limits during wartime. We ate very well, but due to food rationing, we were introduced to the difference between butter and, its novel replacement, oleomargarine. One, *not so fine day*, a hermetically sealed, clear plastic bag, plump full of a pound's worth of solid, white fat showed up on the refrigerator shelf. It had this strange, dime size compartment sealed inside, filled with a vivid orange substance. The solid white fat had to be kneaded until it was malleable, a chore that each of us coveted. The pièce de résistance, the point at which the orange button was compressed, broken open to release the yellow food coloring into the fat, was the provocation for many a skirmish as to who would get the job. Orange swirls faded into a lemon yellow as we kneaded, and kneaded, until it finally, *sort of—maybe*—it resembled the high priced spread. I could barely abide eating it, and hadn't a thought as to the chemical make-up of the food coloring. *I don't want to know! It is too late anyway!*

Our telephone number was 248, or was it Dad's work number that was 248? Whichever! It was a simple three digit number, two rings, the signal to pick up, the black phone a novelty—one of those tall rigs. It had no dial, had a listening thingamajig cradled on the side of the phone, and a cone, at the top, into which one spoke, but it rarely ever rang—our ring. We personally knew the different parties who shared the same line, those who were on the other end of the one, three, and four rings that also rang at our house.

Telephone usage was minimal, not arbitrary, and a privilege, usually with a call to Dad at work. After checking to see if the party line was clear, a real person's voice broke in—a Portland operator with a nasal, singsong request, *"Number pa-leese?"* Everyone could listen-in on party line conversations, and we could hear a lift of the receiver, but a good ear could always tell when a pick-up, or hang up had taken place. This was part of the reason everyone knew everything, about everybody, and in retrospect—great entertainment. The habit was considered bad manners, we not allowed to do that, although, when other parties stayed on for *hours* they got the quickly pick-up the receiver, put-down, three-times-routine, and as a result got ugly. Too bad! Their manners were bad first.

Housework ate up nearly a week's worth of days. Mother's homemaker's attire was made up of a short sleeved floral printed housedress, and a floral printed bib-apron, neither of them color coordinated to the other—ever, not much of a fashion statement—either.[97] Racks and racks worth were readily available at W. T. Grants five and dime store. Everyone's mother wore one with ankle socks and penny loafers.

---

[97] The housedress was the *nineteen and forty's* version of sweats.

The laundry process owned, possessed, and took up one entire day, Monday—the day when Mother did battle with an *Easy* wringer washer, a monster that wrenched her unwilling hands and arms through the wringer's hard rubber rollers when she dropped her guard—especially when doing sheets and towels. The rollers mashed our clothes into unrecognizable forms during the process of squeezing out the excess water, after which, the clothes lay like boards in a heap, while the drain hose was stuck out through the window to empty the washer of dirty water. Filling the tub once again with clean rinse water, the clothes went through the wringing process again, and to think that all of that energy was expended for one—single—dark—load. It's no wonder that radio, and its all day line-up of soap operas was popular listening.

At day's end, she pushed through the door, basket heaped with dried, folded linen on her hip, the scent of fresh air trailing behind her as she walked through the house. She must have dreaded rainy days when the only recourse for drying clothes was to drape them over a fan-shaped dowel hanger that was nailed to the wall, high over the kitchen stove. They dried stiff, scratchy, and had a propensity to cause rashes, especially in diapers and corduroy pants. *These were the good old days!*

Once upon a time, a stone walkway led from the back door of the old summer kitchen, out to an old camp, but now with the building gone, it led us to the middle of nowhere. Some *thing* needed to exist at the end of the walk. Dad set two poles in the ground on either side of the far end of the stone walk. A two-by-eight crossbar was hung between them, on which he strung four clothes lines to the back of the house, a boring, but a practical use of the spot so that Mom didn't have to walk on muddy ground. During the frigid months, her bed sheets stiffened up as hard as a sheet of plywood before the third clothespin was in place, requiring a clothes pole to keep the sheets from dragging on the ground, a feat unto itself when the wind whistled across the bay. One last nuance was added to appease the minor minions. He hung a wooden swing from the two by eight, right in the middle of the whole shebang—*shades of today's aesthetic discipline of feng shui!*

Throughout the week in every island household, certain chores were allocated to a certain day, with a foregone conclusion that Tuesday was set aside for ironing, Wednesday—dusting, Thursday—bed changing, Friday—bread baking and desserts. Saturday, theoretically, was a social day, but in reality was a day to play catch-up. Sunday's blue-laws were liberating to a degree, but the saving grace to all of Mom's scullery work was a knight in shining armor, who often rescued her from the weariness of her duties with one simple phrase, *"Come on Lil, let the kids do the dishes."* Translated it meant, "*Take a break, and come play some music, because I love to listen and you love to play*." He never had to ask twice.

"Music is a Higher Revelation than Philosophy"
Ludwig Van Beethoven

Ivers and Ponds of Boston produced big hulking player pianos that weighed nearly a thousand pounds, one of which sat in the piano room. It was a while before I learned that everyone didn't have a piano room. Just as soon as we were able to reach the player pedals with our toes, and strong enough to pump them, Mom slipped a roll of player music into the mechanism, and the house became a veritable honky-tonk. Music was there for the asking; therefore, none of us ever acquired our mother's adeptness to read and play music. Unlike her, at age five, we didn't have the need to fill a void. I had no voids.

Invariably, the after-dinner soiree for two turned into a sizable social gathering. Neighbors stopped to smell Maria's roses beside the front step, overheard the music, knowing Dad had a reputation for impromptu gatherings, felt quite comfortable about inviting themselves in to listen. Lil now had a major audience and *pulled out all of the stops*, shifting from popular music to the classics, managing to drown out the snipping and bickering going on in the kitchen as we plowed through piles of dishes.

What was wrong with dumping a big pile of silverware into the center of a dishtowel, pulling the four-corners together to make a sack so as to shake the whole pile dry all at once? My newly devised way of drying silverware did not meet my sibling's seal of approval. It evoked a tattle every single time. Snitches! During a musical interlude the politics of sibling rivalry seldom elicited a response from Dad, resulting in a backup strategy, a bit of mass aggression by the other three. They taunted that I was adopted. Proof—my blond, sandy colored hair, and theirs—dark brown, na-a-na-na-na! The adopted thing invariably ticked me off.

Mother swung into *Humoresque*, a classical piece without words—but out in the kitchen, Ann Marie chimed in with words that fit perfectly, that made us giggle and abandon the sniping contest. Within as much time as it took for us to learn Ann's made-up lyrics, in unison, and in company with the piano music, we loudly burst into: *"Mabel, Mabel, if you're able, take your elbows off the table—la-la-la—ta-da-da-da-da, da-a-a-a-a-a!"* Mom's music was a liberally dispensed antidote, a cure-all for sniping, griping, and any basic malaise—and it worked!

Her new Hammond organ was supposed to be a surprise—but the organ salesman slipped the news to Aunt Jo, and before the earth spun another half inch on its axis she was on the phone to Mother. There were not words to aptly describe my father's tone when he found what his oldest sister had done. There were no words, but the flashes in his eyes spoke volumes. We can safely say that Jo was not invited to any musical interludes for a good long time, nor did she get any lobsters for the asking, plus— anything broken, stayed that way! She certainly spit into the wind that time around.

Regardless, the next Sunday, when Mom was just a few feet from the house at church, Dad and two other men negotiated the brand-new and very large electric Hammond organ in through the back door, and into our living room. He couldn't wait for her to get home, had a smile on his face that wouldn't quit, an anticipation that was really worth watching. Imagine if it had been a total surprise.

Music was our parent's quiet place, and oh boy, they needed one. The four of us were a handful. Jean and Joan Baston earned every penny of their baby-sitting dollar the night they decided to invite their friends in to join them. While they were bobbing for apples, from a big galvanized tub of water they'd set in the middle of the dining room, we ran havoc. At first, the teenagers were all up for the chase. Then Joan slipped and tripped into the tub of apples. We hid in places that they didn't know existed, and then—our tomfoolery became not so funny. They couldn't find us. From that point on, only *Aunt* Katy came to sit. She wasn't really our aunt, but a close friend of the family—and she seemed to not find us any trouble.

Usually, just about the time our beds collapsed from our trampoline antics, when our squeals could be heard clear Downfront, the dulcet tones from Mom's organ music reached our ears, as effective as a dose of paregoric. Dulcet tones soothed us to sleep up on our end, but also drowned out the racket emanating from the upper chambers down on her end.[98] The next thing we knew, the sun was coming up. As an aside, we did not get dosed with paregoric, although we did have to endure cod-liver oil and Father John's medicine, and I wondered if Mom bought Father John's because his priestly picture was on the bottle. Those elixirs were *nahsty* tasting. What affliction was Father John's supposed to cure anyway?

***

Carmen and I seized upon Dad's invite for a quick trip to the far *Eastend* on a hazy summer day, a trip that allowed us a ride on the running board of the truck. Carmen, as small as a wisp, stood where Dad could secure her with one hand, as he shifted gears, and steered with the other. We hung onto the inside of the door, and used the other hand to wave at everyone we passed— not a fluttery little hand wave mind-you, but with arm shot straight into the air like a gold medal Olympian winner. This was such a huge deal.

His mission—a quick repair job for Mr. Daley, and while he was up on the ladder fixing something, the white-haired, elderly man engaged us in light conversation, beckoning us to listen-up as he, in a near whisper, let drop a bombshell—classified information, if you please. He announced to us that he was

---

[98] Decades later, with the tubes long burned out and parts now obsolete, the organ sits in the house – a beautiful, polished emblem of their relationship.

actually Santa Claus—in disguise; he of course, on vacation—we now sworn not to tell a soul, because you see—every Tom, Dick, and Harry would be knocking at his door with *lists*—or repair jobs for broken toys from last year's batch—and furthermore— he left the elves at the Pole because they were holy terrors, unruly, and he didn't want them running the island—and by the way, what did we want for Christmas?

There was no beard on his gentle face. Summer shorts and a polo shirt made up his disguise; regardless we sat on his knee and rolled off a list that would choke a horse. Dad was awfully amused by something, but we were too engrossed in this blockbuster piece of information to figure it out. Dad laughed all the way home.

A large herd of antlered deer now forages on the sprawling lawn, in front of, what was Mr. Daley's summer home—about thirty not so tiny deer, so says one of my Eastend childhood friends, Sharon. She found the Mr. Daley a.k.a. Santa Claus remembrance poignant and with her artful and imaginative mind brought me up to date, thought I'd enjoy the poetic symbolism of the grazing island herd. We agreed that Mr. Daley would have savored the miles we've squeezed out of his impersonation.

"No Snowflake Falls in an Inappropriate Place."

Zen

Days—exceedingly short at Christmas time, nights—long and dark as a pocket—islands frozen-in time—desolate in December—all outright absolutes that conjure up a bleak picture of the island in mid-winter, yet nuances played into this scenario that made it anything but bleak. All who sailed into, or by Ponce's Landing, were provided an unexpected pocket of colored lights framed in total darkness; a display that stayed lit all night—every night. My father placed two-lighted Christmas trees on either side of a Memorial that stood *Downfront,* high on a knoll, facing the water. Listed on the Memorial's white façade were the names of all islanders, who had gone to war, gold stars beside the names of those who didn't come back. Atop the peak of the Memorial, he set a big-lighted star, and up the street, a lighted cross attached high atop our chimney, creating a grouping of lights, when viewed from the water—his Christmas card to the island's *Downfront*. He didn't have those colorful memories, but by gosh, he was going to make certain that we did—and anyone else that wandered into the sprit. Of course, the Navy base was just feet away, lit up like New York City—but cold and sterile. I dismissed the Area's blatant existence at that time of the year, found it wanting in respect to the soul of the island.

Island families were not prone to come out on those pitch-black nights until the new moon rose high in the sky, reflecting off the icy ocean, off the white mantle on the back shore, illuminating a large frozen, deep fresh water pond that fringed Harbor de Grace. It never snowed on a new moon. The air was so still and crisp that it froze our nostrils together when we inhaled. That was the setting in which everyone congregated at the Marsh, the ice pond at the base of the New Hill—back when the hill was actually new.

Word got out—somehow. Groups of youngsters and entire families converged upon the scene with skates slung over their shoulders. Someone was always testing a new pair of skates on inexperienced feet and weak, turned-in ankles. Dad climbed the light pole and hooked up an electrical line for a radio to broadcast the strains of big band music, and the muster lasted well into the night. Frozen feet and high spirits were warmed by a huge bonfire, crackling embers that lengthened the hours for the spontaneous diversion from deep winter's cloistered period.

Mom (Lillian) with Roberta, Ann Marie and Carmen

Congregate, daytime activities turned to tobogganing on Rohr's Hill over by South Side Beach, a sport not given to the fainthearted. One could easily become airborne on the extraordinarily steep incline; therefore, any attempt to carryout a successful rapid descent warranted someone aboard that had negotiated the hill it at least once. Even in the summer time this precipice was formidable on foot, with its shifting pockets of gravel and rocks. Forget it on a bike! I stuck to making snowmen.

Dad still owned ancient looking skates from his teen years, *Hans Brinker* skates as we called them, with blades that seemed a yard long. We didn't know that he, Uncle Johnny, and other islanders regularly traveled to Conway, New Hampshire to ski in their youth. To enlighten us as to his athletic prowess, he took us for a spur of the moment skating exhibition at the fresh water Bog over on the crest of South Side beach. The four of us lay flat on the ice, tucked in, side by side, faces down. In one fair swoop he lept over the pile of us. *He—was—good*, and laughed, exhibiting twinkle in his eye—a gratified twinkle.

Neap tide, spring tide, ebb tide, familiar verbalisms, meanings of which filtered into our learning curve, though it was Christmas-tide that was the most quickly assimilated, learned—by heart, by way of our parent's heart. Ann Marie helped us write letters to Santa, and we listened on the radio for him to read our lists, sat on the edges of our chairs in anticipation that he would actually mention our names. He actually did!

Porteous, Mitchell, and Braun outdid itself as the most elegantly decorated storefront on Congress Street in Portland with its several large windows, each depicting holiday scenes: that of an elf's workshop, mannequins attired in old fashioned period dress, huge, brightly wrapped boxes with giant bows, and opulently decorated trees. Real fir trees set atop the overhang at the outside entrance, and a mile of fir-bough rope draped the edge. Adeline Cushing braided the mile of fir-bough rope for Porteous at her kitchen table each year on the island. Their house smelled divine.

Christmas shoppers invariably slowed down as they passed by the store to gaze into the huge windows—then turned to drop change into the Salvation Army's big kettle. Their band and bells added such sweet resonance everywhere we walked. Be the bell ringer young, old, wrinkled, or plump, the face appeared porcelain against the tailored, dark blue, woolen cape, and matching woolen bonnet, uniforms a smidgen on the military side of fashion.

Once through the revolving door at Porteous, the scent of pricey perfumes caught our senses, and the saleswoman with penciled eyebrows apologized and told me that I could find

Evening in Paris perfume up the street at McLellans five and dime store. We slowed down by a crowd of onlookers to listen to the sales pitch of a woman who, while talking non-stop, flipped, curled, and styled her own hair into sensational hairdos with a super-duper hairbrush that was guaranteed *nottoriptearwrinkle, or weardownattheankles*—and she did it without using a mirror.[99] The elevator lady warmly smiled down at us when we spied Santa on a gold throne. He didn't recognize us.

Our Christmas tree set the stage, ushered in the holiday, and changed the entire atmosphere of the house with its woodsy pine scent. One week before Christmas, Dad always took all of us out to hunt for a tree, where we ventured into wooded areas filled with tall dark spruces—places that we never, ever wandered by ourselves—where there were no roads—no water view—so unfamiliar, that I lost my sense of direction and hung close to the crowd. Thus with flakes of snow lazily falling and a gaggle of kids trudging along, groin deep through the snow behind him, Dad searched—and when the tree wasn't perfect, he made it so by hacking an extra branch or two from another. I lost my boot—stuck deep down inside a crusty snow bank. Ann Marie extricated it quickly before my bare foot flash-froze.

Ann had a major mission. Every year she yearned for a small tree of her own, for her room, to decorate all by herself. He cut it for her, but it didn't provide her with any extra gifts on Christmas morning. If she *had* received gifts under her very own tree, guess how many others would dibs a tree of their own too? Dad was no dummy.

One particular year those areas we normally traipsed through tossed us a thorny complication. A lynx swam over from Chebeague, settled into the upper Marsh area, made its presence known with the cry of a banshee, a sound that scared the *bejeezes* out of us. I heard it as I passed by Everett and Annie's house after a day of skating. My heart pounded with every step on the sprint towards home. The woods leading to the marsh were creepy enough as it was without a skulking animal lurking beneath the low branches of a fir tree. Its tenure changed our

---

[99] Not to rip tear wrinkle, or wear down at the ankles.

sense of safety and freedom for a time. One day it was not there anymore—nor were there, come to think of it, any deer roaming around, though there was probably plenty of venison served up during the winter.

With the bare Christmas tree centered in the living room, we raced up over the stairs to the storeroom to retrieve a homemade ladder, one made of rough two by fours, precariously wielding it around, poking holes in the hallway's plaster walls. Standing on ceremony, we all took turns at climbing the ladder once a year to peek into the attic, another dark forbidden place where the tree ornaments were stored. Each large Christmas ball was exquisite, delicately hand painted, as thin as tissue, requiring careful handling, rendering them vulnerable to two or three casualties a season. Before they were strategically placed on the tree, electric bulbs were tested and strung. All eyes scanned the first string of bubble lights, and a big whoop erupted when the first one began to boil.

Ann Marie was selected to put the tinsel on the tree, she the favored because of the way she methodically covered the entire tree, top to bottom, strand-by-strand, each the exact length to the next. She took—forever! Why didn't she just let go a handful of tinsel into the air, to land—*wherever*—and then rearrange, and fluff it up a little here and there? That was my first inkling that she possessed a structured sense of design, and that I was born somewhere to the left of organic.

Mom readied the Christmas party mix, a tradition that would not be offered for another three hundred and sixty-four-days. We dug-in and savored—wondering why we only had this once a year. Who thought up that once-a-year tradition? The recipe you ask? Certainly! It is made up of equal parts each of shelled salted peanuts, raisins, and chocolate bits, a commingling of the salty, sour, and sweet taste in one mouthful, the yin and yang of snacks. Truest to the traditional Christmas treats were Marguerites, a hint of our grandmother, the Spanish confection *almendrados* made from a sweet meringue, flavored with maraschino cherry juice and chopped walnuts.[100] Dollops of the

---

[100] In Spain they used almonds.

mixture were centered on square salted crackers, capped with a cherry, and baked until golden—depending on your oven.

*I am saddened to report that when the fourth generation's votes became significant, and I speak of our children's vote—the youngsters brought up in a junk food era voted the Marguerites "off the island." We will see what **their** children say about it—when they learn how to talk—when they learn how to reason! Until such time, the third generation, the old bitty bunch, will attempt to brainwash the toddlers, every chance we get.*

The final episode of the *Cinnamon Bear*, the culmination of weeks, upon weeks' worth of the fifteen-minute Christmas radio serial played out just before dinner was served on the Eve. Lamenting that the story had come to an end, we were somewhat comforted, because this was the night of nights. The most popular Christmas story of the season was forthcoming. However, the story was not of candle lit windows and home spun warmth, rather, the entire gaggle was transfixed in front of the big radio in the living room by a story that abounds with gloom and impoverishment. *"Once upon a time—of all the good days in the year on Christmas Eve..."* so starts Ebenezer Scrooge's harrowing plight in the dark, cold, dirty atmosphere of Old England. Our imaginations bore witness to Dickens' classic literary work, *A Christmas Carol,* which came by way of Lionel Barrymore's signature voice, and tendency to overact while reading. His voice and the story would forevermore remain the definitive sound of Christmas.

Santa, Dancer, Prancer and the troupe[101] depended on our offering of Marguerites, hot chocolate, and carrots, which were somewhat ceremoniously prepared, placed in the center of the dining room table, with a well thought-out note. Ann Marie headed-up this countdown activity, and we all moved together, from kitchen to dining room, back and forth, in unison, like a flock of swallows, one carrying the cocoa, one the carrots—with an ample amount of budging to keep things normal.

---

[101] Rudolph and Frosty were not yet a part of the scene—at least, not for three or four more years.

Finally, we all thumped up over the stairs and gathered at the bedroom window facing Falmouth, the best vantage point from which to spot Santa. Ann made a big thing out of Jack Frost's ornate, decorative patterns in the glaze of ice on the window, which needed to be scraped off in order that we might scan across the bay. She pointed for us, gave credence to any sparkle in the cold starry sky, giving it life and eight tiny reindeer. Shooting stars only added to the illusion. There he was! We saw that sleigh as clear as day—no question in my mind, and with our inside information, we were quite comfortable that Santa, a.k.a. Mr. Daley, would have no trouble finding us.

Wrestling to get deep beneath the layers of the warm quilts, we had to nod off quickly, because neither Carmen, nor I wanted to be the one responsible for scaring him away—being awake when he arrived. And, damn all those cracker crumbs in the sheets from the Marguerites—the ones we appropriated off the platter before we ran up stairs. Not even they could dampen our determination to nod off.

At the first hint of consciousness, we all tuned-in for some indicator, usually the scent of brewing coffee, the signal that we could make the mad dash, down over the stairs, through the door, and into the warmth and shimmer of the living room. Dressed in flannel nightgowns, our hair and long pigtails askew, we were greeted by a living room that had been transformed into a magical zone. Presents seemed to be stacked, floor to ceiling.

Clamor, paper flailing in all directions, squeals, and clean-up reigned on Christmas morning—followed by Church, and a big turkey dinner, using the best dishes, all planned in the early part of the day. That poor woman must have been exhausted, Dad too from his part in it all. Hardly freed-up from the cleanup, later on that night, Mom made toast with peanut butter and cups of cocoa for the holiday night's unwinding.

Surveying the summer porch, my eyes fixed upon a huge washing machine crate in the corner—one that appeared there two weeks before Christmas, the one with blankets lying over the top. I actually didn't connect it with the season. Obviously, I didn't want to connect it, but Christmas night I most certainly did notice it, when it lay on its side, empty. The box was more than huge—it was gigantic. Any box of that size was fair game, a new playhouse—ta-da! Just as I was staking out my claim one of my siblings appeared through a cloud of sulphur, all gussied up in a cowboy outfit, cap-gun just a-smokin,' insisted the box be turned into a fort—announced to Dad *"I hosied it first,"* and in those-days, unfortunately for me, first hosies mattered!

Saturday Night Beans & Dog Biscuits

"Always alert, never hurt." Portland's *Three-A-Safety-Man*, Arland E. Barnard, imparted his safety message over the radio just before Ann and Pete left for school every morning. Later that night, while we supped, Bing Crosby picked up the slack for fifteen more minutes crooning, *"When the blue of the night, meets the gold of the day."* It was perfectly acceptable to sing in the piano room, at the woodpile, at church, while playing, but interestingly enough, in this highly musically charged house, no one *dasst* break out in song at the dinner table. That infringement of the rules earned you a rap across the knuckles with whatever wooden spoon was handy-by—and there was usually one located in the mashed potatoes down at the head of the table. His favorite saying, along with a rap, was, *"That's for nothing. Now do something."* That's for nothing? Imagine if we really did something. We got the message.

Nor could we complain aloud about the food that Mother had taken so much time to prepare. Nit picking about the meal landed another heaping spoonful of the food in question on our plate. We got that message, too—loud and clear. Carping about the food set before us triggered something in him, we of course, not apprised of the fact that he went without food when he was our age. Sunday night menu, Dad's favorite—was a big antique platter of rice, with a dozen, fried eggs served atop.

Fifty-two times a year we were summoned to the table for Saturday night beans, and fifty-two times a year my father and I locked horns. There were no words spoken, although there was eye language that spoke volumes across the table, a clear understanding, and one that I persistently tried to circumvent. Long after everyone else had left the dinner table, I sat slumped in the high-backed chair, feet dangling back and forth, making designs out of the cold beans in my plate with a fork, my swallow reflex rendered inoperable.

Carmen hung to the other side of the living room door, peeking around the doorsill with saddened eyes; her mouth turned down at the corners, waiting for either Dad or me to make a move. One at a time...ever so slowly...gag!

Down over the hill at Clarke's store, Everett was good for burning midnight oil. To double negative the point home, he was never—*not*—at the store. Clarke's store was always open whenever we were sent with a note for groceries, or to pick up the mail, or when we looked down over the hill from our bedroom late at night. He was married to his business, as well as, his wife Annie, who was the postmistress.[102]

Annie ran the post office from inside the store, and although we knew the combination to our ornate brass mailbox, she usually passed the mail through a small barred window to us. Just after the mailbag was delivered off the boat we stood patiently while she filled an entire wall's worth of brass mailboxes from the other side, biding time with Everett, talking to the chatty parrot on his shoulder, examining a glass on the counter filled with cola and copper pennies that Annie had soaking. The cola had eaten every bit of tarnish off the coins so that the copper shone brightly. I am not sure what Annie's intended message was for all of us—buy cola to clean pennies, or watch out for the rotgut that is being sold. Everett offered us a snack, pointing to the box on top of the candy counter, the box of dog biscuits. Not bad!

---

[102] Annie (MacVane) Clarke

Chapter

10

"The atomic age began at exactly 5:30 Mountain-time on the morning of July 15, 1945, on a stretch of semi-desert land about fifty airline miles from Alamogordo, New Mexico. And just at that instance there rose from the bowels of the earth a light not of this world, the light of many suns in one."
William Laurence—Science writer

Preschool a la Mary Ross 1946

Much to my dismay, I discovered that the basic concept of the new preschool was to not start until everyone else was ready. We sat...and sat...and sat around the table with our red plastic scissors poised, printed outlines of apples waiting, crayons, and mucilage ready to go, but not until Mary Ross gave the signal. She started the preschool for four-year-olds at the Beach Avenue House, a rooming house that Uncle Johnny had purchased. The school was a first of its kind in '46. Through Mary's good heart and intent, we accumulated and salted away such affection for her, and although we had no crystal ball, her good heart and intent would follow us all along our life's path. But...at age three and nine-tenths, not being able to start cutting at will, or drawing free hand annoyed me, in as much as making art was as-good-as-it-gets. Susan Cushing[103] lived just across the field; she and I were the same age, and her birthday was only two weeks after mine. What a coincidence! It was the point at which we decided to be friends. *Good decision!*

Roberta (age 4)

---

[103] Susan (Cushing) Longanecker

***

Hoping that my mission would not be discovered, I sifted books out of the bookcase in the living room, knowing that it wasn't right, but then again, I wasn't hiding the activity. There simply wasn't any paper in the house, and each book contained at least six blank pages, three at the first of the book and three in the back—fair game as far as I was concerned. I do hope none of the books were first editions because every blank page I could find was put to good use.

A couple weeks shy of five, I began kindergarten with Mrs. MacVane. There was plenty of paper hanging about at the new two-room school on the *Westend*, a nice white building located just around the corner from the dump—just before the gravel pit—down the street from the cemetery—and not too far from the New Hill—easy to find. My older siblings had initially attended the Old Schoolhouse[104] with its potbelly stove and outside plumbing, but it was rendered obsolete not long after they started there with Mrs. Hill. The Navy boarded up the one located in the Area and like everything else, painted it brindle green. Because I rarely visited the *Eastend*, I haven't the foggiest as to what good use was made of that one way down there. Someone could easily round out that information, but having so little knowledge about the *Eastend* does highlight how far out of purview the *Eastend* was to a little *Westender*.

Now we had one school for the entire island,[105] and it featured brand-new everything: a water fountain, twelve-foot high windows, heavy, folding oak doors that ran on a track to divide the room in half, and a boiler room that housed a furnace. When the school population rose, as it did during the war, the doors were folded closed to create a two-room schoolhouse. Mrs. MacVane taught grades K through four on one side of the big, folding, oak doors, and her room was scaled to little people, everything close to the floor. Mrs. Hill, on the other side of the

---

[104] The old Westend School was assumed by the Methodist Church and renamed the Ivy Hall. It is a gift shop today, a source of income that is used to help keep the church solvent.
[105] The new school was built in 1945.

218

oak doors, taught fifth through eighth. Her room was a foreign outpost, way out in the back of beyond.

Four of us matriculated together from kindergarten up through to the eighth grade. Susan Cushing was the only girl my age on the *Westend*, very serene, shy, an only child, and not one bit spoiled. Only-children were usually bratty—but not her. Gordon Stewart was frisky, the out door type, and had not an ounce of spoiled in him either. His two older and two younger brothers may have had a great deal to do with that. Buddy Johnson was a year younger than we three, and flat-out brilliant. He skipped a grade and had enough smarts to leapfrog right on by us, but didn't. Now—he should have been spoiled—but he wasn't either. We melded nicely, were an obedient, easy-going bunch. The student body, on a whole, was...*I am looking for a word. We were manageable—that's the word—and without going into a comparative analysis, between then and now, I will chock it up to the era. Although—it is hard for me to imagine, as part of our youthful curriculum, being regularly schooled in "how not to be stolen," to have the constant worry about being kidnapped by a stranger, impacted by a drug culture, terrorists' plots, duck-tape, pollution, and extinction. Imagine going through an entire childhood without those anxieties, and worries.*

Aucocisco – Gem of the Bay

Uptown is a kindred word to *Downfront*, and *Eastend*, hybridized island words, which have evolved over the years. Transit time, to and from *Uptown*, easily chewed up an hour and a half's worth of time—getting to the boat, waiting for the boat, loading passengers, handling freight, making landings, and steaming time—a monotonous stretch for those who made the trip every, single workday. Dad made his job at the Cumberland Cold Storage the more interesting by spending the transit time in the cabin with Captain Earl Stockbridge who ran the *Aucocisco*.

Midnight oil must have been on sale because Dad burned it out back in the shop by the gallon, hard at work well into the night. Obviously, it drove up the price of sleep in the morning; consequently, in order to make the first boat, he and Earl were forced to drum up a triple signal betwixt them. As the boat steamed up the bay from Chebeague and at some point before it approached the breakwater at Long Island, Stockbridge sounded the whistle, a distinct, recognizable sound inclusive to the *Auco.* Mom caught the first blast and rousted Dad out of bed to begin his rituals of readying for work, during which the second whistle sounded, indicating that the boat was coming into Ponce's Landing. It paid us to stand clear of the flight path from the bedroom, to the bathroom, to the back door, where lastly he grabbed his cup of coffee and flew as the third whistle sounded. The lines were being pulled in, and because the plank was already hauled in, most times Dad jumped aboard, his heart rate running at a good clip by that point. As alarm clocks go, the arrangement was matchless, and only once did he not have time to go through all the rituals. That day he simply threw his suit over his pajamas and ran.

We made passage *Uptown,* three times a year to mainland Portland, a trek right up there on the scale of important happenings such as birthdays, Christmas plays, and the ever-popular, annual VFW Fair held at the old school house. There was no other fair as fabulous. Tom Wood, Bill and Lillian Norcross, along with a dedicated lot, decorated the whole nine yards in gobs of red, white, and blue crepe paper, American flags, and colorful streetlights strung for the evening's street dance. Just as with every fair there were a plethora of games, grab-bags, the "wheel" and other games that gave us chance to gamble for great prizes. Summer people always aligned their vacation to popular mid-summer event. This is the level of importance into which we pigeonholed a visit to this foreign municipality we dubbed *Uptown.*

Before we left for the boat, our hair was braided, wrapped atop our heads in a neat crossover pile of plaits. Mother folded a cotton scarf in a triangle, babushka style, tied tightly under the chin, and finalized the process with a series of noisy smooches on our round cheeks, which she seemed to find irresistible—then bid us off at the back door. Filled with visions of Easter bonnets and matching purses, we *troddled* down the walk with Dad to catch the seven a.m. boat. Oh yea, I forgot—there was a visit to the dentist office, too!

Trips with Mother were different than with Dad, spent in the opulent ladies lounge on the main deck of the *Aucocisco*, a long, narrow stateroom that had soft, red velvet seats, mirrors, and an air of elegance. An Italian man and his wife stood in the peak of the bow, serenading passengers with accordions and song during the summer. Unaware that she was participating, Mother's fingers moved with the melodies. Her musical center was always on autopilot.

On this particular early run Captain Stockbridge invited Dad up into the pilothouse of the *Aucocisco* as was usual. Earl was one of the most respected captains in the bay, a handsome and pleasant man with an edge of humor about him. Conceivably, Dad knew him as far back as he could remember, back when Earl was a still a deckhand, before he earned his mate's license in 1909. Therefore, he was a fixture at CBL, as far as Dad was concerned, an old comfortable friend.

They plunked us onto a wide seat that ran the width of the pilothouse in the back of the cabin. Someone on the wharf lifted the rope off the piling, pulled it taunt, and gave it a strong snap, like a whip—sending it right into the hands of the deck hand. Stockbridge reached over and yanked on the bell-pull then let it go. Down below in the engine room, chief engineer, Walter Bean responded to the bell's deep resonant sound by pushing or pulling on the shifting levers, opening throttles to put her into forward. Then Earl reached over to the *jingler,* the signal to speed her up. She shuddered and then began to shake, gently, with the pulse of the engine, as did we for the duration of the trip, as though struck with a slight palsy. It was quite pacifying.

The *Auco*[106] set deep in the water, was the biggest boat in the fleet at that time, rendering us in awe, barely able to utter a

---

[106] The Aucocisco was built just before the turn of the century at the South Portland shipyard in Ferry Village, her engine built by the Portland Company, a favorite of the bay islanders from her start to her finish in 1948. Her large rudder and a big, four-bladed propeller down beneath her stern made her a good handling boat that steered well. She was terrific in all weather, smooth riding, and had a quiet rhythm...like the throb of a heartbeat.

sound. Earl perched atop a stool to the right of the giant wooded steering wheel with one hand on a spoke. I watched and waited for him to give it a big heave, to swing the enormous wheel around a few times to indicate that he was steering the vessel, but witnessed that all the way up the bay he didn't turn it but a spoke either way.

Vessel's horns were quite distinct from a distance, and our ears were sharply tuned to the subtle or blatant differences of the many. Anyone would be hard pressed to apply the term *noise pollution* to the sound of the old boat whistles. It was the same with engines in cars on the island. We never had to look out of the window. Each was unmistakable from the other. The *Auco's* whistle had a superior, musical, mellow sound, but when Stockbridge reached for the overhead rope, in order to blast the horn, Carmen and I about jumped out of our startled skins. The adrenaline shot clear into our fingertips, the wide-eyed response an amusement to Earl and Dad, but it gave us quite a turn, one that required reassurance from the two men.

Dad and Earl fussed with blue packages of Edgeworth tobacco, scraped their pipes with jack knives before filling them, lit, and re-lit the bowls of tobacco with a wooden match that they struck afire by running it across their pant leg. Finally, serpentines of aromatic smoke floated up and were drawn out of the pilothouse window while they talked of the smaller, narrow hulled *Maquoit*—how she played second fiddle to the *Auco*. The sober faced Captain Morrell ran her with that comedic engineer Clarkie—Walter Clarke, an odd paring under which a crew had to work. Dad and Earl pined over the fact that the *Maquoit's* days were numbered. Neither probably wanted to address the notion that the *Auco*, an aging lady herself, might only have a couple calendar years left to ply the bay.

***

Engineer's Lament
"*When in danger or in doubt, run and turn the side lights out.*
Full ahead, have no fear. Stave her up... 'n blame the engineer. "
Coined by chief engineer of the *M/T*
Vincent Tibbetts

Down below in the Auco's open engine room, the workings of the brass engine kept another young passenger spellbound. Bobby Ricker often rode up from Chebeague with his dad, Will—an engineer who now worked for the Casco Bay Lines on the diesel, sister ship, *Emita*. Will's brother, Ray, was hounding at him to go back fishing, because the steamers were getting old and the forty-five dollars a week paycheck was not going to buy them a house any near soon.

Bobby peered down below a grating into the lower part of the engine room where fireman, Jimmy McCabe kept vigil over the steam pressure gauges, shoveling coal into the boiler's fireboxes when the engine called for steam. The chief engineer, old Walter, reminded Bobby a little of Buster Keaton, thin as a rail, with a broad smile plastered all over his face. Bobby asked his father why all engineers of steamboats seemed to be minus fingers, some on both hands. His father's fingers were intact. He, too, chased the moving connecting rods with a long *spigoted* oil can on the Army boats, reached in, miscalculated the stroke of the rod and got nipped a couple of times, unlike others who lost fingers, sometimes lower parts of arms. A seaplane took off from the Navy air ramp on the front on Long Island, the second chance spectacle in one day for the kid.

In time, there were not many engineers remaining who held a steam license like old Walter Bean's, which made it difficult when he came down sick with pneumonia. What to do, what to do! He didn't refuse to go; he physically could not drag himself on board to run the engine. So—with much ado, and no replacement in sight, they wrapped old Walter in several blankets, carried him down to the engine room, slumped him in a chair, like an old dish-rag, and off he went on the five-thirty 'round trip to Cliff, with young Jim McCabe to handle the mechanics. A body with a license is what they needed, and body is about what they got! Walter did live, but it took a stay at the Marine Hospital to put him back on his feet.

Congress Street

Merchandise was stacked high to the ceiling on the shelves at Levinsky's—men's clothing, gas masks, and combat boots, stuff that men liked, but nary an Easter bonnet in the hole-in-the-wall emporium up on the base of Munjoy Hill. Dad told us that Levinsky's father started his business by selling rags from a push wagon when he first came to this country. That struck a note.

On every block, someone hailed Dad as we meandered up Congress on our quest for Easter duds, so many greeted him that it appeared that he knew everyone. *"Where did you get that blond one, Bob,"* they asked, I in hopes that Carmen didn't hear. That was just more fodder to use when plaguing me about being adopted. Carmen hid behind Dad's leg with her finger in her mouth, peeking out as he chatted, then would slip back behind him when they addressed her. I gave them a broad smile, with a front tooth missing, and reveled in having the dime that the tooth fairy left under my pillow.

There was a theme park called Old Orchard somewhere out there, not a place we frequented. You had to take a train to get there. Instead we had Congress Street to entertain us; a bustling place lined with overhanging giant elm trees, teahouses, banks, and stores. Nestled in the midst of it all was the brick home in which the poet, Henry Wadsworth Longfellow lived. Above Monument Square we were introduced to a giant peanut that stood in front of a peanut store clutching a heated box of freshly roasted peanuts, and who politely offered us some. He stood six feet tall, sported a monocle, carried a cane in one hand, and wore a top hat that he tipped to us. It was like being introduced to the President, or royalty—and how come this guy didn't talk?

Next door, at a Cushman's Bakery outlet, Dad picked up an absolutely luscious pastry that he called *slumgullion*. That was his word for a white paper bag filled with broken pieces and end-cuts of chocolate Swiss rolls slathered with fluffy white frosting. Bakery products were a glorious novelty for us, but then again, we had never partaken of an Italian sandwich, didn't have a clue what pizza tasted like, or restaurant food in general. Portland was a theme park unto itself; an adventure all crammed into one day.

He suggested that we save some peanuts for the organ grinder's monkey, a live animal all dressed up in a *cunnin'* little outfit. We crossed the street in order to get a closer look at him. He was on a leash that was frequently yanked, in not too gentle a fashion, by the grinder, an Italian man who stood in front of W. T. Grants and ground music out of a red barrel organ while the monkey drew the attention of any passerby. The animal was terribly nervous, shifty eyed, his teeny stature deceiving as all get out. I didn't dare pass him a peanut. He bit everyone that came near, which was the reason the coin cup was hooked to the organ and not in the monkey's hands.

***

During the autumn trip to town we dropped our Buster Brown[107] shoes off at Dominic Macri's shoe repair shop on Middle Street, a dark, long, narrow, deep place with high ornate tin ceilings. The odor of leather, glue, and shoe polish permeated every nook and cranny—made me lightheaded. Dominic's accent proclaimed his Italian roots, but it was the sparkle in his black eyes that told me about the good nature of the man. Several men had climbed up onto a long narrow platform that set against the length of the wall, seating themselves in the long row of chairs. Each placed one shoed foot on a foot stand, read a newspaper, some chewed on a cigar waiting their turn. Carmen and I watched, absolutely captivated by the deftness the shoeshine guy exhibited with a simple rag and a dab or two of polish as he made quick order of one gentleman's request for a shine. The shiner-person spit on the shoe, finishing it off with a few snaps of the rag. I'd heard about spit shines, but never realized it required real spit.

Round domed buses issued stinky exhaust on our walk up Congress Street, a journey farther up street than we'd ever

---

[107] Buster Brown shoes were brown leather, high boot-like shoes, the type of shoe the well heeled are wearing these days.

ambled before, a quantum leap—for two island neophytes. Actually, our destination was only one huge intersection beyond the pie wedge shaped upper Hays Drug Store, the demarcation line of what I considered the end of Congress Street. Now we were really in no-man's-land, a feeling shared with old Columbus—the feeling of what it was like *not* to fall off the end of the earth.

A surprise meal awaited our hungry bellies just beyond the brownstone Portland Public Library at a Chinese restaurant. The Pagoda's owner and Dad acted like old, fast-friends, and he smiled warmly down at us and extended forth a miniature paper umbrella—a lovely introduction to the first Chinese person that I ever met in my life. He suggested fried rice for us, lobster over Chinese vegetables for Dad. When did Dad acquire such a cosmopolitan leaning for food? It struck me oddly that he would choose something that he ate all of the time, albeit served in a different way—but why not some of those exotic platefuls being served up at the other tables? I took a second look at Dad, this new persona, dressed in suit, tie, and a broad smile.

Every five and dime need that one could have could be found at W. T. Grants. This was the bonnet capital of the world, and now it had a newfangled escalator that provided the elderly population easy access to the upper floors, and children with a novel experience. Heading back down over the damn thing brought my heart rate up to level of a humming bird's. I held my breath, because that first step was never in the right place for me to plant my foot. Carmen was down at the base before I finally summoned up every bit of moxie that I had in reserve to make the leap.

Now back on terra firma, and with a new Betty Grable paper doll book secured, we made a quick stop to check out our foot bone structure in the x-ray machine in the shoe department, slid our feet inside a compartment at the base, and peered down into a small window at the bones of our feet. Imagine—a just-for-the-fun-of-it x-ray machine!

The last tour de force, before leaving W. T.'s wonder works, was to partake of their famous vanilla ice cream sodas. Naturally we first needed to negotiate the tall stools that lined the counter, insurmountable, as they seemed, and spent the first four minutes spinning as we waited for the waitress, who called us *dee-ah*. What a fabulous show she put on constructing the extraordinary creations by pulling down on dispensers that fizzed and *swizzled* water all over scoops of ice cream and vanilla syrup. She offered it up to us in a huge, tall glass, topped with a carnation shaped pile of whipped cream, a cherry, and a broad smile. We were replete in broad smiles when we visited Portland. There must be an explanation somewhere as to why waitresses always sported a frilly, folded handkerchief as though it was a corsage. She was chewing gum, and I looked at Dad to see whether he was going to speak to her about that.

With our new duds finally secured in fancy shopping bags, we knew that the balance of our wardrobe would be made up of Ann Marie's hand-me-downs. They were new to me; she had good taste, I unaware that other families bought more than one new outfit a year for their children. I didn't know the word poor, and didn't have a statistic telling me I was poor. *By today's standards we were just a skip and a jump ahead of it*. Still, he made a fair living, though it was stretched a mite taunt. Life was measures of warm and comfortable—constancies. Constancy is the definitive word—firmness; stability; fidelity; steadiness; consistency. Yep! That's the word! That is exactly what we had.

Just off the island, wide eyed, and very naive, we sopped up every nuance in the general area of the *Uptown* district. Dad had a smile on his face on the walk down over Pearl Street, headed towards Custom House Wharf. We waited to cross Commercial Street, stopped in our tracks while a train slowly rolled over its own tracks, headed west on its way out of town. The engineer waved back and gave a little toot! Dad called us *filleloo birds* for some quirky little thing we did, and I thought that a sweet and endearing term. *Remarkably, I actually fell upon the definition for the term filleloo bird. It is a mythological bird that flies backwards, so as to see where it has been.*

227

The Legacy of Hewie Newcomb

Will Ricker made his way up off Custom House Wharf with a duffle slung over his shoulder, leaving the *Ethylena* at the end of the dock, trudged uptown to his apartment on Shepley Street in Portland, a permanent move from the island for him, Fran, and the kids. He'd left the Casco Bay Lines, forsook the *Emita* and was back fishing, not much to his liking, but he was bent on buying a house. He wanted to move Lainy and Bobby from the Congress Street area, possibly across the Million Dollar Bridge to the lazy town of South Portland, *"The All American City."*

The *Ethylena* was in port now, just long enough for him to have all his teeth extracted, problem enough in itself, but damn his cousin Hewie Newcomb for making matters worse. Years back, when his son, Bobby, was two years old, Hewie shot both sets of false teeth out of his mouth at the toddler in jest, sending the child fleeing home to his mother's skirts in an absolute fright. Although Bobby was almost seven now, he still had this thing about people with a mouth full of gums and no teeth.

Will had a big problem; the false teeth would not be ready for some time, and Bobby would not even come down for breakfast while his father was toothless. Everyday that Will was home Bobby waited upstairs and plaintively hollered down through the register to his mother, *"Is he gone yet?"* Fran clapped her hand over her mouth, had all she could do to keep from bursting out in a gale of laughter every time Bobby's pleas reached down to her through the grate. Will threw his hands up, went back out fishing, time enough to give Bobby a reprieve, and time enough for his teeth to come in the mail.

A Pied Piper's Brand of Home Brew

Dad discovered my samples of primitive art inside his collection of books. The jig was up. Rather than get the dickens, office paper showed up at the house—a windfall, big sheets that were handily transformed into paper doll clothes—in that I rarely cut the ones out of the *boughten* books—too many little square tabs—unnecessary work—not very functional. A couple of licks, as one would a postage stamp, and the new design stayed put on the paper doll—long enough to finish the next frock, anyway.

Children from big families don't necessarily run in packs to seek amusement, and I easily frittered away hours concocting snazzy outfits for classy, Claudette Colbert, singer, Jane Froman, my favorite, Betty Grable, and the newcomer, Elaine Stewart. It got easier as the collection grew to thirty with the addition of fluffy bride dolls, and Katy Keene. Paper dolls were a solitary pastime, the initial indication that there was a creative personality wallowing around in there, another of those "just born with it" things that comes through with the gene pool, right out of the blue—actually, an illustration of my theory for biological osmosis. There truly is nothing quite as impressive as the creative process running at full tilt.

After taking-in a ten minute go-around on afternoon television recently, I gathered, by their reasoning, that those wardrobes created on paper might be substitute for the mish-mosh of hand-me-downs hanging in my closet. That theory dissolved quickly in the light of logic. It didn't run that deeply. My best impression of those moments is that of being absorbed in a pure inventive mode. The more frocks created—the better the results. I liked better results—still do, but the doing—the process itself, always outweighed the finished product. There might be some profound truth in thinking that the journey is more important than the destination. It's not half bad to stumble over a profound truth now and again.

Invariably, we sidled our way into every project into which my father became immersed. He was a magnet, a pied piper. Someone gave him a recipe for lye soap, which called for rendered fat as the main ingredient, but early on he sped up the production, because the rats on the island had discovered the supply he'd saved out in the Shop. After cutting away the section on which they nibbled, he tested it out in the back yard in a cauldron over an open fire. We were insistent that we stir the goopy mess, to have our fingers in it as he poured the hot mixture out in big sheet pans to harden, and then roughly cut into clumsy, hard to handle, four-inch-square cakes. Lye soap was an essential cure-all on the medicine shelf, used for bad cases of poison ivy, an affliction we rarely caught because the shiny plant was easily identifiable—in any season. The recipe simply consisted of boiled rendered fat and lye. The final product was foul looking, smelly—and didn't float!

Shared island recipes sifted from house to house, mayonnaise in the chocolate cake batter for extra moistness, that old passed-down secret island recipe for baked stuffed lobster, another for wine begot from elderberries or dandelion flowers. One would swear the island brewers were sommeliers rivaling one batch against another.

Our contribution was housed in a big crock that sat in the warmth behind the kitchen stove, a fermenting concoction—alive—with yeast, raisins, oranges, and lemons floating atop a frothy liquid. There it sat for a time—puffs of gas actually erupting like pools of active lava, the lid rising up off the top of the crock, ceding the pungent aroma to every corner of the kitchen—a *sicky-sweet* aroma that took our breath away if we got too close. Thankfully, it was seasonal thing—a home brew guaranteed to tear out any man's taste buds—any man who so much as dared honk down a test swig. It made them lose their breath, and then a grimace spread over their face; tears sprang into their eyes, and lastly, the smacking of lips could be heard, a sign that it passed the test.

Summer church turned damp and chilly in the several fall seasons between '46 and '50. Mother's big, black seal coat kept us warm as we snuggled against her during the service. There was nothing to match its warmth—the coat—a gift from Dad. He did not attend Mass, nor were we allowed to fuss about attending church in his presence. He was adamant that we go, and ignored our frail excuses, obviously a man of his word that was given many years before on his wedding day.

Week after week of entertaining oneself through the sameness of a Latin Mass became a flat out challenge. It therefore helped greatly to have the company of one's peers, a youngster from a long-standing summer family. Robbie McCann[108] accommodated me in creatively navigating around the boredom. Like cherubs,

---

[108] Robbie (McCann) Steele

we sang to the rafters when called upon to join in on the Latin hymn—sometimes were successful at rendering the alto pitch. We listened dutifully to the sage wisdom of Father Sullivan, stood, knelt and sat on cue, but there was this long drawn-out stretch of quietude in which my eyelids fell like a late afternoon setting sun.

Huddled in the very back pew, strategically positioned in the shadow of a grownup, we waited for Father to turn his back so that we could test a new candy that had just come on the market. Knowingly she and I embarked upon the commitment of a very venial sin. We divvied, by color, a large bag of tiny, round, multi-colored, thin candy coated, chocolate bits that had the letter M stamped on the top of each, the red ones being the most favored. [109] During the most quiet and reverent of moments in the Mass, the large bag split open sending hundreds of chocolate ball bearings flying. They skittered, and bounced throughout the church until the last one finally settled—like a popped hubcap finally clatters to a long, rolling stop. Try hard as we could to stifle a muzzled, but uncontrolled laughter, it finally convulsed out of us, one that would not abate. Father Sullivan finished the reverend chore, turned around and scanned the pews. His voice boomed as he summoned both Robertas to meet with him following Mass. That one cost us twenty-five Hail Marys, and a modicum of embarrassment. [civ]

Except for the annual Christmas play, none of us saw the inside of the Methodist church and basically couldn't have anything to do with it, except for Dad's requests on the organ for the hymn, *Old Rugged Cross*, in the confines of our house. Words to Protestant songs were not in our repertoire. Secondly, we were not allowed to play church because Mother thought that irreverent, sacrilegious, yet when one of us hauled out a package of candy wafers, which were the size of a quarter—we just couldn't help ourselves. They were perfectly shaped candies with

---

[109] Forest Mar, who invented the little candies with an M on each piece, came by this idea on a trip to Spain where he encountered soldiers of the Spanish Civil War eating pellets of chocolate encased in a sugary coating, to prevent melting.

which to play communion. It mattered not that they were yellow, green, and pink; plus they lasted longer in our mouths than the real-McCoy.

We knew full well that the Hammond organ bench was off limits, but two of us hauled it out away from the organ, anyway, in order to convert it into an altar. Not to worry, we were careful with it. Fancy tablecloths draped over our shoulders made us priestly enough to hand out the confectionary communion, and chant the blessing, *Dominus-s-s Na-Bis-s-s-s Com* on each other, cleansing anybody's sins that came within range of the living room. God help us, should a Methodist playmate be in attendance. Either they, for participating in a quasi-Catholic ceremony—or we, for being sacrilegious, were going to hell for sure. Now what was it Protestants did that we didn't do? They read the Bible, employed lady ministers, and could eat meat on Fridays. Not a single Methodist soul had to say the rosary, give up candy for Lent, or go to confession on a weekly basis. Even our sins were indexed into two categories, venial and mortal. Theirs weren't. Did this mean that we were bigger sinners? I considered a serious theological talk with Dad about this, too, but got waylaid as usual, too easily redirected, and missed out on some salient points of information that I should have talked with him about along the way.

The Spa

Roger's Spa and Clarke's grocery store served different needs and combined, was the hub of the community. Everett Clarke carried groceries and allowed islanders to charge food. He couldn't sell beer, because the post office was housed inside the store, triggering some Federal law in a dusty book somewhere; Roger's Spa could, but not on Election Day—another law in another dusty book. Geneva had rented the store out in the 1940's to a man who tried to make a go of it, evidently with not much success. The front of the island was roused one night to the clamor of a fire Downfront; the Spa was ablaze. Harry Clarke, who lived above the Spa, was thought lost in the inferno, but had, in fact, escaped. It was a total loss—no insurance, but interestingly enough, the man who rented it removed every single thing he owned on the day before the fire. Old man Cushing was hired to move a house from the Eastend—plunked it at the top of the hill at Ponce's Landing and the Spa was in business again.

Geneva Rogers endeared herself to all she met, a wonderful spirit with sparkling eyes, a savvy businesswoman, with the soft edges of a gentlewoman. She had a knack for making every individual feel as though they were the most important thing happening at the moment when she bided a minute or two in pleasantries. Since the age of fifteen, Geneva held down long hours, and while Frances and Margie Gomez played at being waiters at the Cushing Hotel's dining room, Geneva was racking up long hours at John Bickford's Casco Bay Breeze House. Her husband, Sam, was older and not quite as tolerant, with good reason. Working with the public takes more patience than most of us have in reserve, but the mixture of both personalities was essential in keeping the Spa running smoothly. From behind her candy counter she indulged each small child every second they needed to choose from the abundant selection of penny candy that was lined up inside the big glass candy counter. She waited with a small, brown paper bag in hand, poised ready to retrieve two of those coconut watermelon slices and three root beer barrels—*No, no, no—make that three pieces of bubble gum and two waxed lips.* Her candy counter was a study in confectionary ingenuity and we all analyzed every new addition, labored over every choice.

Geneva (Bickford) Rogers

Over at the far counter, a sailor shifted his weight from one leg to the other, tapped his keys on the counter, and counted the wad of bills clutched in his hand. All he needed was a minute to pay for some *cases* of beer, and run. She gave him a sideways glance and returned her attention to me, whose eyes barely cleared the top of the counter, and whose ten cents worth of candy was the important purchase of the moment.

Were a consensus taken of my peers, as to the highlights in their other life, the one in which we stood all two feet tall—three feet on the outside, one can guarantee that the light generated by Geneva, and her candy counter would illuminate the entire island. We are all convinced that the candy was just part of the draw. Geneva's warmth, affection, and the sparkle in her eyes filled the rest of the brown-bag—to the brim; as did her geniality fill our youthful sensibilities.

Her children scooped ice cream cones until they probably wished they never saw another. Those were quite affordable at seven cents, and we fished for all kinds of sodas from down inside the big red cooler filled with ice-cold circulating water— also seven cents. The big band sound filled the air while the paired teenagers, and others, not yet paired, got their nickels worth out of the brightly lit jute box. Most of the boys either couldn't or wouldn't dance, therefore, girls danced with girls, and the few guys who could, were at it non-stop. One boy danced the jitterbug as effortlessly as Fred Astaire, and was much more handsome. His sister was a statuesque beauty, *of the Grace Kelly ilk,* and the dozen red roses she held in her arms the day she was chosen the very first Miss Long Island framed her all-American features. She was not the exception, but the rule. As a whole, this inner circle of teens was extremely attractive.

Quite contented with my dime's worth of candy in a brown bag, I sat scrunched up in the chair and concentrated on picking the rows of little round beads of confection off a foot long strip of paper. That took a while. Meanwhile, the small dance area filled with teenagers and the jute box lit up to a snappy thing by the Andrew Sisters. A record stuck on the one song and everyone eked out another dance before old Sam scuffed across the floor to snap the plug out of the wall.

Quietly watching, crunching and munching—I ate more paper than candy, which is why Dad didn't like us eating it. Tiring of that, I slipped the red-waxed lips over my mouth, not aware of how foolish it looked. Some of the teens laughed, and having caught the image that it presented; I, too, giggled—through the wax lips. It was as close to gum as we were allowed, but nothing close to the sticks of gum that snapped with every chaw. I was in absolute awe of how well the girls finely honed the art, but as tempting as it was, owing to Dad's forewarning it was the better part of discretion not to buy chewing gum. Ann Marie got smacked for disregarding his admonition. I wondered what made him dislike a mouth full of snapping gum so.

Interest waned once the music was silenced. The whole tribe relocated over to the steep bank of the Honor Roll. They could have carried on anywhere to extend their congregate activities after the fling at the Spa, but they chose that spot. Interestingly, their demeanor changed, became more subdued and respectful as they quietly sat all around the grassy incline, earmarks of a youthful brand of veneration. Some stood together at the top of the knoll, up close to the front of the large white Memorial, read all the names of the men on the island that had gone off to war, examined the gold stars stenciled beside those who were killed. Some of the boys there assembled would shortly leave to join the Army and Navy. I was absolutely taken with the whole tribe of them, and hence forth and forever more, to me this group became the *teenage emeritus* of Long Island.

Honor Roll

Each morning someone raised the flag on the Memorial, then furled it each night before sundown. It was never left to set in the rain, or allowed to touch the ground, never thrown in the trash, but rather ceremoniously burned when it had gone beyond use. Islanders stood, with right hand over their heart when any flag was raised, when it paraded on by or at school each morning during the Pledge of Allegiance. It would not be long before Congress amended the Constitution to include *"under God"* in the wording of the Pledge of Allegiance. Changing the Constitution is designed not to be an easy deal. It took a while to **unlearn** *"one nation indivisible with liberty and justice for all."*

No one waited to see if anyone else was going to stand whenever the National Anthem started to play—but stood immediately, with hand over heart until the anthem was completed—and then applauded. The little community of Long

Island was very much a part of the republic, for which the flag stood, especially with the Navy sitting on our front doorstoop.

The teens dispersed, but not before they had planned the next baseball game. The all-American game truly had its hey-day on all of the islands. Teens mustered up an active team of avid players replete with island uniforms, fans, and cheerleaders. Inter-island games were extremely popular, especially with their rivals Chebeague and Cliff Islands. Respectable players one and all, each team drew quite a following, and it mattered not which island played host. Lobster boats full of bait barrels and fans faithfully pursued the heat of the game.

**

Drinking holes phased out when the private clubhouses were no more. No place existed for men to gather, other than in Dad's shop or at someone's fish house. Once a month he, Uncle Johnny, Everett Clarke, George Johnson, and Wood Baston met at a little log cabin that was located between George and Everett's house. It was not a club, as with those in the past with proper names. It simply was the men's night out, one comprised of humongous steaks, drinks, cigars, and a night of cards.

For Sam Rogers and Tucky Woodbury the meeting of the oldfangled crowd was but a short scuffle across the street from their respective homes to a bright stand of birches where they met up with Jake MacVane. Old Jake was a big hulk of man with a long weathered face, who rowed his punt in a different manner than the other lobstermen. Rather than to face the stern, he faced into the bow, inched towards Ponce's, at what always seemed to be a dead low tide, and rather than swing and push the oars, he just dipped them quietly into the water and gave a slight, but strong jig forward. I never saw anyone else do that, then or since. The boulders that they sat on in the birches were well worn—their ritual meeting held without special passwords—just a retreat—away from the women. Wave to one of them, and they all reciprocated. *To this very day, the small piece of turf in the birches bears their transparent image, one that I see each time I look that way—for as long as my brain creates it—or until the birches go. It'll be a while.*

Dearie, on the other hand, was a loner, so named because he sang and whistled as he passed our house each day on his way to the store. We could hear him singing the old, World War I two-step as he neared the house, *"Dearie, life was cheery, in the good old days gone by..."* which is how Ernie Holeman acquired his nickname. We made certain that we pulled a gruff greeting out of him before he continued on his way, and sometimes chimed in on his song. I don't think he appreciated the sing-a-long, and was never certain if he wanted to be bothered. He was a bit snarly. Some had the notion that the World War One veteran suffered from shell shock. He did. I only know that the old curmudgeon never walked a straight line, and followed the well-beaten path down the road, all a catawampus, the same time each day—like clockwork. Dearie didn't visit.

Hat Littlejohn was just the opposite—had the wisdom of the ages in her furrowed face, and a glimmer in her eyes. She was predictably seated in her worn, wide armed rocker when we banged on her back door on our way home from school. I'm not certain why we visited—just because. Her house sat just a few feet from the fire-barn—was grayed and weather beaten, overgrown with tall grass and high bushes, but the pale purple lilacs stood out beautifully against the graying clapboards, the type of house one pictures on an island. Inside, it was chockablock full of timeworn accumulation.

The old woman was attired in a very long dress that reached the floor, which she covered with a long printed apron, taking the out-dated fashion a decade further than did our grandmother. That made it forty years out of fashion, but old timers paid little attention to frivolous fashion—only comfort, and their pocketbooks. She would have looked out of character dress in anything else.

Hat didn't sit at the table; she sat in her rocking chair, which was aligned to the table on her right, much the same as a boat sitting next to a dock. The place was teaming with cats that teetered on windowsills, wafted around her tabletop, and slept beneath the warm wood stove. Everything that she needed was within arms reach there on the table—books, magazines, a corncob pipe, tissues, and a radio, out of which soap opera themes tinkled in the background. On her immediate left, sitting on the floor, but standing level to the wide arm of the chair was a fifty-pound burlap sack of peanuts, into which she handily reached and offered us a handful. At the time, I was unaware that it was Dad who made certain she was supplied. We cracked open shells, ate peanuts with her for a while, patted all the cats, and chatted. She smiled, amused by our little tête à tête, and we left after fifteen minutes, enough of a visit for her, ample for us.

***

Delivering babies was not a calling to which Dad willingly committed himself. Transportation was as far as he wished to go—the same level of commitment as many of the island's lobstermen, though once faced with a woman in labor, all was thrown to the wind. A few years previously, Jack and Josie McCann stood outside of the house at two in the morning, pelting pebbles atop the porch roof, trying to wake someone in the house. He would have been hard pressed to refuse the apprehensive look that was most assuredly on Josie's face, and would not have been able to turn down the apologetic and mannered pleas from Jack. To town they flew, in the nick of time to have Robbie. Two other urgent calls that he received in the middle of the night came from Chebeague, to wit he rowed out to the mooring, jumped in his lobster boat and wailed it over to Chandlers wharf. Mid-way up the bay, on both occasions, the babies made their entrance into the world, delivered by Dad—in the engine room of the lobster boat amidst the fumes from the engine, and that wretched bait smell. One wonders if the baby boys were imprinted by the experience and became lobstermen. I believe they did—become lobstermen.

Noontime arrived—on time—every day—not an easy nonevent to ignore on the island. Both blasting fire sirens on the *Eastend* and *Westend* sounded off, joined by the high pitched, wavering Navy siren in the Area. Bare attention was given to all the commotion, at noon, but if heard at any other time of the day, all eyes took on a widened, stark look and apprehension fill the air. The volunteers raced from all points, jumped aboard the *pumper* that was filled with water from the Marsh. None of the lumbering vehicles moved at any appreciable speed. I don't recollect an island home that ever survived a fire.

Without explanation we were quickly ushered out of the house just before bedtime, all escorted way out into the blackness of the backyard. My eyes locked onto the flames that were shooting up out of the chimney, and there on the top of a very long ladder stood Dad, silhouetted against the flames, his arms folded against the edge of the roof, watching, listening. We stood closely together, eyes wide with anxiety, my stomach quivering from the fear generated by the tunnel of fire in the chimney. Everyone was struck dumb; barely an utterance came from a one of us. It would not have been heard over the fire's hollow roar, which gave off a terribly disconcerting sound. The creosote apparently built up, markedly, inside the chimney, and caught, which meant that it would take awhile to burn-off, a critical time when the intensity of the fire could catch inside, around the chimney. He stayed at the top of the ladder until it died out—and we to our beds, ever so relieved that we weren't part of the statistic. That was close.

Long Island's volunteer fire department was called to the *Eastend* to a house fire just across from the Methodist church where Mame Wallace lived with several foster children. She and the boys watched as their house burned down to the foundation that night, an inferno that consumed the house quickly, incinerated the chimney, letting loose a shower of bricks, one that caught Dad fair square in the mouth, and made short order of all his front teeth. Later that night, he and another volunteer fireman sat at our dining room table, tired and spent, ruminating over the event. We burst into the house to find out whose house burned down. He gave us a nickel to go buy some penny candy, to get rid of us, and we, unaware of the accident, burst in reverse. On our return with the booty, he reached over and took the sweetened waxed teeth that we had bought and popped a pair into his mouth—making light of the injury. I didn't catch the humor in it. It looked like it hurt like the dickens.

"Ring around the rosy, a pocket full of posies—ashes, ashes, we all fall down." Such was the sweet playtime rhyme, hands together, all in a circle, round and round, fall down—until we learned it referenced the rosy symptoms of the Plague of the

1500s, and *ashes* related to the form of burial, putting the kibosh to that lovely little ditty. Instead, let's do the hand clapping game, *"Peas, porridge hot, peas, porridge cold, peas, porridge in the pot, nine days old."* Wouldn't you know! It had a history too—came from the days of cooking in fireplaces, in a big kettle hung over the fire. Every time they lit the fire, they added something to the pot, for days on end...*porridge in the pot, nine days old.* Wasn't that a gross-out? It was time to learn how to play double jump rope with its easy rhythms and up-beat jingles.

My older siblings were long past the let's pretend stage and not much interested in a game of Chinese checkers or paper dolls. I didn't take it personally. At times, even Carmen and I had different energies, therefore sought out other children with which to spend our spring afternoons. Out in back of the old school house the ice pond melted and the water receded, became a road once again, now a short cut from Beach Avenue to the ball field. Carmen, Harry Ross, and Peachie Johnson discovered an exploded rabbit population up there and expended their energies chasing rabbits for an entire afternoon, or two, or three. They got good at it. I heard that rabbits oft times died if given a fright and wondered how they would react if it happened. It didn't.

Blackberry Winter needed to shake-off the last vestiges of the season, and it often did towards spring with a dusting of big, fat, lazy snowflakes atop the spring blossoms, the type of snow that never dallied around very long, a robin's snow as they termed it. Susan's playhouse was a renovated chicken coop, a place that afforded us a haven, should the weather turn. The huge barn offered the same with its lofts, big old desks, and old ledgers that became fodder for pretend secretarial work. In back of the barn there were two tall, very old evergreen trees where her grandfather once hung the pigs after slaughter. The horse and cow stalls were still there, hay remained stuck in nooks and crannies, all remnants of the near past, and because of all the horseshoes, square headed horseshoe nails, and harnesses scattered in amongst everything, it felt as though animals were around the corner, somewhere. There actually were—at least two pseudo types anyway—kept in a carton atop the wood box in Sue's kitchen—fluffy pink and fluffy green, teeny chicks. Stores were filled with the colorful puffballs at Easter, and sold them by the gross. Poor things didn't live long.

We rarely dallied inside anybody's house for long, especially on rainy days. We were up to our yin-yangs in mud, civil engineers bearing garden hoes, digging long rambling troughs in the mud in order to drain the Cushing's driveway of its huge insurmountable puddles of water. A labyrinth of ruts entertained us all afternoon. Unfortunately, we forgot about the dipping temperatures of early spring, the frozen ground by morning, which created a terrain not much different than Donner's Pass. By then it was an obstacle course for her father's old crank-start, 1937 Chrysler to navigate, and his attempts looked like something out of a Mac Sennet Key Stone Cop movie. They called her the *Blue Beetle*.

The weather finally turned, and every evening along about dusk the warm air rang with a choir of peepers, baby frogs born into every standing body of fresh water on the island, and, too, the return of the soft coo of a whippoorwill. I had to stop dead in my tracks to listen, simply hearkening—then burst into the house to pull everyone out to listen too—and they did. Every inch of soil was soggy underfoot. On cue the spongy ground released the water at a considerable clip down roadside ditches, running just beneath a tinsel-thin layer of ice that lay like a bridge atop the ditch, one which we invariably busted with a quick snap of the knuckle to speed up the melting process. A beaver kept trying to damn up the culvert in the Marsh and it brimmed to overflowing.

Geneva Rogers' emergence out in the fields to dig dandelion greens, with a knife and a brown paper bag, ushered in a wave of spring fever. Pussy willows sprouted velvet-like catkins; yellow forsythia laced the fields, indicating that leaves would be forthcoming. As the days warmed we picked Stinking Benjamin[110], in the wooded path leading to and from school, examining lady slippers, and jack-in-the-pulpits. Each orchid and eccentric pulpit was tarried over with the wonder of a curious mind. The unspoken rule dictated that we not pick any plant that

---

[110] Stinking Benjamin - Trillium

was sparse in number, we otherwise happy that a copious amount of sour grass and chamomile were available on which to chew.

The sound of the brass school bell made us quicken our pace along the pine straw path towards school. But we couldn't pass by one particular spruce tree, the only one that exuded pitch, the one with a trunk peppered with pitch pimples filled with pitch gum. We popped a few of them with our fingernails, stuffed a wad of pitch gum into our mouths little realizing, that the resin was a base for turpentine. Two or three chews of the nasty tasting stuff were enough to satisfy our native instincts—and it didn't snap with every chaw—didn't snap at all. We had to run! May baskets were a project of the day. Did Mother know that May baskets were a Druid ritual, a pagan thing—as were the Easter eggs, holly, and pumpkins? I never brought any of it to her attention.

Birthday Cake 101

Mother granted Susan and me permission to take-over the kitchen one afternoon. It was given to us as easily as if we'd asked for a cookie. Sue and I had a mission—her mother Adeline's birthday was imminent; and I discovered that no cake was planned for her dinner table, an incomprehensible thought to my way of thinking. I was aghast! Susan wasn't allowed to cook at her house, only because there were so many grown-ups to handle the job, but at ours, whenever Mom wanted gingerbread on the menu I was delegated the official baker. Sue and I learned things like that during our 4-H meetings down at Harbor DeGrace with Muriel Lowell, and at the parsonage down at the Eastend during Bluebird and Camp Fire Girl meetings, under the guidance of the Reverend, Miss Stimpson. I took it for granted that upgrading to white cake was not such a deal and dove into the process with abandon, greasing two cake pans, measuring our way into the two-layer cake from scratch, whipping egg whites, and standing vigil over the double boiler of white, billowing seven-minute frosting.

She and I skulked up through the field, ever so carefully balancing the decorated cake, lest we dump it at the eleventh hour, but determined to keep the cake cloaked in secrecy from the entire Cushing household. One can only guess the bewilderment it caused as they watched us from the pantry window, walking their long dirt driveway, shoulder to shoulder in cadence towards the house. Transported, as though the cake was made of nitroglycerin, a bit antsy because the top layer was listing very badly, we held our breath, hoping the light crust, which had formed over the seven-minute frosting, would hold it all together. Sue assumed sole responsibility as we neared her house, and just for effect we knocked on the screen door, rather than to just walk inside. Adeline came around the corner with a perplexed look on her face because of the fact that we didn't just walk in, at which time Susan extended our fancy-dancy concoction forward to her mother. We had no idea what we had done by way of this innocent gesture, but had, in fact, hit the mark. Tears sprang to Adeline's eyes. It was the first birthday cake that she had *ever been given in her life* and she was no spring chicken. It was also probably the first cake that she ever ate wherein bacon fat was used to grease the cake pans.

Warmer days upon us, Susan and I kept to this side of the gravel pit and baseball field making a serious project out of catching snakes out in a field, both greenies and brownies. Her father, Walter was none too happy to find that we had dumped twenty or so snakes into the rain barrel to see if they could swim. They can, and we did not—ever do that again. It took a great deal longer to fish them out, than it did to catch them.

A sudden realization took me. Other island households were different from ours. I watched captivated, while one mother did the honors of shaving her husband's scrubby beard, the whole ritual—chair and table in the center of the kitchen, the double shaving mug, shaving brush, straight edge razor, strop, towels, and a basin of water. After his face steamed five minutes in a hot towel, she then proceeded through the whole nine yards, all of which duly impressed me. But the high esteem in which I held her lessened greatly, later on, when at the dinner table she actually reached across and cut his meat for him. That seemed a bit overboard, *even in that day and age!*

Of the Old School

Mrs. Hill retired and with her, the story about the day her undies fell down around her ankles while she was at the blackboard. Poor teachers! They never lived anything down. Aunt Frances, *Mrs. Barrett—as we, her nieces and nephew, now had to call her,* became the upper grade teacher and principal. Mrs. MacVane became sick when we were in the third grade, replaced by a teacher from Portland who boarded on the island, rather than to commute to and from the city each day. We all thought we would not survive without Mrs. MacVane. She, like Geneva Rogers, held the adoration of generations of children.

Mrs. Gallagher was a stickler for math and smoked cigarettes on her break down in the boiler room. Most adults smoked, and I thought it odd that she sifted out of sight to do so, because I doubt that any of us would have given it a second thought had she casually smoked on the playground while monitoring us at recess. Teachers, evidentially, were not supposed to smoke or to partake of *elixirs*.

School had an even tenor to it, sometimes a *same-old, same-old* tenor, but hooking up with the other island children made the trip worthwhile. An inkwell was a point of great pride. Every wooden desk had one in the upper right hand corner, probably a holdover from the old school house. [111] Since ballpoint pens were not yet a part of the scene, we learned the fine art of writing with a proper ink pen, the kind that we had to dip in ink—constantly. It gave us a real appreciation for the generations that were consigned to using a feathered quill pen.

One wasn't given a choice as to where one sat. In a certain grade, we were usually a certain size, and therefore sat at the smallest desks at the front of the room, facing the teacher's desk. Graduate to the next grade and up the row, a bigger desk awaited us, until we graduated to the largest at the back of the room. A half circle of dinky chairs was set up by the teachers desk that

---

[111] Ink Wells - Ballpoint pens, although invented, were very expensive and not yet a dime a dozen.

accommodated each grade's individual class time with the teacher, in reading, writing and 'rithmatic, a busy spot, because each grade was called up for individual attention once a day. Obviously, lessons taught within the half circle were broadcast throughout the room, filtering into our heads as we addressed our own assignments, and for those who could focus, the concept was doable, but for those who could not, they usually became a pain—disruptive. If the teacher didn't handle it, we did. It was hard on a child who ended up being the only one in a class. Depending on his or her aptitude, he or she joined in on the grade ahead, or the class behind. Eight students may have constituted the highest total of any one class.

Ours was a daily twenty-minute walk to and from school at lunchtime, sometimes to a table covered with newspapers on which a full bushel of hot, steaming, cooked shrimp was heaped. January was the month that shrimp came into coastal waters from offshore to spawn—draggers in hot pursuit, *shrimping* the area like there was no tomorrow. Now and again, we took our lunch to school, although we much preferred the surprise that awaited us, each day. The few times that we had to eat at school I was sobered to discover some of the kids had mayonnaise and piccalilli sandwiches, or two slices of bread with mustard slathered on one side. Our leftovers became booty, including the cores of eaten apples, scoffed-up when we weren't looking. A couple of them outright asked for a portion of whatever we had. All the kids knew that the canvassing was less about those particular classmates and more about their parents. When they arrived with no lunch we invited them home with us for tomato soup and grilled cheese sandwiches. Of course, there is the chance that maybe some actually enjoyed mayo and piccalilli sandwiches.

We *Westend* children walked or rode our bikes to school. The boys fashioned make-believe motors on their bikes by wedging a playing card near the spokes so that it created a patter, a whizzing sound. The faster they peddled—the louder the make-believe engine. Obviously, they went through tons of cards, which probably had their mothers scratching their heads when they went to set up the card tables for an afternoon whist party with the neighbor ladies. Whist parties were a big deal, and well attended.

Navy children arrived each day in a genuine bus driven by Burt Russell; one painted a military color, like everything else. We never knew when a new-crop was going to step off the Navy bus, but invariably fresh faces appeared. Uncle Johnny was hired as the regular school bus driver for the *Eastend* children. He appreciated his job, was loyal to it, and to the children. Though gruff around the edges, regardless, the kids had a true affection for him. He wiped noses, buttoned jackets, and soothed skinned knees. He could also bark like a Sergeant. The boys usually straightened away when he gave them the hairy-eyeball. Children, in general, were a constant amusement to him, that is until they got older, became teenagers, and acquired a smart mouth—at which time he systematically disowned them.

We christened the contraption that he drove the *Black Moriah*. It was formally, either a stretch limousine, or a hearse into which seats were built, and it doubled as the island's taxi. The three students who made it to the bus first got the choice

*Uncle Johnny
(Gomez)*

bench seat in the very back and because the bus was so low to the ground, when it hit bumps, the kids in the back seat bounced into the air. As far as the *Eastend* kids were concerned, it was part of the accommodation and he purposefully drove over certain roads, like the "Bunny Hop", one that he knew would produce a roller coaster ride—but not every time—or it would have become one of those *same-old, same-olds*. Once or twice a year we were invited to ride to the *Eastend* with them. We all sang to the top of our lungs—Uncle the loudest of-the-lot. He really didn't know the words, but caught the gist through the rear view mirror, reading our lips, chiming-in a degree behind our verse—pretending that he knew the words all along. *Had everyone been required to wear seat belts in those days, it would have been a non-event, except for Uncle's singing. That road, the one that everyone still calls the 'Bunny Hop," has a perfectly legal name, though I never took time to find out what it was. Someday!*

Four to five miles an hour was all any car traveled on the island's tarred roads, excepting for Old Jim Grey, who it was said was blind as a bat, and drove much too fast. That prompted the warning from Mom that we walk the ditch should we see him on the road. Few women drove cars. Susan's and my mother never learned—never had to learn.

The big city road truck traveled at about two miles an hour and elicited a different response. We knew George Ross was certain to stop to give us an equal amount of attention, as did Uncle Johnny. All of the Islanders in general were generous purveyors of attention, especially to children. Smiling down from the big cab, George anticipated the serenade that he knew was forthcoming, for the hundredth time, and bided patiently while we sang, *"Georgy Porgy, pudding and pie, kissed the girls and made them cry. When the boys came out to play, Georgy Porgy ran away,"* giggle, giggle, our hands over our mouths as though we had said something naughty. We waved to boats, to cars, and greeted strangers politely. Strangers weren't feared. Should we have been afraid? We weren't even cautious. Realistically, that didn't seem to be in the air, not in the mind-set; none would *daast* for the repercussions.

The walk to and from school was unremarkable until the Navy decided to use goats as a way to cut back on mowing the grass inside the fences. The scuttlebutt making the rounds was that the goats were brought to the island because the Commander's wife could drink only goat's milk. Our *"Billy Goat's Gruff"* phase owed to the fact that the animals often escaped from the Area's fencing and presented a formidable barrier when we met up with the herd on the road leading to school. Our greatest problem was the ram's intimidating, territorial nature, his propensity to butt people, which the boys encouraged at every turn, as would a matador in a Spanish bullring.

Over by Jake MacVane's house, good-sized geese were non too friendly either, as we passed by, only they seemed more intent at getting us, wings menacingly spread, and we—lit-out, in a fair sprint. Mother couldn't wait for a change in command, and commander's wife, because her rose bushes were catching hell, chawed right down to the last thorn. Goats preferred thorns.

The school's swings were built so tall that when we played the old game, whereby we jumped off the swing as it reached its highest tilt; we realized that it exceeded a safe vault, though we tested the fates from time to time. Our hands were loaded with blisters from swinging across the new monkey bars, and because the new seesaws had not yet been broken-in, they generated splinters in our butts. In amongst the birches the ground was peppered with conical shaped holes, made with the heels of our shoes for a game of marbles. I never went away with many *keepsies* but was exceptional at making conical shaped holes in three or four turns of my body. *Simon Says*, *Jump Rope, and What Color Am I Thinking About* were a nice change of pace, especially when the blisters on our hands began to hum from too many trips across the monkey bars. The lucky ones who owned the giant economy sized box of crayons faired better at the color game because of the imaginative names the manufacturer tagged each new color. Sky-blue-pink stumped everyone.

The boys owned the outer baseball field out by the blueberry and bayberry bushes. The girls had the one next to the school for softball games and two older girls, from the Eastend, were an even match as captains. When it came to using the bat measure to vie for *first up*, we underlings were never chosen, our hands were too small. The older girls had it down pat—fist over fist, all the way up the bat to the point where the hand was stretched to the limit, from little finger, to the tip of thumb, until it reached up over the base of the bat for the win. Each of those two girls had the ability to crack a baseball clear out to the bayberry bushes, better at the game than half of the boy's team. When either of them took off on a dead tear it was always wise to stay clear of home base, *and* their cast-off bats—stay very clear of them as they tore around the bases. Hell, they'd run you down in their race towards home base, if you were stupid enough to wander into their path. They learned from the best. Bunny Ricker, an *Eastend* mom, wasn't shy about gathering-up the *Eastend* kids for a play-to-win ball game down there—when she wasn't cooking for *Pood*, or washing his bait clothes, or making pies—

or tied up with an important whist game. Today we have soccer-moms. Once upon a time in the late forties and fifties, the *Eastend* of Long Island had *Bun* Ricker.

Bun and Pood! It just dawned on me. I never learned her real name. I wouldn't have known her husband, Pood's, proper name either, had he not made his son a junior. As a young student at the Chebeague Island School Pood actually didn't know his real name—until the teacher asked everyone in the class to give their full and proper names. The others came forth with theirs in an instant. When asked, Pood replied, *"My name is Poodie Ricker."* She said, *"What is your real name?"* He replied, emphatically, *"It's Poodie Ricker!"* His cousin Bea rose to his protection and broke the news. [112] *"Your name is Elliot—'Poodie'."* He was emphatic about his nickname way back then and, *by gorry*, showed the teacher who was in charge—for throughout his life, we could count on one hand the times that he actually reverted to his proper name. As an aside, he always addressed his older brother, Will, by his proper name, Robert. Go figure! The Ricker family did seem to corner the market on nicknames, tagged a neighbor *Ole Puckerfoot*, and an antagonist, *Jimmy-Poopy-Stink*. Now that I think on it—what was Tucky Woodbury's name, Decca Doughty's, Specky's, Buckshot's. and Bunker's? We were the moniker capital of the world, and didn't know it. Personally, I'm glad that *Stinky Ross* ditched his nickname somewhere to the other side of adolescence.

***

Sue, Buddy, Gordon and I matriculated to the big time, to the other side of the oak doors for the fifth through eighth grades with Aunt Frances as our teacher, and contrary to belief, having a family relationship with Mrs. Barrett did not provide me with any favors. What the others didn't realize is that out of earshot from them, she hammered and criticized our actions much more than the classmates who were not related to her. Predictably, her daughter Suzanne, an extremely bright child, didn't have a

---

[112] Cousin Bea – We knew her as Bea Horr

chance in the politics of our peers. Not until she graduated from Wellesley College with honors did they cut her any slack.

We were exposed to a host of teaching tools. Every type of student academic condition lay before one teacher to develop and edify, including Navy brats who melded in nicely, adding a rich flavor of their own to the mix, especially when it came to making geography a reality. Donny Egan arrived from Japan with his family, and our class gained by one. His mom, Bunker Johnson's daughter, married a career Army man. They didn't live on the base. They were *island!* I had a terrible time understanding Donny's strong southern accent, or was it a hybridized military accent I was trying to decipher? I can't imagine what we sounded like to him.

The student population ballooned to fifty-five, half of which were housed in each of the two rooms, needs that encompassed a half-dozen special education children, the fair to *middling*, the bright, and the gifted—one teacher per twenty-five. That's it! Mother was delighted when asked to donate her time at the piano, when holidays rolled around.

A basic plan fit all levels within a grade. The older children taught the younger ones when the teacher was busy, and although homework was not a part of the plan, by nature, some parents helped their own children to extend the basic knowledge of a subject. *Not as structured as other classes in the Portland system, we were more of a precursor to the open classroom, a concept hailed by school systems across the country some twenty years later.* Mrs. Barrett hammered at us when we mispronounced words so that we would not go into the world mouthing *chimley* for chimney, *supposibly* for supposedly—*ain't, yup, acrost* (across), *irregardless,* (regardless) and *lopstas* (lobsters). Thus she worked to extract a vocabulary and diction from us that would transcend island cant. I was not aware that she sparked an undercurrent in me, particularly, for definitive words, and that was all wonderful and good, but lo the day I had to spell the big ones! Mother could picture the words in her head, won spelling bees in both English and French. How did she do that? I would have happily settled for the phonetic alphabet that used symbols. Obviously, the biological osmotic theory, in regard to mother's spelling aptitude, pooped out on me.

Hearing and eye tests rendered us half a day free from the norm, though realistically we were discombobulated for the remainder of the day. A Portland school nurse was there to hand out earphones and test forms, putting us on hold until she gave directions. Our earphones were snugly cupped over our ears, the Victoria plugged in, the needle hung over the record, and she charged us to... wait—wait—wait. Looking about the room, it was apparent that everyone enjoyed the break from the average spate of lessons, all posed with freshly sharpened pencils in hand, an extra one on the desk, just in case, as the nurse carefully placed the needle on the record. A man's voice loudly directed us to, *"Write the number that you hear in the right column! 42...68...93...15...75...22...."* Where did he go? I could hear pencils scribbling away at the other desks, but I'd lost any inkling of the man's voice, certain that the nurse was going to tell me I was deaf as a haddock. *"Now,"* a woman's full-tone voice blasted, *"Write the numbers you hear in the left column...66...13...83...55...71...40..."*

Polio reared its ugly head around Portland and vaccines were disseminated throughout the school system. Doctor Lowenstein came over from Chebeague to give vaccinations, plus DPT shots and we all lined up in the hall to wait our turn. When the needle went in, I passed out, a reaction that seemed to put the face of concern on the good doctor. He said that I had a heart murmur, something that I dismissed—*and have not thought of until this recollection.* Personally, I think it was just an off day. Shots were never a matter of concern for me, though spelling bees were.

Back in '46, the newly created United Nations took up residence in NYC, a move that sparked a lesson in current events. Art accompanied most current-event lessons. We knew one was about to unfold when Mrs. Barrett taped a long, four-foot wide, single sheet of white paper onto a very large stretch of blackboard, paper that she cut from a ream of table covering. We mixed powdered paint in mayonnaise jars, staked out a site beside our best friend, of course, and collectively created some grand murals, a study in how perceptive we all were—or were not—about the world, at large.

Two of us showed inklings of a talent in art, and at one point we were both sent to the Portland School of Art for lessons on Saturdays. One of the cracker-jack, softball captains from the *Eastend*, by far, had the more natural ability, her work free flowing, and skillful. Art was less a competitive activity, more a singular aptitude, and one that benefited all, which may be the reason I leaned towards the activity. Competitiveness was not my fortè, where more people always ended up on the losing side, made to feel badly, or less capable. I did end up winning a game of musical chairs once. The girl that lost to me was so frothing mad at me for budging her out that I offered her the book that I won. The prize didn't mean that much to me. She wouldn't take it. What good purpose came from that exercise, I queried?

I learned from Aunt Jo's generosity, that she had a penchant for the world of art. She paid to extend my Saturday lessons. Somehow, she knew that I, too, would have a penchant—someday. Did we miss out on some of the curriculum that our peers in Portland received? Most assuredly! I do know that we walked away with the ability to learn how to learn, and I personally walked away with an echo in my ear, admonishing me to, never, again in my life end a sentence with a preposition. That one dogs me.

Mrs. Barrett's flair for putting on plays gave us an outlet for expanding our creative juices, writing the plays, and creating the backdrops. The Island responded with full houses at these performances—always full houses. Usually on Fridays, we practiced Christmas plays. My character's part was to utter something cute, and to kiss Santa, an older *Eastend* boy—kiss him on the cheek. I managed to fake it all through rehearsals and allowed Mrs. Barrett to think that I would stick to the script, that is until the night of the play, which was held down at the Methodist Church. At the last moment, I daringly forsook the smooch, blatantly ignoring Mrs. Barrett's frantic hand-language to get on with it. If she complained to Dad, I never heard about it—though it was not ever wise to cross the teacher.

Betty Jane Rich, Geneva Morton,[113] and I were at the water fountain comparing our Christmas wish lists, amidst my slurps, when in all due innocence I referenced Santa as the gift giver. Geneva's face screwed up, in total disbelief, and in all of two seconds she laid waste my lovely imaginings. Just like the scalawag wizard of *Oz,* the curtain swung open on the red suited, portly, old gent—and too, on the vacationing celeb Santa on the *Eastend,* Mr. Daley. Betty Jane, in a futile attempt to intercede, tried to placate the situation, *which was so like her,* but the jig was up. I was ten years old. It was overdue, *but not by much—in those days.*

***

On Saturday, Mother baked, was tied to the kitchen for hours. If we wanted to be around her, we piled big couch pillows down beside the stove, dove in on top of each other, listening to radio, yammering back and forth—more quiet when Saturday's 1950s best programming, *Let's Pretend*[114] and *Big Jon and Sparky* came on the air. Sparky sounded as though he had a tank of helium handy-by, from which he took a honk to keep his voice elf-like.

Somehow she navigated around the confusion, stepped over us to get to the pans, and turned a deaf ear to, *"He touched me! She's looking at me! Ma-a-a!"* Yeast aroma permeated the house, and we all were allowed to thump the bottom of the loaves of bread to test its doneness, talked about the olden days when bread was divided according to status. Workers got the burnt bottom of the loaf, the family got the middle, and guests got the top, or *upper crust.* Not being a connoisseur of *any* brand of crust, if it took being middle class for the rest of my life to keep from eating the bottom, or the *upper crust*—so may it be.

---

[113] Family Connection – Geneva Morton – daughter to <u>Dotty</u> (Ricker) and <u>Specky</u> Morton, grand-daughter to Robert and Annabelle Ricker of Chebeague Island.
<u>Pood</u>, Will (Robert), Ray, Harold, and Dotty—were brothers and sister.
<u>Bunny</u> (Pood's wife) and Specky—were sister and brother.
Their children were the most connected cousins that I ever met.

[114] Let's Pretend - Grimm's Fairy Tales

Amidst the programming, the radio reported the death of Fannie Brice of radio's *Baby Snooks* fame, news that consigned a terrible sadness to the day—a first ever of that kind for me to ponder. Mother's approach to the weepy situation was to redirect, and passed me a big kettle of clamshells to take outside to throw onto the walkway and crunch into bits under my feet.[115] Pushing the screen door open with my foot, our cat, Cinderella, and her three kittens scampered through the opening before the heavy wooden door snapped back on its spring. There was a fourth little fella who hesitated as the door snapped shut—the second great sadness to befall me—all in one day. My spirits plummeted, and surely now I had the blot of a mortal sin on my soul for the suffering the little critter had to endure, a sin that the priest would most certainly hear all about through a rush of tears. That night Dad brought home a pregnant rabbit.

Wintertime didn't slow us down an iota. Eva VanAmburg let us practice in her dining room for an after-school-play that we wrote—just because—we felt like writing a play. Eva wrote a weekly column for the Portland newspaper about the polite society of the island: who arrived to visit, who attended the silver teas, and who served. Has anyone unraveled the reason a person became exalted by simply pouring tea? Invariably Eva closed out her column with the same generic review: *"And a good time was had by all."* She lent us a pile of old clothes for costumes, was actually the only person who ever saw the play, quite amused as she continued sewing on a quilt, or put the definitive touches on another doll. Every bride on the island treasured one of her bride dolls as a shower gift. *I still have the one she made for me.*

There amongst the alders behind her house there appeared a pond along about November, there in a low spot between old Arthur Demmons place and the old school house—one just deep enough for some good skating when the temperatures dropped. It was closer to our home, and a hundred times more shallow than the Marsh. We stayed so long in the afternoon that it is a wonder that we didn't get frostbite in our toes, the hobble home a painful

---

[115] Islanders and the Indians before them used clamshells to solidify mucky areas around living quarters— as did Spaniards on the Costa del Sol.

exercise, sometimes on skates, because if we took them off, the charley-horses were fierce.

Like clockwork—we gimped through the door for our five o'clock radio programs and the charge, *"Mush you huskies!"* a phrase Sergeant Preston of the Yukon used a bit too often. 'Course, The Lone Ranger was *"high-ho-ing"* all over the old west atop *Silver*, and The Cisco Kid was a bit silly, most of it of a boy's mind-set. Actually the programming was gender blind. We never missed an episode—or supper.

Children were the island's social engineers, a self-appointed welcoming committee to any visiting off-islander, or to the newly moved into the community. Susan and I intended to visit two people who moved down recently, but were categorically forbidden to do so by our parents. She and I found that difficult, because they were very congenial. The second time my parents emphasized the directive to stay away, the look in their eyes was unbending, and this time they added that they were communist, a term that neither used freely, if ever. Senator McCarthy was out to get the communist party in that period. The Rosenbergs were put on trial for espionage and sentenced to death. There was a real and present intrigue to which a naval base need be vigilant, a reminder of the integral part the island played in the big picture. We little people of the island tended to forget about that. The newcomer's tenure, at whatever they were *tenuring*—was short-lived. Not long after, they were gone.

Seems as though we just got over a hot war and now a very Cold War was in full bore, one that forced us to practice air raid drills at school. I was not certain, at all, how protected we were by pulling down the school's shades, or how sitting under our dinky desks was going to save us from anything as catastrophic as a bomb. I didn't waste much time worrying about it. That was our parent's job.

***

At night, and on weekends, Dad's shop became a retreat of sorts. It drew a steady stream of island men who walked up the path by the house, ducked under the salted-fish hanging on the clothesline to get out to the shop—a workshop that was chock-full of stuff, wall-to-wall good stuff, hanging from the ceiling important stuff. Even an old Model-T engine sat in the corner. One of his organizational tricks was to nail peanut butter jar covers beneath shelves, in a long row—then filled the jars with specific sizes and types of nails, bolts, do-dads and more stuff—easy to find stuff when all glass containers were screwed into the covers. He was a recycling baron, from the *"Waste not, want not" and "Use it up, wear it out"* generation. The air was blue with smoke, and we kids were all under foot pounding nails just for practice, sawing pieces of wood for no good reason, painting things, and cleaning out corners of the place just to hang around this jovial hub of activity.

Springtime stirred and we again trailed behind him out into the woods, galvanized pails in hand in search of maple trees he eyed for tapping sap. The kitchen oil stove was perfect for boiling it down to maple syrup. The back burners, that were *not* lit, conducted a low heat from the two front burners that were *always* lit.

He gave us impromptu lessons on how to whittle, and what kind of wood to cut for a dowsing stick, coupled with a practical application on its mysterious ability to search out water in the back yard. Dahlias and gladiolas did well out there, grew as tall as we. Whatever he sowed, he planted en masse, and cultivated the dahlias into giant dinner-plate size blossoms, beauties that Mother used on the church's altar. He didn't buy bulbs each season, but wintered them over in the dirt-ledge cellar, a dank place always half filled with coal, and when the run-off was considerable, a foot of water—another of those creepy places.

An eclipse had not happened in a dog's age. The ominous event was upon us and Dad passed out small rectangular pieces of very darkly tinted glass, and swore us to use them, *swore us*—when we looked at the sun's full eclipse. An eerie darkness fell. It was hard not to peek; though the thought of going blind was an adequate deterrent.[116]

In the fall, apple cider was churned out in an old corkscrew apple press. A little fresh apple juice goes a long way; and when we had our fill, the balance was bottled up for fermentation.

---

[116] Eclipse - 30 June 1954 Eclipse was 2 minutes, 35 seconds

During the hunting season he taught me how to use a rifle over at Southside beach. I pinched my finger in the hammer and got a wicked purple blister out of that one.

Ann Marie jumped on the running board of Dad's old truck one Saturday morning to help with a spring ritual of raking up the old grass, and planting flowers in the urns at the cemetery. Our plot was always nicely done. Only one tall granite stone set in the corner, the one belonging to Grammy Gomez. The pieces of Alfred's small gravestone lay against Grammy's. In another corner of the family plot there was a stubborn, sunken patch that would not grow grass. Wouldn't you know! It was directly over where they buried Antonio. Mulling over the problem, Dad said, under his breath, *"Look! He was so bad that the grass won't even grow on his grave."* That took Ann by surprise. He never spoke badly of people, never spoke of his father at all.

The first time that I saw him kneeling beside his bed, hands folded in prayer, I felt terribly intrusive, and was surprised to find out from Mom that he did this every night. I was impressed, and felt guilty because I didn't, and after all, Catholics were supposed to be more prayerful than Protestants. We had miles of beautiful rosary beads to prove it.

As the new manager of O'Brien Trucking Company, another wholesale food-trucking outfit on Commercial Street, Dad's responsibility sometimes called for him to work on Saturdays, and he often took one of us with him, *a forerunner of "Take your daughter to work day."* He gave us our own desk, and typewriter, and then our imaginations took us the rest of the way. We waited for Cinderella, our favorite house cat, the one that he brought to the city to rat the warehouse. We missed her terribly. She changed, didn't come when we called her, and was aloof— preoccupied. Rightly so! The rats on the waterfront were as big as was she. We saw them crawling the rock cribs beneath Custom House Wharf. She had very good reason to be preoccupied.

Larry Naples Diner, an institution located next door to Dad's workplace, was the favorite watering hole for islanders and fishermen on Commercial Street. I took one mouthful of what was actually excellent Italian cooking, but cooked with spices that attack every taste bud in my mouth. After the second glass of water, with hot red pepper tears streaming down my face, knowing that I tried, I really tried—Dad, for the first time ever, did not make me take one more bite.

Chapter

11 ...and The Island Delighted in Itself

First babies are eagerly anticipated in every family, though in this family the fifth elicited the very same response, only there were more of us to do so. In April of 1950 Mom departed for the hospital, leaving Dad to tend us. So certain were they that it would be a boy, that they never considered a girl's name. Predictions were made by how a woman carried the baby. Up front—it would be a girl, if set deep, a boy. I couldn't tell. Mom wore big flowing smocks.

In this same period Dad made a permanent break from city work, boned up on his rough carpentry, electrician, and refrigeration skills, built a substantial amount of traps, and settled into being a full-time islander. It was a big chunk of physical labor to bite off for a forty-five year old man.

The phone's ring drew us from every point in the house, and we huddled around Dad to listen-in on the call that came from the hospital that told us, in fact, that it was a boy, William John, and when Dad hung up the phone, he grabbed our hands, and we all skipped around in a circle. The man was ecstatic.

There was a week's wait before Mom could come home with him, and we had serious work to do before they arrived. Ann Marie and I were sent out into the back yard, the very same day, with the old bassinet, two paintbrushes, and one can each of blue and white paint. I was eight and she was a bossy snit that day, budging into my painting territory, I into hers, and before a half-hour had elapsed the oil-based paint was flying—into our hair, clothes and all over our faces. The kerosene used to get the paint off my face burned, but not half as much as the look in my father's eyes. Our family was no different when it came to spoiling the youngest in the family and as soon as it was reasonable Dad had a *little shadow* who followed him everywhere he went.

Long Island's school began to send its seventh and eighth graders to Portland one day a week. The premise was to begin integrating them into the city schools, to lessen the brunt of those anticipated first days in high school. Ann Marie, Elliot Ricker, Wayne Ladd, Donna Pisak, and Carol Peterson were the initial pioneers that started things rolling at King Junior High. The concept was to familiarize the island children with, at least, a few Portland junior-high students, who would also be attending Portland High School. It would give the island teens a feel for the way single subject classes were managed. They were not long in seeking out those with island roots. Ann Marie made a friend in a quiet city girl, Lainy Ricker who lived on Chebeague years back. Her father, Will, worked on Long Island during the war, ran the *Emita,* and was brother to Pood, her schoolmate Elliot's father. It was practically old home week for Ann, Elliot, and Lainy. Small world!

General MacArthur's swan song, *"Old Soldiers Never Die"* plied the radio airwaves for a great long time, and to the consternation of the country, President Truman actually fired him amidst a political wrangle over whether to, or not to extend the Korean War in '51. War reports peppered each news program with front-line updates, reports that had been a way of life— since forever. When was it not so?

King radio broke with some formats by experimenting with a new Saturday night top one-hundred, song hit program, starting with hit number one-hundred, working backwards to number one—all in a five hour span, perfect timing for Saturday night baby-sitters, with no squeak room for commercials. Sam Conner's huge overstuffed chair set beside the fireplace, a challenge for any nine-year old that had any intention of staying awake. By eight o'clock the house was quiet, the two girls sound asleep and I was curled up in the chair, vowing to keep my eyes opened until the number one song chimed in at midnight. But between the crackling fire and the curled-up comfort level of the chair, sleep crept in before song-hit number eleven made it on air.

Beachcombers 1952-1956

Summer children made shore along about June, and a curious shift ensued. Without so much as a breach of protocol, regular playmates took leave from one another, dispersing amongst the summer children for a contrasted interchange. None of us took the separation personally, because instinctively, we knew the rearrangement to be important, a symbiotic pairing of sorts.

As soon as the weather allowed, we were down on the raft fishing with hand lines, a minute only needed to scavenge the ledges on shore for periwinkles to use for bait. Some people had the knack—some didn't. Ugly sculpin, spiny cunner, or leathery dogfish were all that came up on the end of my line, none good for the table, and all dead ringers of their prehistoric forerunners. Sculpin blew-up when we rubbed their stomachs, a built-in reaction to prevent big, scary fish from lunching on them. Dogfish were no more than two-foot sharks in my school of thought, with two bones that stuck out from each side of the fish, and that meant trouble. We stayed clear of the two bones. I fished very little after I cut into a dogfish for bait, only to have her pups wash out of her gut onto the raft—alive. That was it! Wrap it up!

Our summer pals were children of those who were born just after the turn of the century, a kindred group who embraced and understood the soul of the island. We reconvened our fraternity each year, mainly at our favorite haunt, Fowler's Beach, the white, sandy strand just below Mount Hunger. Comfortably situated in the warm sand up on the rim, the three married Abbot girls, Ruth, Genna, and Doris whiled away the hours with the smaller of their broods—and T-bone, the Kilgore's giant, black, Newfoundland dog. He was a gentle giant, always belly deep in water at the shoreline, as much a part of summer as were sailboats and warm breezes. The women called themselves *The Beachcombers*, a tightly knit group, the watchtower for the more adventurous of us. Mother rarely visited Fowlers, and once we reached a certain age we much preferred she be at home on the other end of a bellow when we burst through the door, announcing to all that we were home. Not that we were in a position to expect or demand such a thing, but her presence in the house gave us a sense of ease; her nearness allowed us to be children. She knew that.

Criterion for any venture was timed on the tide, which made the foray for sand dollars easier on the lungs if we waited for the water to ebb to its lowest point. Otherwise, it was an impossible dive at high tide—too much of the briny deep to deal with, too much like the sea—deep, powerful, and *in-charge*. Shallow was good. A little pocket of the disk-like crustaceans managed to maintain a foothold in their sandy bed, despite the generations of foragers—*and is still there, to this day.* Each sand dollar was fit to burst with Christian symbolism, etched atop with, what looked like, a single poinsettia, and when broken open yielded teeny shells that resembled doves, the quintessential island Christmas tree decoration.

Low tide exposed the treasure trove of the island, the crab pond. It was a nook in which we spent hours prospecting beneath barnacle-covered rocks, under the bed of blue mussel shells, collecting whatever struck our fancy. There were, most assuredly, others like it on the island. We just never visited them.

The most highly prized, chance discovery was the trashed, broken, blue Magnesia bottles, pieces of blue glass worn smooth rolling in, and out on countless tides, pieces that were added to the previous year's array. Baby crabs scrambled for the closest haven, and delicate Chinese hats doggedly hung to the rocks as we prodded at them. There were gobs of empty hats available amongst the blue mussels—no need to mess with the living. We came upon a baby lobster—but only once. He was awful *cunnin'*, and it spawned conversation about the days when they actually swarmed the shoreline, when the Indians summered here. A grownup told us about it. That made it gospel.

A kingdom come fell to us, awesome days filled with sought after camaraderie, idle conversation, seaweed bubble snapping contests, simply gazing outward to sea, and to think, we owned it all—that is until the tide came in up over the huge ledges and boulders twice a day. We then simply turned our attention to all of that water, turned the ledges into springboards for belly whoppers, cannon balls, and used them as an anchor for timid dog paddlers. Water, straight in from the ocean—icy enough to make our skin hurt, chilled us until our teeth chattered uncontrollably, turned our lips blue, a signal to literally bury our bodies in the warm sand dune, just up above the beach for a half-hour. That is the only time we ever went up into the sand dune. Who put all that sand up there anyway? We owe him! *That condition, with blue lips and chattering teeth, is called hypothermia, though we didn't call it anything back then. The parental directive was simple. "When you get too cold, lay in the sand," a directive, voiced only once. No one had to be reminded.*

When the old-timers, *who* ***we*** *knew as old timers*, were young, they said an old-timer, by the name of Fowler willed the use of the beach to the islanders, for an eternity it said—even if the beach passed hands—heaven forbid! Dr. Marchand from Canada owned Southside Beach. He never acted like he owned it. He just owned it—and the islanders continued to use it, as had each past generation, freely, as though public domain.

Like gazelles we were—running the rocks at incredible speeds with nary a stumble or a slither into the seaweed, nimble footed as we flew around the water's edge of Mount Hunger—barefoot, always barefoot. Shoes? Those were heaved in the closet the day school let out. That we never miscalculated the speed and the distance between the rocks, and shattered every bone in our nimble bodies was clearly due to the *Divine Superintendence,* which hovers over Casco Bay. *Today, as I trip up over the top step of the cellar stairs, and stumble headlong into the kitchen, I sigh—pull from this tender memory, and have a good laugh.*

Bernice Veschey, an esteemed member of the Beachcombers who had a lovely cottage on the Ridge Road, was a vacationing art teacher from New York City with ties to the island. An invitation arrived at our house, one she sent to all the little *Westend* girls for an elegant repast, a proper tea party to be hosted by her antique dolls. Ann Marie escorted me and we arrived in our best summer dresses, my dolls gussied up for the occasion, too. They were, after all, the guests of honor and were given seats on little chairs all over the lawn to bide the time with her magnificent porcelain collection. The table was set with a spectacular floral centerpiece, linen napkins, a silver tea set, and real china teacups. This was my first proper tea party, replete with finger sandwiches. I didn't have to hide the bread crust. It was already cut away. My hats off to the chef! The pièce de résistance was a creation I'd never eaten before, an angel cake that was tenderly cut with two forks. Wasn't that a lovely thing to do? Her summer home was really quite intriguing—*in that all of the rooms in her house had sinks set in every corner.*

Hot summer lightening storms had several year 'round residents very nervous, for good cause. Bolts did strike one particular ledge down by the church on the *Eastend*, more often than any other spot on the island. Cars, filled with apprehensive passengers, drove slowly around the island, waiting for the storm front to move through. They believed themselves safe and insulated from lightening bolts, if inside a car, but I never quite understood that if they were petrified of being struck, why did the women always have their recently, washed, wet hair done up in crisscrossed, metal, bobby-pins?

Tillie and Lawrence Rich often ambled by our house on a lightening inspired tour, stopping to bide-a-while until the clouds parted. Tillie carried an invisible pocket of time into which she extracted snippets from the days when she, then the little Ross girl, scampered up the walk to buy our grandmother's candy. She bubbled about it to us through the car window, eyes sparkling, looking up the walkway whilst she drew upon the tender memory. Plainly, she came away from it with abundantly more than a piece of confection. Her fondness for my grandmother was apparent, a partiality which she passed onto her children and grandchildren simply by osmosis.

Certain island families appear to have an extra measure of attachment between them, one that seemingly comes from out of nowhere, its genesis—oft times veiled, as with Susan's and mine. As like as not, ours was forged back when her mother Adeline was orphaned, when my grandmother opened her heart and home to the child to help fill a void. Maria knew well the sorrows of being a parentless child and the emotions of a survivor. Fresh to budding friendships on the island today are Lawrence and Tillie's great granddaughters and Maria's great-great granddaughter, and now they will know from whence this, once upon a time connection was fashioned—between the little Ross girl and an old woman who sold her candy—one smile that challenged the other as to whom was the most pleased—the giver, or the receiver. It was a wise investment on Maria's part, one that the little Ross girl had the presence of mind to reinvest.

Run-A-Way

Uncle Johnny's rendition of *"God Bless America,"* which incidentally, he saved exclusively for bawling kids, was directed at me on a day when a good sob felt worthwhile. His intentional singing was infuriating, but it worked—redirected my attention. Looking straight into his eyes I dramatically declared that I was running away from home, especially away from him and his damnable singing. With the contents of my top drawer inside a busted suitcase I stormed out of the house, down over the hill without nary a protest from any of them. To the contrary, Mom, Dad, and Uncle told me to have a good time. Where else did a small island runaway have to go, but to the end of Ponce's landing—to sit—dangle feet off the end of the wharf—careful not to lose my shoes in the water—careful not to get splinters in my bum, and sat—and sat! Not one single car passed by the *Downfront*, the island very quiet, but for the strident cry of a crow, the bay also empty of traffic except for a one lunger headed towards Portland. Looking in the distance across towards Falmouth, the snow was visible atop Mount Washington. All tolled these clues—including the shoes *on* my feet, pointed out that it was a Sunday afternoon, mid fall.

A visit with someone might be in order, perhaps—far, far away—down on the *Eastend*, but the last time I made the attempt, the breakneck speed at which I took the New Hill was a near disaster. The miniature two-wheel bike was constructed without breaks, so that when it coasted, the pedals continued to turn with the speed of the wheels. My intention was to walk the bike down over the New Hill, but I rode the upper crest a little too long, and it quickly turned into an out of control flight down over the steep hill—pedals spinning so fast that had a foot or an ankle been any where near the pedals, something—on my body would have been badly damaged. Was the bike going to be able to take the sharp turn at the base of the hill, or was it in fact, going to wipe out at the base and end up on the rocks of Harbor de Grace? Hoo-wee! Was I flying! Miraculously, there were no cars coming either way and by Divine Superintendence, the bike made the left turn onto level road—and then wiped out. I walked away from that one with my heart pounding in my ears. I examined *skun-up* knees and tested weakened legs for the long walk home—the long way around. A far-away visit would have to wait for a JC Higgins with a good set of brakes, but if I wanted one of those beauties I would have to get the lead out and make some money.

For now—it was time for my older sister to cease and desist being the boss of me, and I'd had it with the teasing from the others, because one more tease and I was going to pound on someone. A growling stomach signaled the end of the self-imposed exile, the walk back up over the hill, a study in procrastination. Minutes were frittered away in front of the house with Jennifer and Johnifer, Uncle's two mutts—any excuse to keep from trudging up the path with that foolish suitcase in my hand. The amble on by the dining room windows, where everyone was sitting, was inevitable, but done so—not with head down, but with nose stuck high in the air—*resignation with an attitude.* To be an island runaway was an oxymoron, because every inch of the island was home.

Serious bouts with bad judgment rarely brewed among the young people or old people as far as I knew, though one might ask—at that age, how far did I know? Raiding vegetable gardens was the most egregious offence that I knew to happen where policeman, Bunker Johnson[117], discussed it with the parents of the boys involved, and all parties concerned decided that the boys would spend a day at the jail. What jail? Well, I'll be! There they were—two cells, hidden way out behind the fire engines at the fire barn, and here I thought I knew every nook on the island. Bunker was tight-lipped about any nefariousness, but

---

[117] (Bunker) George Johnson

not the island's grapevine, the All Seeing Eye—it never slept, and knew everything about everyone, their grandfather, and the old, twice removed bunch on your mother's side.

Another summer season slid into place and Ann Marie involved me in full-time baby sitting on the mainland, at the beach home of a dentist, only steps from the sands of Old Orchard Beach. Since the age of eight, sitting was expected of us. I learned the ropes, shadowed Ann Marie for two days, and then I went solo. However, this type of sitting asked much more of me than I had to give at the moment, and the couple needed to spend more money for an older person, one who was willing to absorb the dentist's caustic nature, and bratty attitude. Men with bratty attitudes were foreign to me, made me uneasy. Ergo the mainland job was short-lived. Back on the island, Mom watched me unpack the suitcase that was filled one-third with clothing, two-thirds with popular song-hit word books and movie magazines, a slight indication as to the level of maturity of the ten-year old who initially packed the suitcase.

The Worst Storm Since…'38

Fran Ricker was alone in their Portland apartment, comforting a four-week old baby, shoring up her two older children, Bobby and Lainy, throughout a storm of severe intensity, one that dumped twenty inches of snow in thirty-six hours. Gale winds piled the white stuff heavily around their doors, buried the entire coast in twenty-foot drifts. People were trapped on the highways; cars were buried, with a couple more feet atop for good measure. Two hundred people, stranded on Route One south of Biddeford, were rescued by train and brought to Union Station for safety. Those requiring hospitalization were transported by toboggan. Portland was brought to it knees by February of '52's storm. [cv]

Bobby worked to fine tune a short wave radio, listening to the fishermen talk, trying to catch any transmission from his father's trawler, the *Ethylena*, Otis Thompson's able, ninety-foot, Eastern-rigged dragger. News accounts reported seas running at 60 foot. *That is incredible for this area, unless they were talking about far, far off shore. Fishermen would say, "There was not enough fetch 'round heah to make up a sixty-foot sea. Maybe outside—way-y-y outside. Maybe! Realistically, it was more like 20 to 30 foot seas. A wall of water 20 to 30 feet high is nothing' to mess with—and will get your attention some quick."*

Harris Company's trawler, the *Vandal*, broke away from the dock, swept towards, and fetched up on the Portland Bridge, along with the *Alice M. Doughty*, the *Vandal*, another vessel that Will worked on from time to time—new her well. Coast Guard ships Acushnet and Yakutat headed out. Two T-2 tankers, the *SS Fort Mercer* and the *SS Pendleton* had broken in half. They rescued sixty-two from the foundering ships and the water. Five lives were lost. [cvi]

Casco Bay Lines called, looking for Will, needed help with an engine, surprised that Will was not in yet, but not to worry, everything will be alright. Had Fran ignored the news accounts, or Bobby's short wave radio she would have stemmed it a little better, wouldn't have been up all night pacing, actually quite petrified, but she heard it all and a very dark anxiety washed through her thoughts. The clock ticked off the hours; the where, when, what ifs, ran through her mind. What kind of a job could she keep with a newborn if left without a husband? She worked herself into quite a state after a sleepless night, waiting anxiously until the clock reached seven to call his brother Ray, who upon accepting a measure of her anxiety threw it right back at her with the response, *"Jesus Christ, ain't he in yet?"* Envisioning Will at the bottom of the Atlantic, Ray's jolted reaction was not what she needed, nor wanted to hear. As she hoped would happen, Ray easily connected with the vessel and gathered enough news to call back. The boat had lain out all night in the storm, laden with a hole full of fish, waiting for morning. Those were long, thrashing hours in which Will tied himself to the engine to keep from being thrown about the engine room. With a high bow, she jogged into the seas on a slow bell, and was presently making her way in. Nerve-wracking, overdue fishing trips were on a short hawser. That was it! Will was in-for another career change.

Soft-spoken Robert William, Junior—Will, as he was called, didn't make much of a fuss about the trip, but did make an excellent career change, ended his days of commercial fishing in the fifties, when still a young man. His chief engineer's diesel license served him well for a decade as port engineer at Casco Bay Lines, then another near-decade on Lake Champlain running the ferries that ran from Vermont to upstate New York. With a 1,500-horse power, chief's license in his duffle bag, he joined his son, Bobby on the ocean to round out another half decade of his career out of Boston, on the oil tankers Karen Tibbetts and Christian Reinauer.

The man was one in a special breed, one of a unique generation of engineers. He was the type that could stand on a deck and gauge what was happening in the engine room by the vibrations he felt through the bottom of his shoes—a dependable, unassuming man—just the kind of engineer one wants at hand when in the middle of the Storm of '52. It was the better part of discretion though, never to bring up the subject of the South Portland school budget in Will's presence, if, that is, one wished to preserve his soft-spoken, unassuming image.

***

Television did not arrive on the island until I was ten in '52. The snowy, black and white signal, intermittently, came from Boston and on a certain Sunday afternoon, when the signal was coming in strong, Sammy Kuntz's made a spur of the moment call to invite us to the house to watch Lux Video Theater—before the signal dissolved. It was a live play in which the very first image that I experienced was that of a woman being strangled with a scarf. M-m-m-m! That was a bit much for the maiden voyage into the land of TV. I wasn't impressed.

Only a select few had televisions in their homes, and Mrs. Barrett took advantage of the situation, thought that we should be exposed to a once in a lifetime event, the coronation of Queen Elizabeth II of England. Up to that point television was basically filled with a daily dose of the teary-eyed *Queen for a Day,* the stringed puppets of *Howdy Doody,* and *Pinky Lee's* buffoonery. Grades four through eight traipsed over to Vi and John Canning's house on the *Westend,* gathered around the living room television and along with the world followed the pomp and circumstance televised to us live, and on the spot. The boys yawned their way through *the once in a lifetime*, though once they discovered John's girlie calendar in his sitting room, the trip became worthwhile. Thought to be out of earshot, Vi was seething about the game warden, Harold Ricker. John got caught with some *shorts* and Vi raved on, and on—wishing terrible things upon the warden, something about cutting off an important part of Harold's anatomy. She got over it...and we became witnesses a historical English milestone.

Saturday mornings, I usually ran up to cousin, Suzanne's to watch a *Hoot Gibson* cowboy movie on her new TV, little realizing that there was tug of war taking place. Aunt Frances and Uncle Charlie took me aside and quietly asked if I would talk Suzanne into going outside to play. Uncle Charlie wanted to enjoy the big league baseball game that was now being televised. Since when, did adults have to ask permission to use the television? Who was in control here? I didn't work very hard at it, amused with the scenario, toyed with the thought of the shoe being on the *other* foot—of *my father* asking Suzanne to take *me* out to play so that *he* could watch Oral Robert's Tent Show. That would be the day pigs fly.

The air was filled with anticipation when our black and white floor model television arrived at the house in '54, but not filled with quite the same level of excitement as years back when the Hammond organ was squeezed through the back door. We, who were weaned on radio, were enthralled by the pairing of radio voices to the faces of those who made the jump to live TV. We found Jack Benny, Eve Arden, George Burns, Gracie Allen, and a host of others. Yet, this new entertainment tool had a different feel, very different from the island of our own imagination—no better—just different. Our use of the TV was monitored and measured; if we shirked our tasks, Dad simply pulled a tube out of the television and hid it. His ploy worked fairly well. Imagine not having television for the first dozen years of one's life.

That would make a fabulous study. A call to my three island classmates is warranted, for they too were not informed by TV-land during the first dozen, impressionable years of their lives, either. We're twelve years behind the journalese game, with an

outside chance that by being denied twelve years of information,
conceivably we've been left with a warped psyche—and don't
know it. They need to know about this.

Perhaps present day TV can make up for the lost years with its
hundreds of channels, tri split screens, changing lines of
information, rolling scrolls of developing news that crawl along
at the very bottom of the screen. Pundits do a whip-snap job of
talking over, through, and around each other, spin, they call it—
and then there are the small stamps of weather, changing
temperatures, time, and stock quotes handily glued onto any
vacant spot available. Now, that just might do it, though it's a
challenge to keep up with, and absorb the avalanche of
information, and may I apologetically point out a problem,
which could put a wrench in the works. It's just something that I
happened to notice. Excluding the nay saying news, nearly every
program, service announcement, commercial, and weather
report appears to be a teeny bit top heavy in negative
information. Has anyone else noted this, or is it just me? When
did they stop calling a northeast storm, a Northeaster? It's a
Killer Storm now, complete with apocalyptic background music.
What is it, with this heavy dose of service announcements, which
presents us with a brand-new anxiety for each night of the
week—fifty-two weeks worth? They ask if your refrigerator is
killing you; is your furnace killing you—and how about those
killer trucks! Two hundred and sixty new worries per year are
heralded for us to add to our own collection. It's a healthy dose
of angst to absorb, by any measure. Thank heavens for the
commercial break.

Oh-oh! Advertising scare tactic #1: Tire advertisement, which
depicts a car driving in a torrential rainstorm and an image of a
baby's face is flashed across the screen. Guess we know who is
going to buy those tires. Scare tactic #2 warns that you'd better
eat "our brand" of low fat, high fiber "whatever" to keep from
having a heart attack that you might—may—or will develop in
ten years. And cruciferous vegetables are what we need to
forestall the cancer that is lurking out there—or perhaps in
there. Remember cruciferous vegetables...with a touch of lemon
butter,.eaten because they tasted good?

*Well! I tried my best. It was not an easy assignment, under the circumstances. All of that angst clashes too heavily with a mindset that started out in a crib painted with lead-based paint, and would snarl-up with someone who lived in a house atop a ledge that most surely exuded plumes of radon. Hand wringing would not easily align with one who did not have the worry about being stolen, and certainly angst would be in conflict with a daredevil who rode a running board—**one handed**, and took the New Hill on a bike without a helmet or brakes (but only once). Raised without television, and having a disposition that upholds eating dessert first—preferably something covered in dark, bittersweet chocolate does not make one a good candidate for the worrywarts of America. I will be lucky not to be pilloried.*

Edgar Clarke's Night Off
1954-55

Long Island's school children, under the direction of Mrs. Barrett, produced one of the biggest variety shows that ever hit the island, and in anticipation of a large turnout, held it on the big stage at the Navy's auditorium. Part of it was shades of an Al Jolson minstrel show with tambourines and an interlocutor. Other segments were skits, tap dancing, group songs, musical instruments, and vocals. The big dress rehearsal came up a total disaster. On the big night, we all peeked from behind the stage's curtain, out onto a full house, then pulled our act together, and with my mother as the accompanying pianist, commenced to put on a whopping show. Adrenaline is a remarkable chemical and plenty was flowing that night.

Because Cousin Suzanne took dancing lessons at the Dorothy Mason School of Dance in Portland, Aunt Francis made certain that she owned more than one pair of tap shoes, plus a closet full of glitzy recital costumes. Geneva Morton was the other student chosen for her raw talent tap dance number, a chip right off the old block for those who were ever around her dad, Specky when he performed his signature, knee slapping *cloppy* dance. We loved that dance, made him do it every time he came to the house. While Suzanne performed a beautiful rendition of a temperate tap, skip and hop routine, alongside of her, Geneva took off like a shot in the borrowed tap shoes and ill-fitted costume, legs flailing at a hundred miles an hour.

Edgar Clarke, Everett and Annie's son, wasn't going to be stuck with the store that night and miss the performance of all of those kids. He was sold on it, so much so, that he closed Clarke's store at five-thirty to join the sell-out crowd that filled the auditorium. That was unprecedented, for it was the first time that the store ever closed before midnight. During the performances, especially of the littlest performers, the crowd came up out of their seats with a roar, smiles flashing from the front row on the floor, up to the last seat in the balcony—and on that night the island delighted in itself.

First run movies were shown at that same recreation hall. Walter Cushing, the Navy's fire chief, gave us, by invitation only, compliments to see 3-D movie about gargantuan ants with Susan, a treat because civilians could not attend unless by invitation. We looked foolish, an entire audience wearing peculiar, white, cardboard glasses made with one red and one blue lens, glasses that effectively rendered the monstrous ants free to leap out of the screen at us. Hollywood must have been testing out new way of producing colors with a swashbuckling, high sea drama that was heavy in blue. Everything in the movie was blue, Virginia Mayo's eyes, and her magnificent gowns, huge precious stones in her jewelry, the all-consuming sky, and expanses of water. Those Navy kids had everything!

The Navy's bowling alleys opened to island league use, a chance to make a dollar, a job that paid ten cents a set, to clear and set pins. We learned quickly which players sent bowling balls down the alley at the speed of light, the kind that exploded on impact sending pins in all directions—even over into the dead alleys where we sought refuge when the aforementioned bowler came up to bat. Hazard pay was never considered, but was certainly in order. They tipped us instead.

Hurricane Carol, Crinolines & the Esprit de Corps

The equator's ventilating system spewed out hurricanes to plague at us, a wild one hitting the coast in August of '54 while Dad was on business in New York. The fervency of the *Esprit de Corps*,[118] the closely-knit gaggle of summer and island kids was not deterred by the driving winds of *Carol*, in that a dozen of us went where some formidable storm's action was taking place—at back of the island on Southside Beach. Though the storm's center was twenty miles inland, the winds continued to build, had such strength that we literally leaned backwards into it. As though held by an invisible fetter we dared the gale to hold us upright. It took the dare! Our faces were sandblasted, so badly that we finally gave-up on our hazardous undertaking, barged into the wind and back to our respective homes before the rain came down in torrents, and before the wind climbed to eighty miles an hour.

The water pump became inoperable when the electricity went off, something everyone expects to happen on the island—black outs. It usually didn't take much for that to happen, but in these winds it was a foregone conclusion—make ready. Mom did—filled all the pails, pans and containers that were handy with water, but if worst came to worst one of us could run over to Frank and Hulda's and use their old outdoor hand pump. Candles were handy by, in the same spot in the cupboard as always, ready for such an occasion. She could still cook on a kitchen stove that was run on kerosene, but the refrigerator door was off limits, couldn't be opened at every whim. It needed to be kept closed to keep food from spoiling. By the number of trees that came down, it didn't look as though electricity would be back any time soon, possibly for days. The house was pummeled, as was our sense of safety. The mainland wasn't bearing it any better.

The storm reeked havoc all the way inland to Augusta, hammering at towns that rarely saw hurricane action. To the dismay of Bostonians, the steeple atop the historical Old North Church was toppled, hundreds of giant elm trees in Portland, and

---

[118] Esprit de Corps -Spirit of a body of people, group spirit.

274

hundreds of boats were laid waste by its fury in the gristly, above-normal tides, *including* Dad's pretty sleek vessel—the one that had no name. She parted her fasts, and quickly ended up on the rocks at the base of Ponce's Landing, a total loss. He was going to be so sad.

Ponce's Landing was taking on some healthy wave action, and at times, awash. Portland's waterfront flooded out. While tourists and towns-people held their breath, Old Orchard's famous Casino pier withstood the battering of the blast, but how many more before she caves-in. Also busy keeping up with blow-downs, all Naval personnel housed inside *The Area* were better off than most. At least they had their own generator plant.

Deer Point on Chebeague was the storm lookout for a couple of fourteen-year olds. Bobby Ricker and his friend walked their bikes in the ruts of an old overgrown road, through a footpath, up to a spot overlooking the shoreline. When they crested the rocks, they came upon a classical ocean drama, the *Sirius,* fighting the waves, its venturesome skipper working to get the vessel somewhere into another lea. It was snotty at his Chandlers Cove mooring, and knowing him, Bob thought, it was a great excuse to take on the elements, just for the hell of it.

Less than two weeks later, Edna, a more torrential hurricane hit the storm worn area. Between the two giant blasts, mariners were kept ragged trying to render their own and other men's vessels safe. President Eisenhower declared Maine a disaster area. By the second storm the summer people had boarded up and left for the season.

Five punts of progressive sizes were built from wood that Dad milled on a huge, formidable, milling saw out in the back yard, a rig that was a hundred times more intimidating that Mom's Easy wringer washer. The punts were laid in a row, up side down on sawhorses awaiting several gallons of primer; two coats of white oil based paint, and our artistic talent. Never blue paint! Fishermen didn't paint boats blue. The color was deemed unlucky. Carmen finished her job first. My paintbrush was very busy indeed, keeping time with some1955 Latin song hit. It took only three extension cords strung through a window of the house for the company of the radio, perfect backup music for painting boats. Dad and Carmen watched this study in procrastination from the kitchen window—he amused by the antics. My younger sibling, who was less amused, knew what was coming. *"She's never going to finish that boat Sis,"* he said to her, a fact that she could have easily predicted to him. *"Go help her,"* he added. Truly! It would have gotten done. I wasn't out to impress anyone. The day was beautiful. Life was good*!*

I'm surprised that Carmen didn't pull the plug on the radio with that one. But oh how I wish he'd never asked that of her. She never forgot it. I have been forty-five years being castigated—as though his request was my sin—punishable for a lifelong reminder of this relic of a memory.

She and I were a bit fearless and foolhardy when testing the newly built boats. The bell buoy out in the middle of the channel looked like a decent row as we took off in our own respective punt. This would be the day we discovered what a strong current was all about, one that greatly tested our tinsel. It forced us in the direction of Cousins Island and we, more than struggled to reverse direction. We decided to tie Carmen's boat to mine so as not to get separated, but the harder we rowed the more ground we lost, managing only to get back and a-hold of the bell buoy, catch our breath, and contemplate our fate.

All eyes on the front of the island continuously survey the bay and we, glad of the habit, looked over to see a punt headed in our direction, one of the *Esprit de Corps*, Peter Kilgore, a member of the Beachcomber's brood. Carmen's punt was tied off to the buoy, and she waited while I rowed back to the raft at Ponces, in tow behind Peter. She must have looked more capable of hanging-to. I waited on the raft with his dog T-Bone while he went back for Carmen who was an anxious wreck by the time he got back to her. Neither of us dared tell Mother through our embarrassment, although we were certain some islander would. Word always got back. We never pulled that one again—even though it vicariously got the attention of one of the cutest summer boys on the island. In hindsight, there always seemed to be a good side to most problematic situations.

I never saw a punt as small as the fifth one that he built, a perfect size for any five-year old that was handy-by. It was adorable, and was seen all over the place, under Ponces, around the raft. The sight of a five-year old in a punt nearly gave the Catholic nuns the vapors. Cupping their hands to their mouths, they called down from the wharf, *"You come in young man this minute...You shouldn't be out there by yourself."* The response bellowed from below was, *"Keep the faith Sisters."* Where in heaven's name did that come from? On second thought, it had the distinct ring of something Dad would say, but the voice was littler, and Dad was over there on the *Billy G.*

Years and years later, Murdoch and Catherine Newman painted that very same little punt blue, of all colors, filled it with soil and a batch of frothing pink petunias, and set it in front of their cottage. Nice touch!

Bait Barrel Duty

Fowler's beach and my favorite summer gang were put on hold occasionally, on the days when I caught the brass ring, a rendezvous with a bait barrel—my turn to go hauling with Dad. Of the many jobs aboard, baiting traps was a given. Pegging claws was a reasonable task. Measuring for counters a biggie—but toting heavy wooden traps around the boat was out of my league, a limitation that doubled his workload and slowed us down—but I *'spose* that I was better than nothing!

Some days we seemed to be out there just changing the water in the lobster traps, some days there were fair catches. Someone set-over his string of traps, and I watched to see what he would do. I didn't know if they had done it on purpose or if it was an oversight. He didn't seem to care. Grabbing his fish knife, he cut their line, led it under ours, tied two overhand knots, pulled them tight and let it drop, just as quickly as that. I asked the obvious question. They set it over yours; why not just cut the stringer in two halves? He said, *"Fishermen have the memory of a singed cat."* Decent answer!

Just for once on my watch, finding the bait barrel brimming-full of fresh bait, instead of three-quarters empty with very rotted fish, would have been different. Status quo being what it was, I was consigned to hitch up onto the rim of the barrel, balance precariously on my stomach in order to reach the fish at the bottom of the bait barrel. With the bait needle in my right hand, the other way down into the brine, I snagged some red fish carcasses, held my breath as long as I could, skewing fish onto the needle through their lifeless eyes, until the needle was full. Finally I surfaced for fresh air. How many stringers did he say he intended to haul?

Sometimes we hauled quietly, without much of a dialogue; it was too hard to compete with the engine. Other days we bellowed for the entire trip, yakked about fabled subjects, trivia, simplistic occurrences, such as when my bedroom door rattled in the casing, with just a slight clunk, which he said, announced that the wind had turned and was coming off the land, portending a change in the weather. Slight *clunks* were reliable. *"A mackerel sky—will be not more than twenty-four hours dry." "When the deer are in gray coat in October, expect a severe winter." "Hark, I hear the asses bray. We shall have some rain today."* Barring the asses, how does one practically apply all this good stuff? If I had any intelligence, I'd have planned to become a weather person, on the local six-o'clock news.

Traps baited, lined up, and now ready to set, he heaved the first one off the starboard side, put the engine in forward, knocked a couple more off, then we watched as the other seven traps snapped off the stern while the boat tooled along at quite a clip. I prudently stayed up forward, well clear of the trap warp as it whistled off the stern, and believe me—it was humming. It was a fitting time to be awfully careful, a time not to have feet, or any other essential part of one's body anywhere near the line as it came taunt.

The palms of my hands were a mess of scrapes and cuts from the fish bait. Repeated washes in the brine didn't help the situation, smarted like hell. Dad kindly informed me that I was building my character. I shot him a flitting side-glance to silently inform him that I was not as inclined to agree. He caught the glance, laughed, and then pointed the bow towards Portland.

More bait was needed so he hooked her up for a quick trip to the Portland waterfront where Scup Olsen let loose a decent pile of fresh redfish carcasses down a chute onto the deck. I

278

wondered why they called him Scup. One of the fish used for bait was actually called a scup, a *stenotomus chrysops* to a student of marine biology. 'Doubt anyone of that biological ilk ever hung upside-down in a *skanky* bait barrel.

Scup's fish were fresh; their eyes were very blue. I used a pitchfork to heave them into the bait barrel adding a liberal amount of rock salt as the barrel filled. Seagulls amassed overhead, jockeying for a chance to swoop off with one of them—so many filled the space aloft that it was sheer luck that I wasn't *christened*. The frenzy above, around, and below conjured up imagery from the radio program, the one from years back that gave me such nightmares, *The Birds* on Lux Radio Theater. They were persistent!

Waterfront and island nicknames like Scup gave a characteristic flavor to the individual, singular to the person so named. Hen, Specky, or Pood weren't found in the phone book, although Henry, George and Elliot were. How ya doin' Old Chum? Be right with you Old Dee-ah—Old Stock, all gentle salutations applied in lieu of a qualifying tag. Not everyone was amiably addressed. Ole Baastid was a favorite negative, Numb-ass another. Generally, men didn't swear or cuss in the presence of women or girls, and it behooves me to recall Dad ever swearing, or cussing—in front of us or in back of us either.

Hauling lasted all day and I sighed with relief when we put the lobsters in a lobster-car, a big trap built with wide slats that floated off the base of Ponce's. Under the impression the day was done, I looked up to find us headed towards Diamond Island Cove where, on that day, the herring were running. The *Jolly Roger* was at anchor with nets out, dories all over the place, the crew hauling in nets filled with a teeming school of fish that had probably been driven in by some large predator with a mouth full of sharp teeth. Dad must have felt like a mess of herring—the man was forever on a busman's holiday.

Ritchie MacVane, the captain of the boat, had just put some herring on to fry down in the little hole-of-a-galley and invited us aboard to join him. He was fussing because he dropped some of the fish into the barrel of rock salt and couldn't decipher which of them was inedible, so he gave up and fried them all, leaving us with fair warning. The fish had obviously just come out of the water, were cooked perfectly, and so sweet to the taste that I ate to my heart's content, ripping the bones out of the fish in one fair swoop.

I asked about Cow Island and how it came by that name. It was a back-when story...1700s, early 1800s when they penned cows over there. That was a no-brainer, but I had to ask. Unceremoniously, I spit the mouthful of rock-salted fish out into my hand, hoping that the mouthful of salt wouldn't spoil the taste of the ones that had preceded it. My facial contortions set both men into a gale and feigning indignation I huffed out of the galley, up onto the deck, and could not have timed it better. The water was boiling with fish as the men in dories began to haul the nets up tight, the churning fish creating an incredible billowing blanket of iridescence foam. Afternoon light caught the colors of the loose scales that mixed and mingled with the froth, creating a sight like none other that I had ever seen. This piece of New England lore was a once in a lifetime, and I settled comfortably into the railing to see the process of bringing them aboard to completion.

We had to paint punts and buoys, go hauling with him, spend time upside-down inside a bait barrel, cede some of our wardrobe to bait juice, and scrape the bottom of the boat's hull. We joined in on his pursuits, not he in on ours—although we thought the activities belong to us. Men of that genre are not thought of as having been involved with their children, yet as is apparent, he engaged us all of the time.

The "Billy G."

Sundays were the choice days of summer. We flew out of the church door before the last amen, changed into bathing suits in lightening speed, and headed down over the ramp to the raft. Dad was waiting with the *Billy G*, his new, but rather seasoned lobster boat, ready to drop the lines as soon as Mother arrived.

Up to this point we sailed directly across to the deserted Basket Island, which was Dad's favorite spot for a Sunday outing, but someone bought it and that ended that. We tried Cow

Island, but only twice, then rerouted to another uninhabited island on the far side of Chebeague. Moshier's Island constituted a longer ride, but he did not seem to mind, as a matter of fact, he really put himself out for these Sunday junkets, and usually invited another island family to join us. Uncle Johnny brought his wife Muriel, and she brought her two children and her signature sense of humor.

As though we didn't have enough food on the boat—for those not in a lobster frame of mind, and that did happen, the Spa was offering Italian sandwiches, an invention of Portland's Italian community. The sandwiches were first offered by the Amato family at the turn of the century, so say the locals, and were made up of sliced ham, cheese, pickles, bell peppers, diced onions, wedges of tomatoes, and black olives dotted across the top. Every bit of it was stuffed in a foot-long, soft, Italian roll, and sprinkled with a touch of good olive oil. There have been fortunes made from the humble Italian sandwich, a creation that, evidently, is inclusive to the southern part of this state, and not a mile further. It was tried in Florida, but didn't work. The Amato, DiPietro, and DiBiase families come to mind as the forerunners to every corner store that carries them today. Mrs. DiBiase finely chopped her veggies, meat and cheese, which made the sandwich more manageable. Geneva's rendition was exceptional because she sliced everything paper-thin on the meat-slicing machine, including the tomatoes, onions, and green peppers. By doing so, her Italians were light, airy, and when bitten into, the vegetables didn't plop out all over our lap.

A budging contest broke out between Ann, Carmen, and me for the favorite perch, all attempting to claim the furthest point forward on the bow. Dad killed that argument by simply hooking the boat up to an incredible eight knots. Even in this poky state, he managed to make the boat slat against the waves, forcing us to scramble for a place to perch, lest we lose our footing. I wanted to ride in the punt that was in tow, a great ride I thought, skating back and forth in the wake as we breezed down the bay past Chebeague, but he wouldn't go for it. Conversations were limited to bellows due to lack of a missing muffler on the engine, and there was no breathing either, because of the fumes from the exhaust and ripe bait barrels on deck, the very reason we fought for the place on the bow.

Great Moshier's cove was deceiving. Unlike Basket's ice-cold, deep-water access at high tide, the parameter around the cove at Moshier was shallow for a considerable distance, creating a need to anchor far from shore so that the boat would not ground out on an ebbing tide. Anchor in place, the engine silenced, Mom, the lobsters, clams, corn, salads, desserts, and huge pots were neatly packed in the punt for the row to shore. Barring the pots and pans, she gave the appearance of a grand lady in an Impressionistic painting being rowed about the Thames, and just as pretty. Her smile was magnificent.

We children were relegated to disembark the best we could—no diving—too shallow, so we gently slid off the side of the boat into the warm, shallow water, swam until we finally touched bottom, guardedly touched—with great caution. The bottom of the inlet was made up of fine, tan, squishy silt, a place in which conservatively, thousands of horseshoe crabs of assorted and sundry sizes bred and resided. They were shaped like a horse shoe and had long, spear-like tails that stuck straight up in an attempt to ward off, in this case, the intrusion of an army of small feet. We sifted along through the silt and crabs until we made it to shore, never thinking too much about it, other than the cuteness of the teeny ones, and their strange appearance, that of the four-million-year old, prehistoric, arthropod that they were.

Cautiously, too, we gathered wood at the edge of a bumper crop of poison ivy, which distended up over the crests of the entire rocky shoreline of the island, ready to grab at us if given the chance. Dad built a fire in the rocks, on top of which he and Mom engineered a glorious meal, usually of boiled lobsters, corn on the cob with all the fixings. They had it down pat. Alternately, she fried the most succulent tasting raw lobster tails ever known to man in a big iron fry pan over an open fire. These were seemingly average, never-to-be-forgotten moments that culminated when the setting sun sent the signal to pack it up.

***

Wednesday night summer dances at the VFW in 1955-56 were Manna from Heaven; the Teenage Frolics were sent to feed the social welfare of the Island teens. Snappy Big Band sounds of Tommy Dorsey were replaced with the suave, string instrumentals of Percy Faith, Jane Froman supplanted by Patty Page, the Inkspots dislodged by the Platters, and crooners were succeeded by the likes of Bobby Darren. Mary and George Ross, *God love 'em*, took on this responsibility pro-bono-adolescent, just for the good of us, and in the thirteen years that they put on dances for the different generations of teens, they missed only two Wednesdays. They saw it black and white, saw a need, knew how to fill it, and in doing so, invested more than most to give several generations of teens a memory image to carry through life—and they did it—just because.

Along with Bill Haley and the Comets, and Chuck Barry's hits, we made the turn with the rest of the country into the new realm of Rock and Roll. Vestiges of the jitterbug were hanging-to, but about ready to be trounced by the Twist, the cha-cha, and dances of that ilk, those that did not require anybody leading anybody, and nobody holding nobody. But for us, the generation on the cusp—not quite yet, but thanks anyway. Smitten-time was about ready to usurp the tomboy stage in my circle of friends.

For some reason the guys kept to this side of the dungarees and tee shirt look, forsook the macho trend about ready to hit the national scene. The macho trend was not authentic garb unless they folded a cigarette package into the rolled up tee shirt sleeve. Not many of us smoked—yet. Nor—had the DA (duck's-ass) hairdo become the rage. Greased hair caught on with the guys, a look that actually didn't require grease, but in fact, bottles upon bottles of the manly gel, *Slick-um*. We languished in the preppy side of fashion for a time, girls in pedal pushers, cotton summer dresses, full cotton skirts, everything in the closet requiring three crinolines. On wash day, our back yard was filled with heavily starched crinolines, spread out on the grass to dry in the sun. The wardrobe was costing serious baby-sitting dollars and the quest to be in fashion took all of a minute to supplanted old values, cost me my long, sought-after JC Higgins with brakes. In lieu of the bike, money was spent on a poodle skirt, stiffer crinolines, pumps, white bucks, penny loafers and a half dozen bottles of white shoe polish.

As with the generation before us, we poured nickels into the jute-box at the Spa, adopted new dance steps brought to us by summer children, and, too, met every incoming boat. We felt it our duty to be at hand to attend the boat's line should the deckhand miss his mark—our absolute duty to pass the line to the boat on its departure. We had purpose, felt relevant, especially if fog shrouded the wharf. A huge brass bell hung on the front of the waiting room for such purposes. On hearing the Sabino's hesitant approach toward the end of Ponces, one of us grabbed the clapper and began a dialogue with the boat, an interchange between the brass bell, and the resonance of the boat's steam whistle. Back and to, back and to, the Sabino's horn practically upon us, though the boat remained hidden—back and to, until her bow poked through the curtain of fog. The captain quickly gave two bells to back her down then waved his appreciation to whoever carried on the exchange with him.

The Sabino slid into the dock. Down in the engine room a big hulk of a kid was assisting the engineer stoke coal, his first time at it, he said, and thought there was nothing to it—but complained that he had—thus far, singed every hair off both arms. Bobby leaned through a window on the lower deck, blue eyes sparkling back at the bevy of girls who were checking him out—the new guy—one who wore a tee shirt with a package of cigarettes rolled up in one sleeve, wore dungarees, and had a crop of black hair all slick-umed back in a DA. He was one of those Chebeague Island Rickers, a first cousin to the Long Island Ricker and Morton families, but now living in town. When the Sabino departed, we waited for the right moment and lept off a piling into the wake for a free ride on the propeller's wash.

Ponce's Landing was an unconventional hot spot, always packed—half the crowd made up of us, the Esprit de Corps. It was the place to be. Aunt Frances dressed me down for holding hands with Peter Kilgore—down on the wharf—in public! I suppose she had a right. Maybe it wasn't proper, but it seemed absolutely delightful to me. I was certain that she wailed it up over Garfield Street to blather her objections to Dad.

"I'm home," did not elicit the usual response when I blew through the backdoor on a warm summer's night following a

284

night of baby-sitting. Dead silence and an empty house greeted me, an unprecedented event, especially at that late hour. I couldn't settle in, made a round upstairs and down, and finally plopped down on back door stoop and waited—an hour or more, worried, and very agitated by the time the truck finally drove up. They swept up the walk, buoyant. Relieved that there was no problem, I graduated to indignation. They'd been on a moonlight cruise in the *Billy G*, under a hu-u-uge moon, out off the back of the island, on swells as big as all get out. They didn't have to elaborate about it while I was pouting over, what I perceived to be elementary nudges, pushing me out of the nest. "You can't have it all sis, Dad said, especially if you want hair spray, a Victoria, and the newest records."

***

Class pictures of the four 1956 graduates turned out nicely taken by a professional photographer who posed us beneath the birches in front of the school, with Gordon, Buddy, Sue and me in new duds—in shoes that gave us blisters. I'd never seen Gordon and Buddy in a suit. Spiffy! Store racks were jammed with dubby looking pastel taffeta dresses, each requiring an umbrella's worth of crinolines, and I searched until I unearthed a pink one that didn't look like a Sunday school dress, one that was, of course, color coordinated to Susan's blue creation. I longed to

Long Island Class of '56 (l to r): Bud Johnson, Roberta, Susan (Cushing), Gordon Stewart

be barefoot, but that was the least of my worries. We had to get real summer jobs and sure up for that daily trip to the city, to high school in the fall.

Ann Marie worked three summers for a well-to-do family on the mainland, and now that she had graduated from high school, Dad and she lined me up for the same job. Liken to the tinsel on the Christmas tree, everything that she did had a two hundred percent result, raising the bar for me. So with a shaky ego, I left my family, the island, let go of the Esprit de Corps, and tested my underpinnings.

Homesick! Was I ever! Binoculars helped, eyes pinched as I gazed across to the island at boat time, straining to pick out the recognizable forms on the wharf. They were there—poised atop a piling, ready to bail into the wake of the Casco Bay boat. I caught a glimpse of Dad on the *Billy G*, out hauling traps, and again on a Sunday just as they headed back into the dock after a trip to Moshier. A sudden twang plucked at something inside my chest. Growing up had little to do with feeling lighthearted and contented. Dad was smart to expose us to this grand way of life, to separate us from the island for a bit, and the forty dollars a week wasn't anything to sneeze at in 1956. The time had come to settle and begin to absorb the surroundings.

Monhegan race day was a gala affair in Casco Bay. Sailboats of every size and description converged, obliterating my view of the island. I knew that they would all be sailing past Fowler's Beach, tacking in close enough to talk to the kids out on the rocks. This was certainly a different perspective from which to view the beginning of the race, but I was not convinced it was a better one.

The younger men of the affluent family invited their close friends to sail with them, one of which was a vocal, and a very colorful Maine Maritime graduate, a master-captain, and very Irish. Good choice! Colorful stories! They swarmed all over the deck to make the sailboat ready for the traditional race, in which they'd entered in the first class, and then prepared to embark on their call to excellence, but not before a rousing game of touch football, and a traditional smorgasbord, for which the head of the family traditionally cooked a humongous steak outside on a grill. The cook was relieved of the duty that day. She didn't cook beef, or grill foods.

Nominal amounts of domestic work were expected of me when the maid and cook were in a pinch, but my major task was to don a bathing suit and swim with the twelve grandchildren, when they visited—appreciative that only four were invited over at any given time. For enlightenment, the staff made certain that I absorbed great gobs of etiquette and some stuck before my eyes glazed over. The worst offence that one could commit was to disclose the chutney hors d'oeuvre recipes to anyone, especially to my employer's dowager sister. Never heard of the word chutney, let alone knew what it was—to my inexperienced pallet. Let's see—the label read: North India—fruit, raisins, mangoes, sugar, vinegar, and lemon juice—a nicely packaged, very expensive relish that tasted oddly like the big crock of macerating fruit behind Mother's kitchen stove smelled—like home brew!

Learning curves had me on the run for a while. The maid taught me to serve borsch—from the left of the guest—with my right hand—to react when a guest laid the fork and knife upside-down across the top of the dinner plate, which was the unspoken signal to take the dish away—whoops—from the right this time—no-no-no, again with the right hand. Though I ate in the kitchen with the maid and cook, the manners in the formal dining room were in-force—sit straight, napkin folded in half on lap, left hand in lap, wait for the hostess to start. Remember, the soupspoon dips from the back of the spoon, right hand brings the spoon to you. In other words, Roberta do not lean over the plate—and don't slurp. It took forever to eat a bowl of soup. I much preferred the Chinese, pick-the-bowl-up routine—though I never employed the practice in their presence. During the three years there, I learned a whole new group of social graces that were spread amongst other useful tools and poignant discoveries.

Cook was straightforward, a softhearted young woman from Germany, my mentor from the get-go. She was quite successful at transforming work into a quasi-finishing school that rendered my week's pay an added benefit. Towards the end of the three-year tenure we discussed Carmen as my replacement, and they expressed contentment in having another three years with the same family of girls they'd employed now for six years running. Quite innocently I asked Cook why she prepared such a limited menu, exclusively chicken and fish, never beef—with an expectation that she would talk in terms of diet. Her voice took on a low and hesitant tone, and her answer puzzled me, as she made it clear that she never cooked anything else—ever. The air in her hometown of Auschwitz made her ill when she was a child, she said; the smell of certain foods made her ill. She looked for awareness, some kind of recognition on my face, but it was not there. The look on her face made me stop asking.

The significance of that conversation did not hit home until a few years later, when the Eichmann trials began in 1960, and when we looked into the face of a truly depraved man, Adolph Eichmann, a man who had lost his soul. The news was riveting. Incomprehensible ravages, within the ravages of World War II were coming to light, all of them new to me. Cook came to mind immediately. The reality of the person that I came to know during summer work didn't square at all with the horrific dichotomy that surrounded her in the beginning of her young life. She would have been too young to be culpable, but was, none the less handed a heinous legacy. Though I never saw her again, I was left with a profound awareness, and a gossamer connection to six million souls, an imposing link, which I felt, need be sustained, but how? For all of their sufferings, what paltry atonement did I have to give but a perpetual dignity in the hallowed places of my heart and mind? I made room.

Summer adjourned, and Dad arrived in the *Billy G* to fetch me. He gently slid up alongside of the private dock and tied her off. His overhauls, duck billed hat, and rolled down hip boots were in sharp contrast to the squire's golfing garb, but as far as I was concerned he was a sight for sore eyes. Graciously, he was invited to sit and visit. Each man settled into an Adirondack chair, sipped on a scotch, conversed quietly with humorous overtones, sitting into each other, respectfully, each comfortable in themselves and the moment. It crossed my mind, that at the core of it all, I had the good fortune to have gracious and responsible men about me thus far—good fortune, indeed!

By the end of my three-year tenure, I had a good sense of what the old, and the nouveau riche were all about—education, family, beautiful homes, and social standing. Their gentility was very comfortably borne, as a genteel nature is supposed to be. "New Money," the nouveau riche did not always know how to carry into effect the art of being wealthy, the decorum, etiquette, and bearing—all of which one could possess—even without wealth. I speak to the social graces that were deemed a sham, and disposed of the 60's. I miss them, and am curious. Had social graces continued to be a way of life, would small-claims and family courts have become as over-run as they are today? What is the basis for the majority of the cases brought before a judge in the lower courts, but a rampant lack of civility and offensive manners, in one form or another? I digress.

Fowler's beach embraced a new group of children with young mothers, who were attempting to augment their lost social life with the company of each other. The Beachcomber's, the ladies now devoid of small children, reinvented themselves, and came out the other end as a mature in-group. Women do that—reinvent themselves every five years, to preserve a young-at-heart attitude and an interesting mind.

Their cocktail parties, hors d'oeuvres, and dinners were elegant—replete with fresh flowers from their gardens, the good silver, bone china, and crystal. Definitive implements appeared from nowhere, cobalt blue-glass swizzle sticks with which to stir drinks—in cobalt blue-glasses, using the pinkie-finger-in-the-air-method. Dinner napkins with tatted edges were pulled from the linen closet, and diminutive silver spoons were stuck in a salt well at each setting, along with crescent shaped bone dishes, to put bones in, and place cards that leaned on sterling silver do-dads. A tea cozy tightly covered an elegant silver teapot that held tea balls filled with loose tea, which was surrounded by sugar/creamer sets, complete with teeny, sterling silver tongs for sugar cubes, and a dish of lemon wedges. Aunt Frances seemed to have three of everything to choose from when she entertained the girls. They met regularly at each other's homes—well into their seventies and eighties. I believe that those wonderful summer repasts were a gift to one another—and maybe, a bit of a throwback to their simplistic lemon, cobweb, and peanut parties in the days of their youthful energies.

***

Carmen and I lollygagged up the walk to the house, knowing full well that our activities had become entertainment to the widow Mountfort. We never made it to our door without seeing a tuft of white hair reappear in the corner of her big kitchen window. Now with Frank gone, the cat population exploded to about thirty. Elderly and childlike, she spent a large part of her money on cat food, the kitchen tabletop an expanse on which she directly fed the hordes inside of her house. Mom sent us over to get her for supper, not that she idly passed over the call to her house. She plainly couldn't deal with the fleas that met, and devoured her at Hulda's back door.

Hulda was not the only lonely that broke bread in our home by virtue of Dad's spur of the moment invitations. Mother always cooked enough for an army. Decca Doughty arrived and meekly offered up a quart of shucked clams to sell to Dad, and on the spot, was invited to dine with Tucky Woodbury—who shuffled over from across the street, with the aide of two canes, and Carl Marshmire, who walked down the street—with the aide of one cane. All were there to enjoy Lillian's home cooked meal and an hour's worth of old songs at the Hammond organ. I suspect that we all enjoyed the company, because we hung right in the midst of them for the entire evening.

Hulda died in the sixties; Mountfort's Inn was condemned, dismantled, the wood cut into small manageable pieces, it now the source of fuel for our wood stove. Each time Mother fed sticks of it to the fire she offered up an apologetic burnt-offering, stick by stick, until it was gone. *"If Hulda and Frank ever knew it would come to this"*—she said sadly. It bothered her.

Chapter

12 ..."Uphold the Blue & White"

Portland High School Fall 1956

Fifteen hundred students noisily navigated as we four, wide-eyed naïveté were swept up in the tide of moving masses, our introduction to a huge city school, but no more, no less than had been experienced by the generations before us. The initial impact was much like jumping feet first off a piling at low tide—arms tight to the body—toes pointed. Had it not been for a sympathetic, mite of an Italian girl from Munjoy Hill, the maze of hallways would have led me in circles. Sandy and I compared notes in homeroom, I of the thought that the math equations being asked of us were trick questions, when in fact they were too simple. Before noon, our curriculum was changed, I to college preparatory with two periods of art added—imagine— two whole periods of art a day with art teacher, Barbara Wallace. Sandy was one of the few who came to the class with a serious talent, a wonderful organic note that ran throughout her work. Socially, I was in awe of how she threaded in and out of a variegated group of classmates, was not the least bit cliquish, though she ran with the tightest of cliques, teens that knew each other from kindergarten. Her boyfriend was the absolute cream of the crop.

The transition was a rite of passage, and every island plebe struggled through the initiation. Why certainly, it was a cultural shock! Susan, Gordon, Buddy and I disappeared into the noise and haste for a time, and then resurfaced in the afternoon at the *Porthole*, on Custom House Wharf, looking as though we'd been wrung through Mom's *Easy* wringer rollers.

Work chewed up the previous three summers so that I had not seen much of the summer gang; therefore, I was elated to see Peter Kilgore's familiar face in the hallowed halls. Surrounded by a mass of friends, he shown popular amongst his peers, more than excelled in his studies, was an athletic star, and what-is-this? At age thirteen, the less than accustomed greeting was my first encounter with the *great divide* between freshman and sophomore, between high school social standing, *in which he was swimming*, and of which *I had none to that point*. Worst of all was the divide between city and island. It would seem that a high school education taught more than a series of academics. I would have to speak to him about this when I found the opportune moment.

*I found the opportune moment, but not until we were in our fifties, midst amused reminiscence of a night that the basketball coach caught us on a date at Vallees Restaurant—the night **before** a big game. Did Peter ever catch hell! Throughout our respective life's path, a lesson that we both had good sense to learn was the art of preserving a very tender lifelong friendship, one borne on Fowler's Beach, with the big, old, black Newfoundland dog, T-Bone as witness.*

Ancient mythology, algebra, geometry, Shakespeare, band, and the *Teen Clickers* filled the ensuing years to the brim. I stayed *Uptown* overnight to join-in on the crowded environment of the *Seven-Eleven* dances, each Friday night at the YWCA, *the place* for Portland teens.

In our sophomore year, Portland High was just one school, of the many in the country, in which the entire student body had their fingerprints taken by the FBI. There is quite an art to taking fingerprints. I recall thinking that having my prints safely ensconced somewhere would secure my identity. It was an era in which the majority trusted local authority, and obviously, the FBI. *Our prints are still on file in some dusty vault, and though today's mind-set would be rankled about First Amendment rights, for the most part, my disposition lingers.*

A rumor was floating around the night before the Portland-Deering Thanksgiving Day football game—one that involved the Deering mascot. Why—someone ran off with the ram, the poor devil. What kind of shameless, incorrigible, heartless, tricksters would do something like that? Was anyone watching the bulldog mascot? Did he need watching? The game was highly charged, and worth the muddy splatter all over my white bucks and white band uniform, but the walk from Fitzpatrick Stadium to Casco Bay Lines with an alto sax was a killer.

They waited dinner for me on Thanksgiving Day, which was thoughtful. I walked through the door, tears streaming down my face, sobbing that we'd lost to Deering—we LOST, and what did I have to endure during my abysmal state of wretchedness—but Uncle Johnny—tuned up in his most bombastic rendition of *"God Bless America."* How old, I asked, did one have to be before he relented?

Pretty clothes remained high on the list and a transition in style welcomed-in plaid kilts, which were worn *above* the knees with matching tights, and coordinated sweaters, *the* new look that replaced the calf length straight skirts and the crinoline look of '56. Conformity reared its conventional head, and we, in lockstep, spent the dollars it took to do so. Dad took me to the bank to cash in a twenty-five dollar War Bond that Uncle Johnny gave me when I was born, *all of which* was needed for a fluff of a blue gown that I wore to a ball, my first one. I don't recall my date, though he would have been a good dancer, my criteria at the time, yet I recall how I paid for the gown. Go figure!

> "What made us friends in the long ago when first we met?
> Well I think I know.
> The best in me and the best in you hailed each other
> Because *they* knew,
> That long ago before time began,
> Our being friends was a part of God's plan." Unknown

Unknown's poignant words could easily have been written with my mentor, Sandy, in mind. This year's Christmas card from her counseled me to search for glad feelings in unexpected places, and to feel at peace wherever my wanderings take me; remarkably similar words of advice she offered-up in "Freshman Alley," forty-four years before. Though at that time, it may have sounded more like, "Don't worry Bert—go anyway. Doesn't matter if you don't know anyone. You'll have a great time."

She and I regrouped for our fortieth PHS class reunion, and my husband, knowing full well my penchant for table-hopping, opted to give Sandy and me a girl's night out. A fair showing of those who "upheld the blue and white" came together to strengthen some bonds and to check out those who weathered best the march of time. Our classmates truly seemed more like family, at that stage in our lives, and none, within our circle minded the imprints that the passing years had left on our faces. Oh, there was one that whined openly, felt disconcerted by the aging process that met him at every table, a mirror, and a reminder that he had entered the winter of life. But if he listened closely, those old friends were better than plastic surgeons in that regard, in that they beheld the face from across the years and responded to the spirit behind it. Spirits are extraordinarily constant, and appear to be ageless. This is good!

Winter Solstice 1956-60

Naval activities and personnel were cut back considerably in the Area, which ceded the island back to itself somewhat, and in the dead of winter it assumed a more isolated atmosphere, likened to a bear going into a den when its pulse slows, when it sinks into a deep sleep. The people didn't, but the *rock* did.

Usually no cars were out on the roads at night, no tracks found in the new snow. Everyone was hunkered down. A curtain of flakes fell lightly atop an island's worth of undisturbed snow, since there simply were not many of us there to do much disturbing. Of course, the gong of the bell buoy, and the sound of the wave-action on the back shore at Southside Beach were ever present, but both were so much a part of the tenor of the island that I didn't hear either of them, unless I actually stopped to listen. What did break through the silence, as Carmen and I headed up Garfield to pick-up cousin Suzanne, was the blat of the foghorn on the end of the Navy pier, and Portland Head's muffled tone in the distance. We met Tommy Pisak and Susan trudging up Beach Avenue, and all of us converged on Buddy's with the ingredients for homemade pizza. His parents were out for the night and although his mother didn't mind our taking over her small kitchen, it was not certain just how happy she was with the remnants from our homemade crust, left on the countertop after a hasty departure. We had to meet the *Eastend* kids at the old schoolhouse and couldn't waste a minute. Any of us could have shown up with a platter of crabmeat rolls, or peanut butter sandwiches, but by gory, we were going to be like those city kids who were the regulars on *The Dave Astor Show,* the local TV dance program. We strove through the door with passable pizzas in hand—and a massive amount of energy to expend.

Now, we didn't just barge into the old school. The church let us use the former place of learning, with its squeaky floorboards and original blackboards—avail ourselves of it whenever we asked, but of course, accompanied by a few rules from Mary Ross. If the church elders happened to worry, they needn't have, for in mid winter's social bleak climate, we were so ready for a dose of self-administered trustworthiness for this simple interval of self-indulgence. The old wood stove was stoked up nicely thanks to Sharon. The Eastend kids were already there. Someone manned the Victrola, an updated model that accommodated 78, 45, *and* 33&1/3rpm records, the kind that played a single record at a time, although it skipped terribly under the weight of our dancing over weak floorboards. Tommy was very tired and went home early.

Thereafter, the country became caught up in the riveting game shows, especially the infamous *Sixty-Four-Thousand Dollar Question* with its wide-eyed contestants who stood in an isolation booth, sweating, and answering extraordinary questions. Dad had a feel about the show—knew that before they entered the booth, some knew the answers! To the one who turned out to be the biggest offender in the hoax, he'd mock, *"Think hard now, come on!"* I threw one of those tisks his way. How could he tell just by watching them, or was it that I couldn't believe that such a lie was perpetrated on the whole country. Verily, I became a believer when it blew wide open and the crap hit the fan.

Though I didn't know this at the time, Dad mirrored his mother's posture when it came to preserving a space to enjoy some favored programming, his two most favored being *Oral Roberts Tent Meetings*, and *Bishop Fulton J. Sheen.* When he settled in the living room to watch the two programs, he was *not* to be disturbed. Just like his mother and her NY Metropolitan Opera, he wasn't!

***

Six books, a cumbersome saxophone case, and a purse weighted down the ninety pounds that supported it all on my trudge uphill on Pearl Street, and the several blocks to high school each morning—then back down over, at the end of the day, in rain, sleet, and snow. *This was 1959, a BBS, (a Before Backpack Story) a hardship story, the kind of story that one lays thickly onto one's own children when they rail over a four-block trek to school. Why doesn't that work on children?*

Until I reached the other end of Freshman Alley in the afternoon, I'd forgotten that I'd not eaten, as was the case most days. George's delicatessen was handy-by, just a block away, with its wonderful Jewish food, and George, with his white, paper, army shaped cap, busily situated, fair and square in the middle of what seemed to be a mountain of blintzes and wurst. George was the type of restaurateur who answered fire alarms at two in the morning, and was found at every conflagration laden with free coffee and sandwiches for the firemen.

Stepping up to the glass enclosure, mouth salivating, I ordered my usual liverwurst with mustard and mayo on white, potato salad, and kosher pickle. While he performed his magic, I searched for my money, emptied my purse, turned every pocket on my person inside out only to find it necessary to turn to him, with a stark look on my face, and explain that I had to cancel the order for lack of funds. I must have looked hungry as a waif, because he said, paternally, *"You eat! You pay me tomorrow."* I did—and, I did—the next day! On the spot, of course, I initiated him into that exclusive club of gracious men that I continued to have surrounding me, and now along with the firemen, and the city's population, I shared a common affection for him. Satiated, and with blood sugars now on the rise, I continued the walk with my cumbersome load down onto the much-traveled Custom House Wharf, a juncture at which I always felt home-free.

Captains Earl Stockbridge and old Ross Kent could run Casco Bay blindfolded, had a maritime talent that gave us all a sense of well-being. If either of those two men was in the pilothouse, we jumped aboard without a concern. I never contemplated the expanse or depth of the water we sailed upon twice a day. Had I done so—I might never have stepped foot off the island. Come to think of it, some people actually never did leave the island. None thought it out of the ordinary. In fact, maybe there was something extraordinary about never stepping foot off the island, because the many residents that lived independently to a ripe old age hardly left their homes, let alone visited the city.

An era ended when the biggest steamers grew weary. The *Maquoit's* bones lay between the Diamond's, the *Emita's* off Rings Island in Newburyport. They salvaged and junked the *Aucocisco*, which left the smaller diesel *Gurnet,* and the jowl hulled, steamer *Sabino* the only remnants of the resplendent fleet of a once upon a time in Casco Bay.

During the fall, winter and spring's rough weather, we sat in the wrap-around seats in the stern area below deck of the *Gurnet*, our feet propped beneath us to keep them dry, while water washed in a shallow tide, back and forth on the deck of the cabin. She invariably took on water through the sliding doors up towards the bow. Seated in a folding chair in the center of the deck, I didn't fair well going over the Sound on one of those blowy days, tipped over, books and all into the water on deck when the boat took one broadside. Great way to start the day!

Casco Bay Lines began to replace the old wooden steamers with steel hulled, cold, uncomfortable, noisy, diesel vessels that whined and screamed all the way up the bay, not much more seaworthy than the old ladies of the fleet, but required smaller crews, more economical to run. Is it clear that I never bonded with those—those—*those* piles of metal fatigue? They had the audacity to name them after the *Auco* and *Emita*.

Something was not quite right about one of them, the *Sunshine*, until it dawned on me that the passenger's cabin sat below the waterline, a floating tomb, a tragedy waiting-to-happen, and the only boat in my life that I was uneasy climbing aboard. Its career was short lived, thank God, when she ran aground off the end of Diamond Cove in a dense fog, wedged in tighter than *Zip's you-know-what*, and—thank you, thank you, thank you—unsalvageable!

No radar was available when fog crept in-between the islands. We'd tool along at a slow bell on the *Gurnet*, the deckhand pacing from port to starboard, listening for—anything, while the captain worked the boat's coordinates from the compass inside the cabin, clocking the minutes it took to go from one buoy to another. I felt better being on the upper deck, listening too, rather than below in the passenger cabin. Crossing Hussy's Sound, the captain sent me out in the point of the bow to *sound*. In the murky hush, the blast of the horn was amplified, twofold. I anxiously awaited the horn's resonance to bounce off Great Diamond Cove or Pumpkin Nob, peering into the wall of mist for—anything, when to my relief, the horn loudly reverberated back on the heels of itself. I simply pointed towards Diamond Cove—certain that the Captain caught the instant echo at the same moment. It didn't hurt to have an extra set of ears in the bow, if only an island kid who knew when it was time to serious-up. That was one of them.

Thou Shalt Not...

Jeezuscrise 'mloss nevabinonthusoneb'fore! *"What did he say?"* I asked, trying to make sense of the string of words that just spilled out of the mouth of an old Chebeague Islander who had just stepped off the plank onto one of the new tin CBL boats. Bobby Ricker, one of the deckhands stared off into space for a few seconds. A smile breached his lips. He translated, *"He said,"* 'Jesus Christ I'm lost, never been on this one before.' It required someone who'd been raised down on Chebeague to translate that one—and even he struggled a bit.

Cursing within the earshot of a man of the cloth resonated like fingernails over a black board. Therefore, they toned it down to a cuss, animated cusses at that, *"Suffrin' Crise, Smokeen' Crise, and Jumpt-up Holy Old Keee-rise."* They even tacked a middle name to one—*"Jesus H. Crise!"* The H is one for the trivia buffs to decipher. If one leans-in and listens very—very closely, most usually, it is not a curse one hears, but a petition—as with the term *Christer*, used to describe the terrible storm of 1898—as well as Ole Chum's outburst for the near accidental demise of a man and his horse—likewise with Ray Ricker's exclamation upon hearing that his brother, Will was still out in one of the worst storms ever. Those don't sound in vain, but more an informal prayer. Highly informal, I admit—but, non-the-less, a *would-you, at-this-moment, PLEASE-pay-attention prayer.*

Everyone had a Maine accent—we were reminded often enough by off-islanders who poked fun and tried to mimic the familiar twang, but without much success. The accent could easily be rendered by simply talking through lightly clenched teeth, dropping the G off every word ending in *ing*, running all the words together, and using the *a-a-h* sound liberally, as in the vernacularisms, *dee-aah, sto-aah,* and *caahn't,* a Bostonian way of saying cannot. A spoon under the tongue made the results even better if someone wished to get Downeast about it. We used *dasst,* for don't dare, a word not found in the dictionary, although it was a perfectly legal word to us.

But the heaviest Downeast accents came from deep inside cloistered communities, such as one over on the Westend of Chebeague. It was a language unto itself. Depending upon what *shire* or *ham* it originated in England, we were privy to vestiges, and residue of those adventurous souls who came over before the Revolutionary War. I listened up whenever I heard the heavy singsong cant, because nine times out of ten, there was a very dry wit, and a fair amount of *wisdoms* behind the heavy dialect.

Not a Spleeny One Amongst Us

Bitter winds and salt spray built a treacherous walkway of ice on the slips at Ponce's Landing, difficult to keep sanded with two incoming tides a day washing in and out covering the slip in a rounded-over, thick glare of ice. Even Clarke's Hill and the hill leading to Ponces were non-negotiable, at times. On occasion we fell and slid down the length of the slip—but always caught ourselves on something, usually the gangplank. Unfortunately, the schoolbooks skittered over the thick blanket of ice and continued the descent, a meager offering to the god, *Poseidon,* for our deliverance. We arrived at school, only to be informed that school was called off for weather. Wouldn't you think that Mr. Reich could have called one of us before the boat departed?

No two landings were ever the same. We just *adored* the ones made on a dead-low tide, whereby we all had to climb up to the hurricane deck of the *Gurnet*, the topmost deck, the only deck that lined up with the wharf—where they threw out the freight plank, a wide plank that had no railings. It was the no railings part of it that made me suck-in and hold my breath as I skittered across. Strong northerly winds made landings tough at Ponce's. In the four years of travel, if the captain thought it best, we stayed aboard and got off at Cleaves Landing on the *Eastend*, then walked the three miles home. Though transporting us was not his responsibility anymore, when Uncle Johnny took-in the unfolding scene at Ponces, he followed the boat and was waiting for us at Cleaves with his school bus. Knowing him, he'd been watching the weather, surmised what would happen, and was on hand to see it through.

Cleaves, by this time, was condemned—planks had rotted, were missing, leaving huge gaps. Casco Bay Lines no longer provided service to that dock, but on that one very blustery occasion, we were given the choice. In a single file, we disembarked onto the skeleton wharf, following the lead, as one would through a mind field, picking what looked to be the strongest path. The *Eastend* kids felt more secure in their steps, probably because they played around the wharf, or fished off it. Susan and I, on the other hand, held our breaths until we reached solid ground.

Now and again, Cleave's was unapproachable due to ice. In that situation we stayed aboard, made the run a few miles out to Cliff Island, hoped conditions would subside within the hour's turn around, and use an extra hour to do homework and to flirt with the deck hands. In my case, it was mostly to flirt with the deck hands.

Huge swells posed an interesting impasse. When the boat rolled away from Ponces on one of them, and was thrust back in on the next wave to ram the wharf—broadside, no plank was ever set out, or it would have been destroyed. Like a band of parachutist, they lined us up single file; waited for the boat to roll

300

into the dock, and just before the critical moment of impact the deckhand shouted, *"jump!"* Evidentially there wasn't a *spleeny one amongst us*. One by one—we took the unconventional, ungraceful leave, because a refusal to jump meant another trip to town and another trip back after dark, with the outside chance the last trip could be canceled altogether. Everett Clarke watched from the back window of the Clarke's store up on the hill, observing that the boys budged to the head of the line, jumped first, and before the girls had begun the process, traipsed up over the dock without so much as a backward glance. Plebeians!

Tommy Pisak was diagnosed with acute leukemia, battled the heavy end of the illness from the get-go, and went on a downward spiral so fast that there was hardly any time to grasp the gravity of his terminal state. We entertained hope, but he slipped from our midst. As though we were tossed a hot coal with only bare hands with which to make the catch, individually none of us wished to handle the grief alone—hence, we sought the insulation of the group. Following his funeral, we crammed into a huge corner booth at Theodore's Restaurant on Commercial Street trying to make some sense of it, a form of unseasoned counseling that we offered each to the other—one that fast approached ripening under the weight of reality.

***

Two fifteen-year old Portland boys made up Cap'n Stockbridge's crew on the first and last run down the bay. Bobby Ricker landed the job in order to get back to familiar surroundings after his dad, Will, snapped up the stationary engineer's job at Casco Bay Lines. Any minute that Bob wasn't compelled to be someplace else—and school qualified as iffy in his mind, he was at the Custom House Wharf, or on those boats. By five a.m. the freight shed was a flurry of activity when both deckhands arrived. Old Tavern Farm and Oakhurst Dairy trucks stacked cases of milk into labyrinths, deposited blocks of ice in a pile. Cushman and Nissen's bakery trucks unloaded bread and pastries. Guy Gannet dumped newspaper bundles in a heap. The boys loaded it all on the boat while Stockbridge warmed the

301

Emita Two's engines; the lines were pulled and off they steamed—all three packed in the small cabin.

The first rays of the sun climbed in the East as they headed for Cliff Island, the last island on the run, and the first to deposit their children on a school day morning. On the way back up through the bay, they gathered teenagers and commuters from Chebeague, Long, Trefethen's at Peaks, and Great Diamond. Each group of islanders sat segregated from the others, in the same way each island was segregated. People were friendly enough. Why, three-quarters of them were related!

Kay Carr was waiting on Diamond Island wharf to pass aboard a brown paper bag filled with homemade donuts that she had just plucked out of the hot fat—earmarked for the crew. Cap'n Stockbridge would pass-up on them. His ulcer was kicking up. Kay, and her husband Dan, a retired Portland policeman, were the corner posts of the sparsely populated island, met every boat, delivered the papers, and taxied if needed. A mailman arrived at Diamond on the ten o'clock to deliver mail, on foot. She and Dan were regulars for Catholic services on Long. They were close to us—like our own—or were we Dan and Kay's?

Deck hands flirted with the girls, the girls with the deck hands. Stockbridge told Bobby Ricker, *"Stay away from that little Gawmez girl, because her father is Spanish, has a two edged sword, and if he misses you with the forward swing, he'll finish you off with the back swing."*

It was late in the day, along about dusk. The *Aucocisco Two* sailed by the breakwater headed for Ponce's landing where Uncle Johnny stood with the bag of mail. Stockbridge lay in the bunk of the pilothouse immobilized by an ulcer attack—suffering. He put Bobby at the wheel and Jackie on deck to handle the lines alone. The fifteen-year-old turned and said, *"I can't do this Cap."* Hitching up on his elbow, Earl pointed in the direction the boat needed to go and groaned, *"Yes you can, just head her for the further end of the dock."* Out on deck, Jack's work was cut out for him. He had to hit (lasso) that piling with a rope—and on that day, Bob gave him the longest, far-reaching shot of his rope-throwing career.

"It was not the most masterful piece of seamanship, Bob recalls, but the wharf survived." Bob was one of the seventh generation Rickers to spend his life on the ocean since Wentworth Ricker stepped ashore out there on Chebeague in 1778. Islanders trusted Bob's maritime instincts when, at eighteen, he ran as captain on the Casco Bay Line vessels in the late fifties, early sixties. One of his champions, then retired Spa owner, Geneva Rogers, was certain to be on the Westend point of Long Island during storms, there explicitly to watch him negotiate the major swells that were rolling in through Hussey's Sound, praising him on every wave that he took. He never knew that the eyes of the island also kept him within their aegis.

During his career as Master, he'd honed his abilities, could turn the coastal tanker, "Vincent Tibbetts," on a dime, and bring the vessel in to the dock so quietly, that until the engine shut down, there was no clue that the ship was tied-up. He, like his paternal forbearers, earned the trust of crews—no better gauge of a man's mettle. He was, and actually still is at this writing, a walking, talking case for my theory of biological osmosis, a boatman to the marrow. I'm curious if that is why his first mate, himself an ocean Master, referred to him as "Captain Master." His small children endearingly called him "Captain Daddy." His wife never called him late for supper.

At the Base of Ponce's Landing

"Nothing is constant but change"—so goes the adage, one that might not be thought a maxim to which an islander would ascribe to life. But if one has lived on an island, the vista is obviously far-reaching, and is in a constant state of flux—a concept not hard to translate into human terms.

The base of Ponce's Landing was more the portal, than a piece of real estate, was a genre painting of our family's life's path, beginning with Maria and Antonio's immigration onto Ponces, where they set roots and worked mere feet from its base. Mother and Dad met there, and five separate times raced down over the wharf to usher us all into the world, some born at a time when World War II held a joint tenancy of the shoreline with the civilian pier. Dad's boat, the one with no name, wrecked at its base during the height of a hurricane, and Ann Marie touched mortality within feet of the same. We left the den and followed our father onto the wharf for our first exposure to the mainland, used it as one would a hawse pipe through which we crawled to and from bait barrel duty on the *Billy G*—used it, too, for Dad's splendid Sunday family junkets. Ponce's emerged as *the place* for our teenage gambits; and thereafter, it became a spot where we bided, and marked inordinate amounts of time awaiting transit to high school. Thinking back on those grayed, old planks, and pilings, the tiny patch of real estate actually alluded to the ingress into childhood, and the egress out to, and beyond the age of majority.

Tides of change are a given; however, the swiftness and degree of change can throw one off balance, put one onto a hard list, where the only recourse is to hang on tightly until the wheel of time, and a sea anchor's worth of understanding levels conditions. Dad told our youngest brother, *"I'm going down to the store...will be right back."* But he never came back. He died suddenly on that snotty day, in June of '59, died at age fifty-two in the act of living, just as he rowed out on a very low tide to deliver a can of fuel to a floundering sailboat full of strangers, doing what he thought was right. As he readied to throw them the line, he dropped from life. The turning tide gently delivered him, in the punt, onto the shore at the base of Ponce's.

In an instant, we learned the finer points of what profound sadness was all about, a sadness that settled in as a permanent fixture, and became a part of the greater whole. I really never became *un-sad* about his parting. He left too much of a void. Mother was Grace under pressure, made it through the initial stages, but she was truly not prepared for life without him. The two oldest had just left the nest. Carmen and I were adolescents. Out in the back yard his 'shadow" sat alone on a stump with his head in his hands, trying to grasp the unthinkable—a heart-breaking scene. The following day, on Mom's birthday, a shining new set of copper bottom pans was delivered from the Casco Bay boat—a gift from Dad.

The island community, as it is wont to do, too, became cloaked in the very same deep sense of loss. At the funeral home, the depth of their loss became all too visible; for the first time in my sixteen years, I saw grown men cry. A nun imparted solace to Ann Marie, telling her that although he was not of the Faith, that they would pray that his soul reach heaven. Listening off on the sideline, I chewed on that one for half a minute. It was about like chewing on a wad of dulse. To my way of thinking, his spirit was safely ensconced in wherever it is that enlightened souls abide, and he ascended very nicely on his own steam—but thank you anyway.

Hard pressed to fill the huge void, we compromised by looking to those places where we could quickly recapture his essence. Freely, it reflected in the faces of the island, often cropped up in family mannerisms, and can still be found in nooks and crannies, from the *Eastend* to the *Westend*, places where he invested his patronage and expended his spirit. Nevertheless, it was a *catch, as catch can* until we fathomed that his intrinsic nature abided in his legacies, and within each of us. We were favored, more than most, to have had him in our lives, if only for a trice. The finality of his passing abruptly closed a door for all of us in the family, because it was evident that, never in time, nor in this incomparable fashion would circumstances ever again align to create another epoch such as the one through which we had been seasoned thus far.

"All mankind is of one Author,
And is one volume;
When one man dies,
One Chapter is not torn out of the book,
But translated into a better language."
Donne 1573-1631

Bob Gomez and the "Billy G."

A Promise

In the East the waters play on the shores of Casco Bay,
Where giant ships of commerce come and go.
In the West the mountain high, reaching upward pierce the sky,
Its summit always capped in winter's snow.
Built upon a point of land richly blessed by nature's hand,
Fair in beauty with its wooded islands nigh.
Is our Portland in her hour leading on to fame and power?
Our own dear school Portland High.

Portland High School song-1860

I'm so-o-o sorry. It truly is embarrassing when someone breaks into his or her old high school song, especially one that sounds like the version that Rudy Vallee sang through a megaphone, back when only guys did the cheer leading. Does anyone today know who Rudy Vallee was? Not to worry! They didn't in 1960 either. I'm not certain where Rudy Vallee was in 1860, but when he attended Portland High School, the above aforementioned verse was part of the school song, and on the school's hundredth anniversary in 1960, the original version was first on the slate for us to sing.

The senior class was separated into six groups, sixty to a group, three hundred sixty—total. Each group rehearsed the hefty repertoire, in six-part harmony, separately. It was torture—didn't make much sense to most, until the day that all six groups congregated in the assembly hall balcony and sang the pieces together for the first time. We were blown away—couldn't believe that we were capable of the harmonics that flowed when nearly four hundred of us lifted our voices.

High school graduation day—still bleary-eyed from all of the finals, I called Mom from the city to tell her how crammed the day was, nothing but a blur, with more rehearsals, the graduation itself, prom, dinner, and the prom party at Crystal Lake—too much really. She informed me that a dozen red roses and a dozen white roses arrived on the morning boat. I searched my memory, didn't have a clue as to who would care enough, or had enough money to send me roses. She found the cards and read them to me, and what I had dismissed from my mind happened a year before on the boat as we headed for Portland. Old Jensen, a Navy security policeman, who boarded next door at the Mountfort Inn, engaged me in an odd conversation shortly after Dad died. Probably thinking that without my father's influence, that I might not take the remaining year of school seriously, he said, *"If you finish high school, I will send you a dozen white roses on your graduation day."* In my mind there was never a question that I would graduate, never the less, it was truly a kind gesture. I politely accepted his bribe. A sarcastic voice from behind us said, *"If **she** graduates, I will send her a dozen **red** roses!"* I looked around. It was that young captain, that smart aleck Bobby Ricker. I got the message—and an entire year later, on graduation day, a dozen long stemmed ***red*** roses.

Casco Bay Lines Engineer Ray Estabrooke
(left) and Captain Bob Ricker (right)

EPILOGUE

Will The Real Ole Deah Please Stand Up!

New Year's Eve was upon us, the beginning of a new millennium, the year 2000. A ripper of a northeaster was blustering its way towards Maine. So what else is new? Grocery stores were filled with bread, milk, and battery shoppers. The heavy drum of overly dramatized music heralded each weather forecast as the storm advanced, menacing music that is used by the media—and gets everyone more on edge—unnecessarily, I believe. Inclinations to visit Mom at the island, to celebrate, do a little dance—and hold-up through a big, bad storm with her and Carmen all merged as the fun thing to do. I made plans to go a day early, and to beat all of those packed-together isobars [119] that I saw on the weather map.

Driving on past my front yard, headed in the direction of the new Casco Bay Transit Authority, I made a mental note that the bared Japanese quince bush that I propagated from my grandmother's on the island, a forsythia bush, which came from the same place, and the *Hulda* roses, would certainly benefit from the protection of the expected foot of snow. Slips from the island roses now pepper my property and are spectacular along about the Fourth of July, set there as an appropriate way to remember the island, its former and present heirs and assigns.

A pile of music books, earmarked for Mom, filled two-thirds of my suitcase, different levels of music lessons for her to teach classes that she offers to any island child who wants to learn. She plays for school activities, weddings, memorials, and services at the Methodist church, as well as her own church. At age eighty-eight the passion remains. Mulling that I still have a problem packing a suitcase properly, I rolled the heavy load over to the ticket counter.

Chris and Steve McDuffie were going in the same direction, toting a huge cooler of food, enough to get them through the New Year repast at their Beach Cove cottage, planning, they

---

[119] Isobars that are closely packed on a weather map indicate very high winds.

309

said, to welcome in the new millennium with my cousin and his wife down at the *Eastend*. Opening their summer home in the dead of winter is a new activity in recent years, one that many have taken up quite regularly. It is a glorious idea. The school's new library commands their attention these days, and everything is moving forward under their watchful eye. We spoke affectionately of George Ross who had just passed away, and I well understood Steve's sadness. As though it a winged bird George's warm smile and the old rhyme, *"Georgie, Porgy, Pudding and Pie,"* made a glide across my mind's eye. Steve's eyes spoke to the remorse that we shared in having to let go of a tried and true constancy.

Skies were graying, the islands slate blue with rivulets of white snow at the water's edge. We passed by Fort Gorges, a juncture where a metamorphosis invariably takes place, not a Peter Pan thing, and not a conscious bid. I simply regain my identity—am Roberta Gomez again—happens every time— happens to anyone who is an islander.

The boat crossed Hussy's Sound and approached Long Island. I scanned the winter landscape of Fowler's Beach, Mount Hunger, and the buttoned-up cottages that lay in dormancy on the *Westend*. A poem unexpectedly presented itself, one written by my old friend, Peter, an entreaty not difficult to honor in the least. He eloquently requested of the reader to please tenderly hold the thought of his walk amongst us. Each and every time I sail by Fort Gorges and head down the bay it is a done deal. With each eyeful of seascape, regardless the season, invariably, Dad's nature along with Uncle Johnny, Adeline, Walter and all the others quietly slip into my thoughts—and contentedly abide. There's plenty of room.

Who put the lighted cross on the Catholic Church this year? It's a lovely Christmas card scene for those of us making the approach to the island. There is something affable about a pocket of colored lights on the front of the island in the winter, especially when it comes on dark.

We passed on by Ponce's and landed at the new, spacious, cement Mariner's Wharf that was built in the general area, where three Navy docks once stood. Long Island is now a town, an entity unto itself, seceded from Portland—brave hearts all. Three military jets flew low over the celebrants on that July day of independence in 1993, a symbol of the island's newfound autonomy. Cousin, Mark, Aunt Tilly's grandson, was its first city father-chair of selectmen. Maria would have burst her buttons with pride for his achievement, as would all of the grandparents of the other involved shakers and movers so have been.

Every half a minute a salutation came my way on the walk up the windy pier, indeed a welcomed sound to a reputed expatriate. *God love 'em*, for continuing to consider me an islander! For all my born days I've never felt anything other than one. I noticed that the wharf wasn't moving under me, as did Ponces on a blowy day. Mom was going to enjoy the supply of copper cleaner that I bought for her forty-year-old pans—the ones Dad gave her for her birthday in June of '59—the shiny ones neatly stacked in her cupboard that she cooks with every day.

Sharon stood on the porch at Clarke's store, she now a gifted pillar of the community. It was plain that she would be a leader back then—when she checked the fire in the wood stove at the old school house to make certain it was near out, turned the lights off, and locked the doors after the mid-winter dances. Her community out-reach program has been an inconspicuous, but an enormous success, which encompasses the Fisherman's Wives Association, one that aids families who lose their husbands and fathers to the sea. Though the tools she utilizes are different than those used by the MacVane women, it is the very same mind-set that benefited my Grandmother in her time of need, a measure of the island's unfailing idealism and vigilance, one towards another. She and I made a promise to get together, a promise neither of us can ever keep. Yet we continue promise making as though it might change one year—maybe when we get old. Excuse me! We are old! That we are not successful in an effort to regroup affects the friendship little. Like a good book, we just pick up where we left off.

Smiles flashed warm greetings inside Everett Clarke's store, the one and the same that was rebuilt after the big fire of 1914. I spied Everett's picture propped up in the corner, another of the old baseball team, and delighted in the varied greetings thrown my way.

Carmen did a lovely job decorating out-side the homestead. Miniature lights were threaded all through Maria's Japanese quince bushes to illuminate the walkway up the side of the house, the same clamshell walk, though they lay buried beneath inches of soil laid down by the years.

***

Late that night I stood on the back stoop, under a curtain of unrelenting snow, scanning the darkened sea while the storm made it presence felt. The quince branches were thickly blanketed by this time and the tiny lights cast a wide swarth over and under the billows of snow that clung to them. The whole bush snapped to the whims of the wind, a barometer of the moment.

The aura of it all hoisted a memory of a year ago, to be exact, of an early morning when I sat at the computer at four o'clock scrolling through some scanned old black and white photos of the island and its people. My objective, at that early hour, was to find something of interest to paint in the studio that day. I found two that I tarried over—just two. One was a tiny photo of the Rich's house on the Eastend, where Lawrence and Tillie Rich, their children Alma, Betty Jane, and Larry lived. It had diapers hanging on a clothesline that draped off the side of the house, probably Larry's, and a few ducks in the foreground. Compositionally it was right-on. I made note to paint that one. I then stopped at an old high school picture of Harry Ross, thinking it would be fun to tack some years on the youthful face, place a odd looking hat down over his head, which was a part of his character these days—make the old dear look as he is at present—white hair and all—then went on with the day.

A late afternoon radio news broadcast cut sharply into my thoughts, made me snap to attention and stand in place. It reported the sinking of a fishing boat, *Two Friends*, out off Boon Island the previous afternoon, a day of furious winds. This was the first I had heard of it. They must have been in the shoals, I reasoned, a treacherous place to be in those winds. A young

312

fisherman, Larry Rich's son, Shawn was saved. An instant prayer rose up out of me.

That night, watching the local news, my husband and I were riveted to the lead story. The other two fishermen, who were aboard had perished. I was expecting to hear that they were young men like Shawn, but when their names were made public my heart sank along with the "Two Friends." The other men were Shawn's dad, Larry Rich, and the captain, Harry Ross.

The most difficult part of the newscast for me was Harry's distress call to the Coast Guard. I heard his soft controlled voice, and closed my eyes when it rose with a strong roll of the boat. This was a hard one that left us sick at heart, a loss that would deeply affect the whole island and fishing fleet. At the end of the newscast, we remained absorbed in conversation for a long time. It was such a sorrowful moment. They had too much to live for and were both such good souls.

Like the strike of a match, I came to attention. I'd forgotten, completely forgotten—sat up straight, and turned around to my husband, probably looking for an explanation and said, "You will never believe what I had up on the computer screen at four o'clock this morning!"

***

Carmen's son shoveled us out the next morning before we had risen and then sifted off into the ether on a five-day fishing trip before we realized he was gone. With him gone for a few days, this day would be full of loose dangling ends for his five-year old. She pulled in the slack of one of those dangling ends by arriving at the back door at breakfast time, with designs on me— and a back yard banked in snow—sticky, snowman building snow. There was a small shovel inside the door, a perfect trowel with which to sculpt a creation. I called in the chips on the high average I had in three-dimensional design at the Portland School of Art, and in no time we had the base packed high. Her young mom plunked the head atop its shoulders. Carmen barked from inside—charging us not to build it so close to the back door. The little one locked eyes with me to see what I would do, if in fact, I would *miss-mind*. I grabbed a crooked branch, stuck it into the sculpted shoulder, and packed snow all around it to form an arm

313

locked in a frozen salute—to my sister. Mother smiled from the kitchen window, entertained with our shenanigans, and we posed proudly for Carmen's video camera beside the finished keeper of the gate.

The word out was that it was basic black and tux for the New Year celebration at the VFW hall that night, a hall that Dad helped build, on the same spot where the old Cushing Pavilion once stood. I had half of it right—black turtle, black slacks, black shoes with a huge fisherman net sweater and to add a shabby chic dimension—thermal long underwear beneath it all.

Late that evening, Carmen and I found that the line of cars parked at the VFW led clear up the road to the ball field. Sorry! There is no ball field any more. In the same way as I continue to call that old hill, the *New Hill*, I continue to call prime waterfront property the ball field. Either way, the footing was treacherous and like the legions of TV service announcements that incessantly warn women our age about osteoporosis, I warned Carmen that we needed to protect the lack of density in our bone masses by creeping down the steep, icy incline to the hall. The concept set us into a fit of laughter.

The city-based band was talented, had a full sound, some brass, and sounded as though they'd practiced a great deal. Through the sparkle and glitter of the decorations, most everyone was, in fact, dressed in black—a distinctive New York vogue. A large Baby Boom contingent was ensconced. Word was traveling the grapevine that Everett Clarke's business had been sold, now out of the family. They're probably just plainly tired. It was a good long run. Roger's Spa already changed hands a few times before it became a restaurant with a New York frame of mind. I wonder if they season lobster with garlic and balsamic? Daow! They wouldn't! Would they?

A few of the Johnsons arrived with the family matriarch. It was her first New Year party without her husband, Bud in fifty years; sadly, he had recently passed. Had Bud been there, he would have invariably touched on a fit of melancholy—he'd have made mention of the days back when he and the young Horr girl were sparking, reminding me of just how fond he was of my father for helping to co-ordinate the winter gatherings.

"Those skating parties at the Marsh, Bert—bond fires—music, those were the days. Gawd, you know I miss him awful?" I believe he did. His words were keepsakes. That is a tender link I will miss.

Others of Bud's generation all sat in a small group, the *teenage emeritus* from the forties, those that congregated and danced to the jute box at Rogers Spa so many years back. One would expect to see elderly on the faces of those who spent their youthful energies in the 40s, but comely is closer to the mark. I looked into knowing eyes, contemporary demeanors, and into comfortable, spirited natures that are deeply involved with the island's growth.

Old Zoeth, who lived on the island in the 1800's, and *his* son Zodie, who beat many a path up the banks of Harbor de Grace in the 1900s, would be heartened to see their progeny reemerged with the island. We are all gladdened for a continuance of their quiet charm in, yet another generation of gentleman fishermen.

One of the Stewart boys waved from across the room—just moved back to the island after forty years away, happy to be home and any one of us could speculate that it took him all of a minute to settle-in. I inquired about his younger brother, my old classmate from the island's grammar school. Gordon was fine and would be coming back for the deer season. He bungees back too, like our other classmate, Buddy, just to touch base, to reconnect. The fourth in our class, Susan, has been here all the while, involved with charting the direction of the community. Cushings, whether they be from the clan that landed two hundred fifty years ago, or those present today, have certainly finely honed the art of chart making.

Someone remarked that as close as we were, collectively, not many of us married each other, but instead, married off the island. Sue, Gordon, Buddy, and I are still married to the same mates with whom we originally promised *for better or worse*. There it is again, *the law of opposites*. Asked what I thought was the secret of these long-term parings, I hedged. One has to have bounteous amounts of *sooth* to be a qualified soothsayer. I'll check with the other three and shoot for a consensus.

I introduced myself to the newer members of the summer community as Lillian's daughter, no more than that was needed, and listened as they talked of their newly purchased summer homes and businesses, alert to the level of energy on display, exactly the element needed for such undertakings. I wondered if any had yet caught on to the connected community that abides here, maybe—maybe not. In general, I had the sense, that though slow on the up-take, following the secession, the island had just recently made one of those sharp turns again.

Effervescence fizzed through the phone line the next morning, from the other Long Island—Long Island, New York. My niece, Mary Susan, the one who sparked this meandering mosaic, called the island to lend her lively brand of holiday greetings to everyone and touch base. Her call seemed to bear a likeness, a whisper of the family's past inclinations to stand at the back door and holler, *"I'm home!"*

***

Back at my home in the city later that night, with the fireplace kindled, I recounted the whole weekend to my husband Bob while we toasted each other with champagne. This is our fortieth anniversary year, one in which to plan something special—a cruise maybe? Pardon my derelict manners. I speak of Bob Ricker—the one whose children called him Captain Daddy, the fella who remembered the red roses back in '60, Will and Fran's only son, grandson of the fisherman who rode out the November Gale of '98, great-grandson of the old stone slooper Stephen—on back to the oak-tree planting, Revolutionary soldier, Wentworth on Chebeague. On second thought, a cruise may not be such an easy sell.

He pointed out that there was a message on my answering machine wishing me a happy New Year. The voice belonged to my oldest friend on the planet, Susan. It is reassuring to start out the year with a time-tested constancy. This holiday season left me very satisfied indeed.

I checked the calendar. Five years have passed; time now to recycle that priceless piece of advice given to me by the Beachcombers, which means its time for a reinvention. In the last notable re-inventive mode, I started this book. Five years before

316

that, I tooled down to the Coast Guard Office in Boston and acquired ordinary seaman's papers in order to cook aboard an oil recovery ship, one of those found opportunities that does not often present itself. Of all careers from which one has to choose, I find it an intriguing parallel to have embarked upon a culinary calling in the maritime field, one and the same as my grandfather. Fortunately though, no symptoms of pitch-knot-*itis* seem to have made it through the osmotic curtain with the career. *"Bread & Butter!"*

The Rock, The Stock, & Its Heirs & Assigns

We who take a sabbatical from the island are never asked to surrender the label, *Islander*. On the contrary, it is ours for life— is actually a dowry that we take with us of acquired ingrained sensibilities, of strong bonds that we have with those who live there, the *stock*—and with the island itself, the *rock*. We are the heirs and assigns forever of an irreplaceable spirit borne in a particular season, one that has accompanied us through our adult life experiences. It is a remarkable crony to have alongside— *abs'lutely* remarkable!

The island will metamorphose with the winds of fortunes, in the interim it will continue to breed its own sense of community just as it did with those who first settled the island and the bay. The younger generations are now the conservators and don't need our paths or footsteps to find the way. Some of ours might not have been compassed that well—or they don't apply in this day and age. Though I do wish that they could have experienced some of what we had—especially the times when a hosie and a handshake was binding, when constancy was a given, and spirituality was nurtured. That mindset has been displaced—is considered too naive in some circles, too gullible for this worldwide community in which we all now abide.

Regardless, the course has been set. The younger generation requires new ways of getting from here to there, and ways of garnering happiness. We can't lead them to that anyway, although—a bit of illumination to shine their way while they work at it—just when it comes on dark—wouldn't hurt.

I heard a millionaire describe what he considered happiness. It's a good one! He said, *"Happiness is: Something to do, Something to love, and Something to look forward to."* I ruminated long on that little gem. That was not just a bit of illumination he shone my way—it was a power plant's worth— an ageless bit of advise, applicable in any season—one of such value that I'm tempted to toss it over there—over at the base of Ponce's Landing. I'll just leave it handy-by for the island's heirs and assigns to discover on their own—a bit of philosophical sustenance as they work to conserve a nonrenewable way of life—something to sure them up should their foundations ever become unhinged—then ardently wish them well.

I ought to get going; a serious thought about a reinvention awaits me. Hang on! I can't forget my island dowry and the bag of something to do, love, and look forward to. I never go anywhere without *a-one-of them.*

***

We'll bunch up later, ole de-ah!

ACKNOWLEDGEMENTS

Brunswick Historical Society
Brahms, Ann (Author of: *The Key Is Under the Flowerpot* and *Nana's House*)
Cady, Ann Marie (Gomez)
Chaney, David – State of Maine Parks and Services
                Park Mgr. Eagle Island 1986-98
Colby, C. William – Historian, Spruce Head Island
Eagle Island Historical Society
                The Friends of Peary's Eagle Island,
                PO Box 70, Bailey Island, ME 04003)
Evergreen Methodist Church
                Notes by Henrietta (Dyer) Cushing 1903 to 1907
Frappier, Captain William (Author of: *Steamboat Yesterdays On Casco Bay)*
Gomez, Antonio Jr.
Gomez, Lillian (LeBlanc)
Green, Phyllis
Harpswell Historical Society
Horr, Robert (Rocky) & Terry
Keene, Able Seaman, Bruce
Long Island Historical Society
Longanecker, Susan (Cushing)
MacVane, Donald
Maine Historical Society
Mainella, Mary Susan (Cady)
McCann Family – Captain Carl, Margaret, Dorothy
Pinette, Retired, Captain Joseph
Portland Public Library
Ricker, Frances (Savage)
Ricker, Captain, Robert (Bob)
Ricker, Chief Engineer, Robert (Will)
Ricker, Suzanne (Graphic artist)
Robertson, Carmen (Gomez)
Ross, Kay
Ross, Mary
Stephens, Virginia
Tiechert's, Harriet (Nelson)
Tillman, Marjorie (Gomez)
Wood, Olan (Spunk) and Gail (Rogers)

ENDNOTES

Archival news accounts make up much of the anecdotal accounts and narration.

i	p. 20	"Swift"	Portland City Directory	1871
ii	p. 20	Wentworth Ricker	U.S. Pension Office	1778
iii	p. 20	George Ricker	"Ricker" W.M.B. Laphain 1877	1706
iv	p. 22	"Newcomb"	Portland City Directory	1875 -1885
v	p. 23	"Alice"	US Merchant Steam Vessels 1884 p.285	1884
			Washington: US Government Printing Office	
vi	p. 23	John Sears - 1640	History of Portland	
			by Willis	1865
vii	p. 23	Long Island Population	Portland City Directory	1830
viii	p. 24	Methodist Church	Long Island Methodist Episcopal Records	1856
ix	p. 24	Schoolmistress	Portland City Directory	1852
x	p. 24	Long Island School	Portland City Directory	1850 -1871
			Historians - Susan Longanecker	
			& Mrs. Hickock	
xi	p. 26	Charitable		
		Organizations	Portland City Directory	1871
xii	p. 26	Portland 1871	Portland Press Herald (29 May 1982)April	1871
		Fire 1866 – Alarm System		
		Sebago Lake Water		
		Ulysses Grant 1871 - Trains		
		Shipping	Portland City Directory	1871
xiii	p. 27	Portland 1871	Portland Daily Advertiser	1870
xiv	p. 28	Birth - Maria	Maria Campos Baptismal Papers	1871
			Long Island, Maine Historical Society	
			LIHS 2000.14.6	
xv	p. 28	Antonio's Place of Birth	Immigration Papers – Azores	1893
xvi	p. 28	Antonio's Parentage	Vital Records	
			Marriage Information 09 Dec	1921
			Microfilm State of Maine Portland Library	
xvii	p. 29	Parent's Pottery Craft	Maria Campos Baptismal Papers	1871
xviii	p. 29	Estepona	Estepona Official Site Costa del Sol, Spain	1998
xix	p. 31	Earthquake 6.8 mag	Andalusian Institute of Geophysics 25 Dec	1884
			Important Earthquakes	
			University of Granada	
xx	p. 31	Earthquake Map	Terremolos Historicos Del Sur De Espana, [IAG]	
xxi	p. 32	Storms	Daily Eastern Argus, Portland, Maine	
			Jan	1893
			Microfilm files, Portland Public Library	
xxii	p. 32	Lt. Peary	Daily Eastern Argus 11 Feb	1893
xxiii	p. 32	Spanish Navy	Rough Article -Mary Siteman Doughty	
			Long Island,	
			Maine Historical Society 24 June	1905
xxiv	p. 32	Azores	Immigration Papers	1893
xxv	p. 33	SC Grace Davis	Marine Journal report Portland Transcript	
			21 & 28 March	1893
xxvi	p.34	Cigar Ad	Portland Daily Press	1870
		Deeds-Ponce	Registry of Deeds Book 418 P.157	1875

Page 107   **CHAPTER FIVE**

Page 127   **CHAPTER SIX**